Immigration Policy and the Terrorist Threat in Canada and the United States

Immigration Policy and the Terrorist Threat in Canada and the United States

edited by Alexander Moens and Martin Collacott

Fraser Institute

www.fraserinstitute.org

2008

Editing and production: Kristin Fryer
Design: Lindsey Thomas Martin
Cover design: Bill Ray
Front cover images: Dino O., Fotolia.com; Tomasz Trojanowski, Fotolia.com; Izabela Habur, iStockphoto.com.

Date of issue: May 2008
Printed and bound in Canada

Immigration policy and the terrorist threat in Canada and the United States / edited by Alexander Moens and Martin Collacott.

Includes bibliographical references.
ISBN 978-0-88975-234-4

Contents

About the Authors

James Bissett

James Bissett is a former Canadian diplomat and Ambassador. He served as the head of the Canadian Immigration Service from 1985 to 1990. He is now retired and living in Ottawa.

Martin Collacott

Martin Collacott is a Senior Fellow at the Fraser Institute, where he studies immigration policy, the treatment of refugees, and related issues involving terrorism. Mr. Collacott has 30 years of distinguished service in the Department of External Affairs for Canada. His assignments included Director General for Security Services. While in this capacity, he was responsible for the coordination of counterterrorism policy at the international level. He has represented Canada's Department of External Affairs in Indochina, Hong Kong, Lagos, and Tokyo. During the late 1960s, he served as the Chinese-speaking member of the Canadian negotiating team that established diplomatic relations with the People's Republic of China. Later in his career, Mr. Collacott was appointed High Commissioner to Sri Lanka, Ambassador to Syria and Lebanon, and Ambassador to Cambodia. As part of these assignments, he had major responsibilities regarding the delivery of immigration and refugee programs.

Glynn Custred

Glynn Custred is a professor emeritus at California State University, East Bay. He has done ethnographic field work in South America and has written on both the Canadian and the United States-Mexico borders.

Stephen Gallagher

Dr. Stephen Gallagher is the Program Director of the Montreal branch of the Canadian International Council. He also lectures at McGill University. He has taught at the University of Calgary, the University of Manitoba, and Concordia University.

David Harris

David Harris is a lawyer and is President of Democracy House, a Canadian non-profit organization dedicated to the advancement of democracy in a secure world. Canada's *Maclean's* magazine has called him "one of Canada's leading experts on terrorism." A former Chief of Strategic Planning of the Canadian Security Intelligence Service (CSIS), Mr. Harris recently appeared as Counsel to the Canadian Coalition for Democracies before two terrorism-related Commissions of Inquiry: the Air India Inquiry and the Iacobucci Internal Inquiry.

Mark Krikorian

Mark Krikorian is the Executive Director of the Center for Immigration Studies (CIS). He is also a regular contributor to the *National Review*. He frequently testifies before Congress and has published articles in the *Washington Post*, *The New York Times*, and elsewhere. He has appeared on *60 Minutes*, *Nightline*, *The News Hour with Jim Lehrer*, CNN, National Public Radio, and on many other television and radio programs. He received his BA from Georgetown University and his MA from the Fletcher School of Law and Diplomacy at Tufts University. He also pursued graduate studies at Yerevan State University in then Soviet Armenia.

Salim Mansur

Salim Mansur is a professor of political science at the University of Western Ontario. He is also an academic member of the Center for Security Policy, Washington, DC; Canadian Director for the Center for Islamic Pluralism, Washington DC; Senior Fellow with the Canadian Coalition for Democracies; and a nationally syndicated columnist with Sun Media.

Alexander Moens

Alexander Moens is a professor of Political Science at Simon Fraser University in Vancouver and a Senior Fellow with the Fraser Institute's Centre for Canadian-American Relations. He is the author of *The Foreign Policy of George W. Bush: Values, Strategy, Loyalty* and *Saving the North American Security and Prosperity Partnership: The Case for a North American Standards and Regulatory Area.*

John J. Noble

John J. Noble served in Foreign Affairs for 35 years in a variety of positions in Ottawa. He also served as Ambassador to Greece, Minister to France, and Ambassador to Switzerland and Liechtenstein. He has written extensively about Canadian-American relations.

Christopher Rudolph

Christopher Rudolph is Assistant Professor of International Politics at American University in Washington, DC. A specialist in international relations with a particular focus on international migration, he is the author of *National Security and Immigration*. His work has appeared in leading academic journals, including the *American Political Science Review*, *International Organization*, *Security Studies*, and *International Studies Review*.

Jan C. Ting

Jan C. Ting is a professor of Law at Temple University Beasley School of Law in Philadelphia. He is a former Assistant Commissioner of the United States Immigration and Naturalization Service. In 2006, he was the Republican Party nominee for the United States Senate in the state of Delaware.

Acknowledgments

The editors would like to acknowledge the thorough editing and source checking done by Michael Cust, MA candidate, who interned with the Centre for Canadian-American Relations at the Fraser Institute.

This volume began as a series of papers presented at a conference in Toronto in June 2007, titled, "Immigration Policy, Border Controls, and the Terrorist Threat in Canada and the United States." Both the conference and the edited volume have been supported generously by the Barbara & Bob Mitchell Fund and the Aurea Foundation.

We would like to thank the many people at the Fraser Institute who have worked energetically on this project in all its stages. A special thank you goes to Mark Mullins, Executive Director of the Institute, for his unwavering support. We would also like to thank Leah Costello, Arby Yeo, Dean Pelkey, and other members of the team in Vancouver and Toronto for organizing a flawless conference. Finally, we appreciate the hard work in the final production process done by Kristin Fryer with the support of Kristin McCahon.

Introduction

Alexander Moens and Martin Collacott

In June 2007, the Fraser Institute held a major conference in Toronto, Ontario, titled, "Immigration Policy, Border Controls, and the Terrorist Threat in Canada and the United States." As co-chairs of this conference, we introduced the theme and purpose of the conference by referring to recent events: the planned millennium bombing of the Los Angeles Airport and the attacks of September 11, 2001. These two events brought to light how terrorists are able to manipulate the immigration and refugee policies of Western democracies. Subsequent strikes and uncovered plots in Europe, Canada, and other countries have demonstrated the need for us to re-examine the security threats associated with immigration and refugee processing, and the threat that may arise from migrants, new citizens, or the next generation who do not integrate or identify with the values of their new homelands.

While immigrants can make significant contributions to their new countries, the possibility that they may use the host country as a place for recruitment, fund-raising, and a staging ground for terrorist attacks, abroad or in the host country, poses a clear and present danger. The long border and dense trade relationship between Canada and the United States adds to the complexity of managing this threat.

The purpose of the conference was to inform the public by describing the terrorist threat as it truly is. At the conference, we examined and compared the government policies of Canada and the United

States, as well as European countries, that are designed to deal with this problem. Our objective was to analyze strengths and weaknesses in these policies and to formulate recommendations that would provide a better balance between immigration and national security.

The ten chapters in this volume all arose from this conference. We brought together a mixture of Canadian and American experts to address the following issues: terrorist threat assessments; national security and civil liberties; immigration, refugee, and asylum policies; border controls; and Canadian-American initiatives to produce a smarter and more secure border. The chapters reveal that the challenges of dealing with groups or individuals who are planning terrorist acts, recruiting supporters, and providing financial or logistical support to terrorist movements overseas are still very much present in Canada and the United States. The threat has not diminished, and the possibility that determined terrorist groups will at some point be able to find cracks in our armour remains very real.

Most of the authors in this volume (as well as the editors) may easily fall victim to charges of being anti-immigrant, xenophobic, or alarmist with respect to the terrorist threat. But in fact, none of these authors is opposed to effectively managed immigration or allowing genuine refugees who pose no security threat to enter the country through a well-vetted system. All believe that the vast majority of immigrants pose no danger, but are simply seeking to improve their freedom and prosperity. However, given the stakes raised by terrorist attacks, even a small minority of threatening individuals should warrant major attention and policy adjustments. The security issues raised in this volume pertain to the increasing risks posed by Canada's largely open-ended immigration and asylum systems. In Canada, both systems are heavily influenced by special interest groups and political parties that are vying for political support from limited but influential segments of the electorate. The general principle of immigration and the importance of keeping our borders as open as possible to the movement of commerce are not being challenged. Rather, this volume seeks to demonstrate that the current state of immigration and refugee policies leaves much to be desired from a security perspective.

The purpose of this book is, first of all, to raise awareness among the public and among government officials that Western policies regarding migration, non-integration, and their relation to public safety need to be re-examined. In Canada, trying to open up public debate is a David and Goliath struggle as Canadian academic and non-governmental organization (NGO) elites are nearly universal in their opposition to a critical consideration of immigration issues.

We have organized the issues addressed in this book into four themes. Usually there are one or two Canadian contributors per theme and one American contributor.

Daniel Stoffman, a well-known Canadian writer and author of *Who Gets In: What's Wrong with Canada's Immigration Program* (2001), leads off with the first theme ("Mass Immigration and the Growing Threat of Terrorism") with a chapter that debunks popularly held myths and images of large-scale immigration among Canadians. He questions whether high levels of immigration actually offer solutions to labour market shortages or to the social and fiscal challenges faced by a society with an aging population. Stoffman also describes how immigration patterns in recent decades have changed. He outlines how continuously replenished and increasingly large and less diverse immigrant communities pose greater challenges in terms of integration and security risks, whether sponsoring terrorism abroad (Tamil Tigers) or cultivating home-grown terrorism (Sikh and Islamist). He cites specific examples, such as the terrorist plot discovered in Toronto in 2006, to explain why these trends constitute an acute danger.

Salim Mansur, who teaches political science at the University of Western Ontario, follows Stoffman with an exposé on how the recent threat of jihadist terror has brought to the fore the dangerous nexus between large-scale immigration and limited levels of integration among some immigrant communities in Western societies, including Canada, the United States, and the United Kingdom. For example, this nexus has created fertile ground for the radicalization of young Muslims by jihadist influence, as the latter has grown into a global network. Liberal democratic societies, which emphasize pluralism, multiculturalism, and tolerance, have much work to do in finding ways to deal with this emerging threat.

Mark Krikorian, the Executive Director of the Center for Immigration Studies in Washington, DC, demonstrates that intake levels of all categories in the United States are so high that the immigration, asylum, and visa systems are simply overwhelmed. Being overwhelmed means that many of the security checks that should take place do not, and, as a result, potentially dangerous individuals are not detected or prevented from entering. The system overload and subsequent vulnerability, Krikorian asserts, has become an element in the strategy of some jihadist groups who wish to attack the United States.

Under the next theme, "Troubled Immigration and Refugee Systems," Stephen Gallagher and James Bissett offer detailed accounts of how imperfectly Canada's refugee policy system actually works. The most obvious flaws—the virtually endless opportunities for review and delay and the near-impossibility, in many cases, of deporting a person whose refugee claim has been rejected—will raise the eyebrows of many readers who are being exposed to these issues for the first time. Gallagher, who teaches at McGill University and Concordia University, shows that the dysfunctional refugee system has, in effect, become a parallel immigration channel through which most claimants are eventually able to become permanent residents and in which immigration eligibility has been replaced by self-selection. He also shows that, in comparison with Great Britain, Australia, the United States, and most other Western democracies, Canadian practices and processes are uniquely lenient.

Bissett, a former Canadian ambassador and Executive Director of the Immigration Service, explains how Canadian politicians are reluctant to fix known flaws in the system for fear of losing votes from immigrant groups. In fact, vote-seeking practices, multiculturalism, and liberal immigration and refugee policies have become very much intertwined. As a result, many politicians have become extremely reluctant to designate certain groups—particularly those with deep roots in ethnic communities—as having terrorist connections if they risk losing electoral support by doing so. Bissett also outlines how some of the measures taken by Canada in the wake of 9/11 to tighten public security have begun to erode in recent years.

Glynn Custred, a professor emeritus of anthropology at the University of California, East Bay, focuses on the porous southern border of the United States. Just as Canadian elites and governments are reluctant to shore up their immigration and refugee systems, American officials in the Bush administration have been dragging their feet on closing the border to illegal migration. Similar to Krikorian, who argues that the sheer number of entrants must be brought down before some level of security can be re-established in the visa and migration system, Custred believes American authorities must fix the border before any programs to enhance the flow of commerce can be launched.

The next theme in the book, "Balancing Liberty and Security in the New Environment," addresses the important question raised by many scholars and critics of governmental policies in both Canada and the United States since 9/11 of how basic civil liberties, as well as respect for cultural diversity and openness to newcomers, can be maintained in the face of the new threats of terrorism. Jan C. Ting, a professor at Temple University in Philadelphia, offers a detailed legal and political analysis of why increased security need not permanently reverse or undo civil liberties.

Under the same theme, David Harris sounds the alarm about the imbalanced state of affairs in Canada. As a lawyer, Harris sees only lop-sided concerns for civil liberties, multicultural correctness, and a complete lack of threat awareness among Canadian academics and many senior government officials. While intelligence and law enforcement officials may be doing a good job, they are not receiving clear policy guidance from the political leadership. Harris' plea for a hard-nosed recognition of the jihadist threat to our way of life is aimed at raising public understanding and concern. In his words, "if the government fails to restrict the enjoyment of some liberties in the face of infiltration and growing threats, one might expect to see other liberties ultimately going unenjoyed."

Stoffman, Gallagher, Bissett, and Harris all point out the short-sightedness of Canadian politicians and political parties in their failing to address the serious flaws in Canada's refugee and asylum systems and the lack of security in its immigration system. These authors realize that, in addition to existing systems of patronage and "pork barrel" politics, political parties in democratic countries are continuously seeking new ways of securing electoral support. The issue remains, however, of whether a government can afford to jeopardize national security and public safety for the sake of pursuing votes at nomination rallies and national elections.

The final section of the book, "The Challenge of Strengthening the Canada-US Border," looks at how these issues impact the border between Canada and the United States. There are a number of other border issues that are not examined in any detail in this book, including the border's inadequate infrastructure and insufficient manpower to screen the massive flow of trucks that carry over $1 billion in trade every day between our two countries. The main focus of this section is how security, as it relates to migration issues, affects border controls and regimes.

John Noble, a former Canadian ambassador who is now a distinguished senior fellow at Carleton University, describes the various efforts to improve the border and make it "smarter" that the United States, acting alone or in concert with Canada, has taken since 9/11. Likewise, Christopher Rudolph examines the range of initiatives launched in North America recently. Rudolph, a professor in the School of International Service at American University in Washington, DC, argues that there needs to be better cooperation between the two countries in terms of basic intelligence sharing.

Both Noble and Rudolph explain why the European example of open borders (the Schengen Accord) and a common perimeter policy do not provide useful templates for North America. There are too many differences and sensitivities on security and immigration issues to expect much progress on the perimeter concept, beyond joint customs officers in selected ports to inspect inbound container cargo. The American propensity to continue to add additional border enforcement will not provide more security. By the same token, until American authorities are satisfied that Canada will share its assessment of threats and will act accordingly, the United States will continue to put in place whatever measures it considers necessary on a unilateral basis.

Noble and Rudolph agree that simply increasing security and screening at the Canada-United States border will be enormously costly and will not improve security, per se, as the vast majority of traffic contains no threat. Moreover, the cost to commerce would be prohibitive. Instead, both governments and policy makers must realize that a smarter, more cooperative, and more coordinated perimeter effort is the key to achieving greater border security in the post-9/11 era. Progress thus far under the Smart Border Accord remains modest. What is clear, however, is that, regardless of what challenges the United States faces on its southern border in terms of illegal migration, Canada and the United States need to find more harmonization in security, visa, and asylum measures. Their aim must be to create a system of mutual recognition and shared security criteria, which would alleviate the need for certain border checks and thereby improve the flow without diminishing real security.

In our final chapter, we review the main flaws and weaknesses in Canada's immigration and asylum systems and their impact on North American security. We evaluate the broad themes raised in this volume and make general recommendations for reform. In closing, we make a call for a comprehensive and independent review of Canada's immigration and refugee determination systems.

Immigration Policy and the Terrorist Threat in Canada and the United States

Chapter 1

Truths and Myths about Immigration

Daniel Stoffman

Canada has the highest rate of immigration per capita of any industrialized country (Statistics Canada, 2003: 6). The doctrine that high immigration levels are essential, not only to our prosperity but also to our very demographic survival, has become entrenched in Canada. The combination of these two factors makes it difficult, perhaps even impossible, for Canada to control unwanted immigration. By unwanted immigration, I mean immigrants who pose a threat to the existing population because they are criminals or supporters of organizations that wish harm upon the people of Canada and other Western countries.

Many options for stopping unwanted immigration have been offered. For example, it has been widely acknowledged for more than a decade that the Canadian refugee determination system needs a major overhaul to make it less susceptible to abuse from fraudulent claimants, some of whom pose security risks. A lower acceptance rate, similar to the rates of other refugee-accepting countries, would deter some illegitimate arrivals, as would increased detention of claimants considered unlikely to appear at their refugee hearings and failed claimants considered unlikely to leave the country voluntarily.

Of course, not all immigrants who pose a threat to Canadian society arrive as refugee claimants. Some come through the regular immigration stream. More rigorous scrutiny of immigration applications submitted to Canadian officials abroad would help minimize the number of immigrants who may pose security risks. As well, Canada's new policy of arming border guards, which is being implemented gradually by the federal government, has the obvious benefit of deterring violent individuals who are trying to cross into Canada from the United States.

But none of these reforms would reduce unwanted immigration as effectively as a simple reduction in the annual immigration intake. Because the current immigration level is so high, it is not possible to screen every newcomer thoroughly. Canadian officials cannot always verify that the newcomer actually is who he or she claims to be. As a result, it is inevitable that dangerous people will gain admission.

Generous, yet moderate, immigration levels prevailed in Canada until the annual intake was raised and made permanent by Brian Mulroney's Progressive Conservative government in the late 1980s. Successive federal governments have maintained that policy, despite the rise of international terrorist organizations that target Western countries. As a result of this policy, each year 260,000 immigrants enter Canada, a country with a population that is one-tenth that of the United States. If the United States had legal immigration on the same scale, it would be admitting 2.6 million immigrants each year instead of one million (Camarota, 2007).

If Canada were serious about reducing its vulnerability to international terrorism, it would return to the more moderate levels of immigration it once had, similar to the levels that other major immigrant-receiving countries, such as the United States and Australia, maintain. But Canadian governments have tied their own hands by adopting beliefs about immigration that prevent a return to normal levels. Moreover, successive governments have viewed high immigration levels as a winning proposition from an electoral point of view, even though a recent survey indicates that 62% of Canadians want greater restrictions on immigration (Pew Research Center, 2007). Since no Canadian political party advocates a reduction in immigration levels, voters who feel strongly about the issue have no option at the ballot box. Consequently, governments are free to ignore public opinion. They seem to believe that an expansive immigration policy will please ethnic organizations whose leaders will respond by marshalling support for a government that implements such a policy (Stoffman, 2002: 76–93).

As a result, Canadian immigration policy, once managed in the national interest, is now too often manipulated by politicians seeking re-election. A recent example of this can be found in an internal report prepared by Canada's diplomatic mission in India, which describes the results of a decision made in 2004 to open a Canadian immigration office in Chandigarh, the capital of the state of Punjab (O'Neil, 2007, Oct. 19). According to Richard Kurland, the Vancouver immigration lawyer who obtained the document, the office was opened to reward Punjabi-Canadians who were clamouring for better immigration services. "Liberals yearned for Indo-Canadian votes, and even though officials advised that Chandigarh was a hotbed of false documents, Liberal politics trumped logic," he told CanWest News Service. "And now Canada's immigration system gets to pay the price for Liberal pragmatism" (O'Neil, 2007, Oct. 19).

The price, according to the report, is a flood of fraudulent immigration applications, including many from self-styled nannies with no training. "Fraud is omnipresent in Chandigarh and is found in every sort of document," the internal report states. "This office has identified over 160 'nanny schools' in the Punjab. While some … are bone fide schools, there are a considerable number lacking facilities, equipment and students—but having large graduating classes" (O'Neil, 2007, Oct. 19).

In 2004, Raj Chahal, who was an advisor to Jean Chrétien while Chrétien was Prime Minister, told *The Vancouver Sun* that the Chandigarh office was opened despite the objections of both Citizenship and Immigration Canada and the Department of Foreign Affairs. Both departments advised that the resources could be better employed in other parts of India and Asia. The cost of opening the Chandigarh office and then running it for five years was reported to be $25 million (O'Neil, 2007, Oct. 19).

There are a number of false beliefs that are helping to prevent reform of Canada's immigration policy. The conventional wisdom in Canada is that we are desperate for more immigrants because we have a low birth rate and the boomer generation is getting too old to work. Unless millions of new immigrants move to Canada, all of us will become poorer because a smaller work force will not be able to sustain the welfare state that supports the elderly at the current level of benefits. The reality, by contrast, is that neither economic nor demographic justifications exist for accepting any negative consequences resulting from the immigration program.

Major studies in Canada, the United States, and Australia have found that, as a fraction of GDP, the economic gains from immigration are minuscule—certainly not large enough to justify maintaining a large immigration program. In a major study, the Economic Council of Canada summed up the Canadian literature as follows: "There is little or no effect of immigration on the per capita income of existing residents" (Economic Council of Canada, 1991: 22). The disconnect between immigration and economic prosperity has been evident throughout Canada's history. "A historical perspective gives little or no support to the view that immigration is needed for economic prosperity," the Council stated in its report. "In the 19th and early 20th centuries, the fastest growth in real per-capita incomes occurred at times when net immigration was nil or negative" (1991: 19). An Australian study on the economic effects of immigration by the Committee for Economic Development of Australia supports this finding. It failed to find any significant impact other than that immigration made the overall economy larger (Economic Council of Canada, 1991: 22).

A 1997 study by the National Academy of Sciences on immigration's impact on the American economy concluded that the fiscal burden of providing government services to new immigrants was greater than any economic gains attributable to immigration (Cassidy, 1997, July 14: 42). The modest gains that immigration does deliver, as American economist George Borjas has demonstrated, are the result of lower labour costs (1999: 87–104). In other words, the most significant economic impact of immigration is the reduction in the costs of goods and services that results from depressing wages. Whether one views this as good or bad depends on whether one is a wage earner or a wage payer. Immigration, Borjas explains, induces a substantial redistribution of wealth, away from workers who compete with immigrants and toward employers and other users of immigrant services (1999: 13). Workers lose because immigrants drag wages down. Employers gain because immigrants drag wages down.

These wealth transfers may amount to tens of billions of dollars each year (Borjas, 1999).

Immigration makes the economy larger because more people are producing and consuming goods and services. But that doesn't make the average person any richer. It is obvious that no relationship exists between population size and average incomes. If it did, the people in countries such as China, India, and Indonesia would be the wealthiest in the world. However, population growth—or the lack of it—does influence a country's economic development. Economist David Foot points out that, because of differences in fertility rates, the economies of China and India will develop quite differently in the future. Because China has below-replacement fertility, it will experience worker shortages that will drive wages up. When that happens, China will no longer be a low-cost competitor in the world. "China is going to gradually become a rich country in per capita terms," argues Foot. By contrast, if Indian parents continue to have three or more children, "there's always going to be a pool of cheap young labour, so wages are always going to remain low" (Foot, 2007, Oct. 8: 28).

As the work of Borjas, Foot, and others demonstrates, population growth, whether it results from natural increase or immigration, has a powerful impact on wages. Strangely, however, this topic is rarely discussed in Canada in relation to immigration policy. Stranger still, politicians who claim to represent the interests of working people often advocate increasing immigration levels, a policy that would actually increase downward pressure on wages.

A political consensus exists in Canada that extremely high immigration levels are necessary because the Canadian population is aging. However, populations are aging in all industrialized countries—and most developing ones, as well—and yet no other country contemplates a per capita immigration intake comparable to Canada's. In fact, no evidence exists to support the peculiar Canadian myth that population aging in combination with moderate, rather than high, immigration levels will spell economic doom.

In 2002, Marcel Mérette, an economist at the University of Ottawa, produced a study on the economics of an aging population. He found that investments in human capital—education and training—that accompanied aging in seven industrialized countries actually increased economic growth more rapidly than would have occurred in the absence of aging. Why? Because a better educated workforce drives technological progress, the real engine of economic growth. Innovation blossoms when resources grow scarce. Just as higher energy costs lead to advances in fuel efficiency, so also does labour-saving technology accompany labour scarcity (Mérette, 2002: 3).

Populations all over the world are aging because fertility is decreasing while longevity is increasing. The notion that immigration is an antidote to the aging phenomenon is simply wrong. Only an astronomical, and entirely impractical, intake of exclusively young immigrants would significantly decrease the average age of Canadians (Stoffman, 2002: 106). Even if Canada were to double its already high immigrant intake, the impact on the average age of the Canadian population would be minimal. Moreover, China and India—the major immigrant-sending countries—are enjoying rapid economic growth and, consequently, are providing good opportunities at home for the same young, well-trained workers that Canada hopes to attract. Thus, in the future, it will be increasingly difficult to attract such people as permanent immigrants.

Canadians will have to accept that Canada, like the rest of the world, is getting older and that this phenomenon is manageable. Other countries, such as Italy and Japan, that are older than Canada have adjusted to an aging population and a slow growing workforce, and have managed to keep the buses running and the hospitals functioning. This has been accomplished through moderate levels of immigration, the education and training of young people, maximized labour participation rates, and increased productivity through the use of technology. Slower labour force growth, concludes Mérette, is offset by greater investment in human capital and rising participation rates. "As a result," he writes, "growth in the effective labour force may not drop much with population aging" (Mérette, 2002: 12).

There are many examples of successful adaptation to labour scarcity. European countries, which have less available low-cost labour, were a decade ahead of Canada in automating fee collection at parking garages (Stoffman, 2002: 114-115). Another example is the production of grapes to be dried into raisins, one of the most labour-intensive agricultural operations. In

California, bunches of grapes are cut by hand, manually placed in a tray for drying, manually turned, and manually collected. Australia lacks a large supply of cheap farm labour, so farmers developed a method of growing grapes on trellises. This new system reduced the need for labour and increased yields by 200%. This more productive method has been slow to spread to the United States because the availability of cheap labour acts as a disincentive to farmers to make large capital investments (Krikorian, 2004).

Perhaps the most powerful and prevalent economic argument for high immigration levels is the notion that Canada needs a large number of newcomers to do the jobs that Canadians will not do, such as cleaning houses and offices, caring for children and the elderly, and driving taxis. Yet Canadian-born people work in mines, fight fires, and collect garbage. Why would they accept these arduous jobs and yet refuse to do others? The answer is obvious. There is no job that Canadians will not do. However, they expect to be paid well for it and to enjoy good working conditions. When people say that Canada needs immigrants to do the jobs Canadians will not do, they are really saying that Canada wants immigrants because immigrants have no choice but to accept wages and working conditions that no one else will accept. That is not a justifiable use of the immigration program.

An excessive immigration intake does no favour for newcomers to Canada. The economic performance of immigrants has fallen as the number of immigrants has increased. In 1980, immigrants were 1.4 times as likely as Canadian-born people to have low incomes. By 2000, they were 2.5 times as likely to be poor (Picot and Hou, 2003). In 2007, Statistics Canada published a report entitled *Losing Ground: the Persistent Growth of Family Poverty in Canada's Largest City* (2007a). It revealed that the number of families with children in Toronto living below the poverty line increased by 9.7% to 92,930 between 2000 and 2005. During the same period, the number of poor families in Canada as a whole shrank by 5.1% (*Toronto Star*, 2007, Dec. 31). Toronto differs from the rest of Canada in another important way—it receives 40% of all immigrants to Canada (Statistics Canada, 2007b). In the context of the data on falling immigrant economic performance, it is clear that the growth of poverty in Toronto is closely linked to a mismanaged immigration program.

A return to moderate immigration levels would improve the chances for newcomers to become successful in the Canadian economy. It would also bring other benefits, including more manageable growth in major cities, higher productivity, and more rapid per capita economic growth. A more moderate immigration level would also decrease Canada's vulnerability to international terrorism by making it possible to screen newcomers more carefully. The Canadian government not only lacks the resources to do thorough checks of 260,000 people, it even lacks the resources to check immigrants who come from terrorist-producing regions. In 2006, Jack Hooper, the deputy director of the Canadian Security and Intelligence Service (CSIS), told the Senate national security committee that 20,000 people had come to Canada from the Pakistan-Afghanistan region since 2001 and that, because of a lack of resources, no security checks whatsoever had been done on 90% of them (Gordon, 2006, May 30).

Immediately after the terrorist attacks of September 11, 2001, travelers shunned air travel. Six years later, planes were filled to capacity and airline profits were soaring (Pae, 2007, Oct. 19). The fearfulness immediately following 9/11 may have been irrational, but there is no reason for Canadians to be complacent merely because six years have elapsed since the attack. Canadians have been victimized by terrorists in the past and there is no reason to believe that they will not be attacked again. In 1985, Sikh terrorists who were based in Canada murdered 329 people, most of them Canadians, by planting a bomb on an Air India jet en route from Canada to India. The attack on the World Trade Center in 2001 killed 24 Canadians. In 2002, Osama bin Laden named Canada one of al-Qaeda's targets. An al-Qaeda training manual published in 2004 stated, "We must target and kill the Jews and the Christians ... The grades of importance are as follows: Americans, British, Spaniards, Australians, Canadians, Italians" (Bell, 2006, June 3).

Canada's immigration policies also have consequences for other nations. Ahmed Ressam, the Algerian refugee claimant who intended to blow up the Los Angeles airport, is often cited as an example of how Canada's laxity endangers the United States. When he was arrested while trying to enter the United States in 1999, Ressam had been living in Canada for five years, even though France had warned the Canadian government that he was a terrorist and even though he had not bothered to show up for his refugee hearing. During that time, he had travelled to Afghanistan for training and used a false identity to obtain a Canadian passport (Stoffman, 2002: 9). It would be wrong to assume that Ressam was not a threat to his host country, as well as to the United States. During his trial, he testified that he and an associate, Samir Ait Mohamed, had plotted to detonate a bomb in a Montreal area with a large Jewish population, but had dropped that plan to concentrate on the Los Angeles attack.

The most prominent case of an attack on Canadian soil that might have occurred had police not prevented it is the alleged plot of a terrorist cell in suburban Toronto, whose members were arrested in June 2006. Some were Canadian-born, while others were immigrants from various parts of the world, including Egypt, Somalia, and Afghanistan (Bell and Patrick, 2006, June 4). They had allegedly planned to use massive bombs to attack the Toronto headquarters of CSIS and the Toronto Stock Exchange. There was also an alleged plan to attack the Parliament buildings in Ottawa and to behead Prime Minister Stephen Harper. Most of those who were charged lived in parts of suburban Toronto that had significant populations of Muslims. One member of the Muslim community, Mubin Shaikh, played an important role in the arrests of the 18 suspects by acting as an informant to CSIS. In an interview, Shaikh explained his motives: "This is home for me. I can't have things blowing up in my backyard. There are values that I live by—it's not that they're Islamic or they're Western; it's that they're human. That's what it comes down to" (Le Goff, 2004: 3).

It is natural for immigrants from the same cultural and linguistic backgrounds to settle in the same neighbourhoods. They have always done so. In a free country, people have the right to live where they choose, to speak whatever language they choose, and to maintain their culture. The difference between the current situation and the past is that immigration used to come in waves—a group would come from a particular country, such as Japan or Portugal, and then that influx would stop, either because Canada reduced its immigration quota or because fewer Japanese or Portuguese wanted to come.

This does not happen any more. Canada now has relentless immigration, year after year, from the same places to the same places. As a result, large self-contained communities are created and are constantly replenished. The majority of the residents of these communities are good people who want to build prosperous lives for their families. Most, like Mubin Shaikh, are law-abiding citizens who abhor violence. But some are not, and the larger a community is, the easier it is for groups that are hostile towards Canada and the West to operate secretly within these communities and to develop support networks.

Canadians rightly pride themselves on the cultural diversity of their major cities, but the reality is that Canadian cities are not diverse enough. Out of 194 countries in the world, just 10 of them account for 62% of all new immigrants. That the majority of immigrants arrive from a small number of source countries is nothing new. During the first major immigration wave between 1867 and 1914, 40% of new arrivals to Canada were from the British Isles (Le Goff, 2004: 3). What is new today is the relentlessness of the immigration flow and its size. In the past, immigration levels fluctuated according to the government's estimate of the need for new workers. Since the time of the Mulroney government, however, Canada's policy has been to maintain high levels of immigration, regardless of economic conditions. Moreover, because certain family members of existing residents can enter Canada by right, communities that are already well-established continue to grow rapidly.

Most immigrants leave home in search of better economic opportunities, which is why most source countries are those in which large numbers of young people compete for jobs and earn lower wages. Rich countries with older populations are not significant sources of immigrants. Thus, Italy and Japan no longer send many immigrants to Canada. Eventually, because of demographic changes, the number of immigrants from current major source countries may diminish. But in the meantime, creating a more diverse intake would require a change of policy in Canada. If that were successfully achieved, there might be a larger number of ethnic communities, but they would also be smaller and, perhaps, more integrated into the broader community.

The constant flow of new arrivals from the same places to the same places is not the only hindrance to integration. Another obstacle is the confusing rhetoric surrounding the policy of multiculturalism. Canada is not really a multicultural country because cultural practices that clash with basic Canadian values are not permitted (Stoffman, 2002: 119–150). Canada is a liberal democracy in which all persons are equal, regardless of gender, race, religion, or sexual orientation. Yet many immigrants arrive imbued with the cultures of countries that are not liberal democracies and do not value or accept individual freedom. In addition, a whole range of practices that are allowed in other countries—such as circumcising young girls, eating dogs, and carrying handguns—are not tolerated in Canada. Yet, because the policy of multiculturalism is so ill-defined, it is understandable that some immigrants are confused with respect to what they can and cannot do (Stoffman, 2002).

Moreover, from a security perspective, the ideology of multiculturalism may hinder law enforcement. Advocates of multiculturalism rightly insist that people of all backgrounds must be treated with courtesy and respect. However, there is a danger that the officials responsible for safeguarding all Canadians will be overly sensitive with respect to linking security issues to the immigration program. If we are afraid to confront problems caused by undesirable immigration, how can we possibly control it?

Martin Collacott (2007, May 8), a retired Canadian diplomat who was responsible for coordinating counterterrorism policy for the Department of Foreign Affairs, believes the sacred cow of multiculturalism may have been partially responsible for the success of the 1985 Air India bombing.

> Official multiculturalism policy, with its privileging of tolerance above all else, prevented our authorities from fully investigating and thwarting the terrorists' plot … The government's look the other way policy allowed Sikh militants to intimidate the Sikh community at large … Even during the Air India trial, supporters of the accused were still able to threaten witnesses for the prosecution.

A striking case of "looking the other way" occurred when those accused of planning to commit various acts of terrorism were arrested in Toronto. Mike McDonell, Assistant Commissioner of the Royal Canadian Mounted Police, claimed that the suspects "represent the broad strata of our society. Some are students, some are employed, some are unemployed" (Austen and Johnston, 2006, June 4). Based on his remarks, one would expect to find a diverse assortment of people in that group of suspected terrorists— men and women of all ages, from a variety of religious and cultural backgrounds. But in fact, all of the suspects were Muslims, either immigrants or the offspring of recent immigrants, all were male, and all but two of them were in their teens or twenties at the time of the arrests. Several of them attended the same mosque.

In other words, there was little relevant diversity among these suspects. Rather than representing the "broad strata" of Canadian society, these men fit the same narrow profile as those who successfully committed mass murder in the subway in London, the trains in Madrid, and the World Trade Center in New York. Yet McDonell's attempt to pretend otherwise is understandable. In "multicultural" Canada, racial profiling is unacceptable. Our intelligence and security agencies, argues Collacott, "are being told to operate with one hand tied behind their backs. They will be excoriated if they fail to catch the terrorists and equally lambasted by activists if they show too much zeal in pursuing their leads" (2007, May 8).

If the police are unwilling to state the obvious because they are afraid of offending someone, then the safety of the general public is compromised. Law enforcement officials must feel free to speak frankly about the dangers posed by radical Islamists who think it is right to kill "infidels" anywhere, including the more than 32 million infidels who live in Canada.

Fear of causing offence has also led the media to fail to inform Canadians fully. *The Toronto Star*, Canada's largest daily newspaper, refuses to publish the race of suspects being sought by police for criminal acts, although it is doubtful that the *Star's* editor, if mugged on the street, would decline to mention the skin colour of his attacker when informing the police. A public opinion poll conducted in February 2007 provides another example of media surrender to multiculturalist sensibilities. The poll found that more than 80% of Canadian Muslims were satisfied with life in Canada and 73% of them thought the terrorist attacks allegedly being plotted were completely unjustified. The headline on the CBC web site read, "Glad to be Canadian, Muslims Say" (Corbella, 2007, Feb. 18). It is not surprising that a majority of Muslims thought the attacks were unjustified. But the real story, which is surprising, was that 12% thought the attacks were justified. This means that 12% of the Canadian Muslim population of around 750,000–900,000 thought it would be justifiable to explode massive bombs in Toronto and Ottawa, for example, killing thousands of innocent people in the process. By reporting the results of the poll the way they did, the Canadian media tried to shield the public from this information, presumably so as not to embarrass the Muslim community. This is the "see no evil, hear no evil" approach that says, If all immigration is good immigration, then how can there ever be unwanted immigration?

A steady stream of supporters of the Tamil Tigers, one of the world's most murderous terrorist organizations, have found a haven in Canada. The Tigers, who are fighting to carve a separate Tamil state out of Sri Lanka, are the world's most accomplished suicide bombers. They have used that tactic to murder a Sri Lankan president and a former Indian prime minister, as well as several moderate Sri Lankan Tamil leaders. Hundreds of ordinary people, who were in the wrong place at the wrong time, also died at the hands of the Tigers—their bombing of a bank building in 1996 killed 90 people (Waldman, 2003, Jan. 14). Rohan Gunaratna, a research fellow at the Center for the Study of Terrorism and Political Violence at the University of St. Andrews, told *The New York Times*, "Of all the suicide-capable terrorist groups … they are the most ruthless" (Waldman, 2003, Jan. 14).

Tiger supporters came to Canada because the Immigration and Refugee Board offered automatic refugee status to anyone who claimed to be a Tamil from Sri Lanka. These claimants didn't even have to prove that they had ever been to Sri Lanka (Stoffman, 1994). After immigrating, some of them used Canada as a place to raise funds to commit terrorist acts in Sri Lanka (*CBC News*, 2005, Nov. 30). Nevertheless, federal Liberal governments were so eager to cultivate support among the fast-growing Tamil community that they refused to ban the Tigers as a terrorist organization, even though the United States and United Kingdom had already done so.

When Paul Martin, who would later become prime minister, was criticized for attending a dinner sponsored by a group associated with the Tamil Tigers, he was unapologetic. Such criticism, he claimed, was "not the Canadian way" (Collacott, 2007, May 8). This is one example of how a dysfunctional immigration and refugee system, in combination with the notion that minority cultural groups must be immune from criticism, makes it difficult for Canada to control unwanted immigration.

Only an infinitesimal percentage of the immigrants and refugees who come to Canada wish us harm. But, as tragic events have shown, it takes only a few to kill and maim thousands. However, Canada can reduce its vulnerability by taking the same sensible approach towards immigration and refugee reform that would be justified even if a terrorist threat did not exist. First, immigration levels must be reduced. All the adverse impacts of immigration, both economic and social, stem from excessively high numbers. The sharp increase in Canada's intake in the 1990s has been followed by an equally sharp increase in the rate of poverty among new immigrants. Moreover, when a relentless stream of immigrants who speak the same language arrives, self-contained communities are created, integration is impeded, and social division may result. Finally, an excessive immigration intake creates overly rapid growth in the major cities that are the destinations of most newcomers. This growth benefits the real estate industry, but not the population as a whole.

As well, fixing the refugee system would allow Canada to direct more of its resources toward genuine refugees, while deterring fraudulent ones. Because Canada does not share a border with a refugee-producing country, there is no reason why large numbers of claimants should show up at the Canadian border. They come because of what migration experts call the "pull factor." The ease of gaining refugee status in Canada attracts economic migrants who may not qualify under the regular immigration program or may have to wait for years before being accepted. Because Canada is not close to refugee-producing areas, its role in refugee protection should be to choose from among the millions of people in refugee camps who most need permanent resettlement and bring them to Canada. In 1986, Canada won the United Nations Nansen Medal for its work in resettling thousands of such people. Reducing the pull factor by implementing normal international standards of refugee selection would free up resources that could support an increased focus on such resettlement. As a side benefit, officials could better ensure that these refugees posed no security risks because they would be preselected by Canada.

Immigration is an important national tradition. While immigration is not a prerequisite for economic growth, those who immigrate bring with them new energy and new ideas. Over the past 50 years, they have helped transform the major immigrant-receiving centres of Toronto and Vancouver from dull provincial outposts into cosmopolitan cities brimming with vitality. But because immigration is not essential to economic growth or demographic survival, there is no justification for accepting any negative consequences resulting from the immigration program. One such consequence is an increase in our vulnerability to international terrorism. We can never become invulnerable, but a return to the generous but moderate immigration program that Canada abandoned in the 1990s would make Canada a safer place.

References

Austen, Ian, and David Johnston (2006, June 4). 17 Held in Plot to Bomb Sites in Ontario. *The New York Times.* <http://www.nytimes.com/2006/06/04/world/americas/04toronto.html>. Accessed December 7, 2007.

Bell, Stewart (2006, June 3). Never Mind Foreign Terrorists, Why is Canada Growing its Own Extremists? *National Post.*

Bell, Stewart, and Kelly Patrick (2006, June 4). Alleged Canadian Terror Plot has Worldwide Links. *National Post.* <http://www.canada.com/story.html?id=de3f8e90-982a-47af-8e5e-a1366fd5d6cc>. Accessed December 19, 2007.

Borjas, George (1999). *Heaven's Door.* Princeton University Press.

Camarota, Steven A. (2007). *100 Million More: Projecting the Impact of Immigration on the US Population, 2007-2060.* Center for Immigration Studies. <http://www.cis.org/articles/2007/back707.html>. Accessed December 19, 2007.

Cassidy, John (1997, July 14). The Melting-Pot Myth. *The New Yorker.*

CBC News (2005, November 30). Tamil Tigers Illegally Fundraising in Toronto: Community Member. <http://www.cbc.ca/story/canada/national/2005/11/30/tamil051130.html>. Accessed December 7, 2007.

Collacott, Martin (2007, May 8). The Perils of Multiculturalism at 31,000 Feet. *National Post.* <http://www.nationalpost.com/news/story.html?id=abff3264-91a0-4d5c-b118-ba4ba1f43ce3>. Accessed December 7, 2007.

Corbella, Licia (2007, February 18). Disturbing Reality Buried. *Calgary Sun.*

Economic Council of Canada (1991). *Economic and Social Impacts of Immigration.* Economic Council of Canada.

Foot, David (2007, October 8). The Human Factor. *Canadian Business.*

Godfrey, Tom (2007, June 21). Toronto Gains Say on Newcomers. *Toronto Sun.* <http://torontosun.com/News/TorontoAndGTA/2007/06/21/4277740-sun.html>. Accessed June 22, 2007.

Gordon, James (2006, May 30). CSIS Admits Security Shortcoming. *National Post.* <http://www.nationalpost.com/news/story.html?id=306b2a86-a000-4c92-9adc-366ce1f40be7>. Accessed December 19, 2007.

Krikorian, Mark (2004). *Jobs Americans Won't Do: Voodoo Economics from the White House.* Center for Immigration Studies. <http://www.cis.org/articles/2004/markoped010704.html>. Accessed December 6, 2007.

Le Goff, Philippe (2004). *Immigration to Canada: What Policy for What Purposes.* Library of Parliament, Parliamentary Research Branch. <http://dsp-psd.pwgsc.gc.ca/Collection-R/LoPBdP/PRB-e/PRB0350-e.pdf>. Accessed December 6, 2007.

Mérette, Marcel (2002). The Bright Side: A Positive View on the Economics of Aging. *Choices* 8, 1 (March). <http://www.irpp.org/choices/archive/vol8no1.pdf>. Accessed December 6, 2007.

O'Neil, Peter (2007, October 19). 'Nannies' Exploit Visa Office to Come to Canada. *National Post.* A13. <http://www.canada.com/nationalpost/news/story.html?id=1f4a6265-6e8e-46d7-829c-89547220f22e>. Accessed November 22, 2007.

Pae, Peter (2007, October 19). Airlines Squeeze Fliers as Profits Soar. *Los Angeles Times.*

Pew Research Center (2007). *World Publics Welcome Global Trade—But Not Immigration*. Pew Research Center. <http://pewglobal.org/reports/display.php?ReportID=258>. Accessed November 23, 2007.

Picot, Garnett, and Feng Hou (2003). *The Rise in Low-Income Rates Among Immigrants in Canada*. Statistics Canada, Business and Labour Market Analysis Division. <http://www.statcan.ca/english/research/11F0019MIE/11F0019MIE2003198.pdf>. Accessed December 6, 2007.

Statistics Canada (2003). *Canada's Ethnocultural Portrait: The Changing Mosaic*. Statistics Canada.

Statistics Canada (2007a). *Losing Ground: The Persistent Growth of Family Poverty in Canada's Largest City*. Statistics Canada.

Statistics Canada (2007b). *Immigration in Canada: A Portrait of the Foreign-Born Population. Census Year 2006*. <www12.statcan.ca/english/census06/analysis/immcit/pdf/97-557-XIE2006001.pdf>.

Stoffman, Daniel (1994). Open Door Travesty. *Saturday Night* (November): 52–60.

Stoffman, Daniel (2002). *Who Gets In*. Macfarlane, Walter & Ross.

The Toronto Star (2007, December 31). Frances Lankin Exposed Reality of Toronto Poverty. A6.

Waldman, Amy (2003, January 14). Masters of Suicide Bombing. *The New York Times*. <http://query.nytimes.com/gst/fullpage.html?res=9E06E1DB1231F937A25752C0A9659C8B63>. Accessed March 31, 2008.

Chapter 2

Immigration and Muslim Extremists in the Post-9/11 World

Salim Mansur

The most important means of countering Muslim extremists in the Western world in the post-9/11 era of Islamist terrorism are intelligence-gathering, policing, and security services. In addition, there are other means within the wider community that can assist this frontline work. These means include the "war of ideas" that must be waged against extremism within the Arab-Muslim world and in Muslim communities in the West through our media and within our education, social, and political institutions. This chapter will focus on what I describe as an exercise in the "sociology of immigration" as it helps to explain the origin and growth of extremism in Muslim immigrant communities in the West. Such a discussion of this aspect is often neglected. The nature of immigration to Canada and other Western liberal democracies needs to be re-examined, as does the extent to which immigration and extremism—in this chapter, Muslim extremism—are connected.

About immigration

There is general agreement in the study of immigration on the nature and causes of migration. Civil unrest and wars, socioeconomic inequality, and poverty are among the main "push" factors in the movement of people across natural or political boundaries. Market needs in terms of skilled and unskilled labour, demographic needs in terms of sustaining or increasing population levels, and the benefits of rich economies are the "pull" factors that attract people to move from depressed zones of the world to prosperous zones.

Canada has been well-served by immigration at various stages in its history—for example, during the populating of the West in the early part of the twentieth century. While questions have been raised regarding the net economic benefit to Canada in the last 25 years, as the earnings of immigrants have fallen well below those of Canadian-born and earlier immigrants, Canadians in general have not taken issue with immigration policy on economic grounds. The view of immigration as a negative-sum phenomenon has been based, for the most part, on culture and race, rather than economics. But since the 1960s, any merit of such arguments has been mostly discounted in the liberal democracies of Europe and North America in favour of economic arguments.

However, here we may recall the warnings of Enoch Powell, a British Member of Parliament, which were most compellingly stated in his deeply controversial speech of April 20, 1968, at a Conservative Party gathering in Birmingham. Four decades later, his speech is remembered mostly for being considered inflammatory by his peers. But the main point of Powell's speech was to show how unrestricted immigration was inexorably and unalterably changing the nature of British society. For Powell, it was about numbers: "bearing in mind that numbers are of the essence: the significance and consequences of an alien element introduced into a country or population are profoundly different according to whether that element is 1% or 10%" (1991: 373–79). Powell's warning went unheeded and he was removed from the Conservative's shadow cabinet. His political career never recovered from the controversy created by his remarks, even though there was much support for his views among voters. Today, Powell's words have a haunting presence in Britain, which was rocked by "homegrown terror" and suicide bombings in London in July 2005. That particular terrorist attack was perpetrated by Muslims extremists who were born in England.

Comparative profile of immigration in the second global century

Let us consider briefly some salient features of immigration to put the consensus on the subject in context, and show why security concerns have placed this consensus under siege since 9/11. In this discussion, I will rely on the work of Jeffrey Williamson (2005) and the figures on mass migration he compiled. Williamson points out that the world is experiencing the second "global century," which began around 1950. In this view, the first global century (based on years for which figures are available) began around 1820 and ended with World War I. During the first global century, barriers to trade and to the flows of labour and capital came down and helped spread prosperity. Between 1914 and 1950, there was a retreat from the gains of the first global century as a result of wars and economic depression. In the second global century, increased and concerted efforts have been made to repair ruptures after the first global century. The end of the Cold War has accelerated the pace of the second global century as globalization has become an irreversible phenomenon.

In terms of immigration, or mass migration from poor to prosperous zones in the second global century, Williamson notes that the annual increase of immigrants to North America and Europe was gradual until the mid-1970s, after which it rose sharply to one million immigrants per year in the 1990s. As Williamson writes, "the absolute numbers by then were similar to those reached during the age of mass migration about a century earlier, but they were smaller relative to the destination coun- try populations that had to absorb them" (2005: 1). His figures reveal that, contrary to popular belief, the number of immigrants entering the United States as a percentage of the population remains well below the peak reached in the first global century. As Williamson notes, "the annual immigration rate fell from 11.6 immigrants per thousand in the 1900s to 0.4 immigrant per thousand in the 1940s, before rising again to four immi- grants per thousand in the 1990s" (2005: 1).

As the proportion of foreign-born people to native population changed, the effects of the immigration flow were felt in the host country. Between 1965 and 2000, the percentage of a host country's total population com- prised of foreign-born people increased from 6% to 13% in North America, and from 2.2% to 7.7% in Europe.[1] The source-area composition of legal immigrants to the United States during this period also shifted dramatically. More than half of those who immigrated between 1951 and 1960 originated from Europe, around 40% were from the Americas (of this number, more than 25% came from Mexico), and just over 6% were from Asia. Between 1991 and 2000, the source-area composition showed a sharp decline from Europe to approximately 15%, from the Americas an increase to under 50% (Mexicans accounted for half of this number), and a dramatic five-fold increase in immigrants from Asia to 30.7%. In the same period, the number immigrants from Africa also rose dramatically (more than six-fold) from 0.6% to 3.9% (Williamson, 2005: 4).

The figures for Canada provided by Statistics Canada are comparable to those in the United States. In 1961, 85.71% of immigrants to Canada were from Europe and 2.0% were from Asia. In 2001, 42.0% were from Europe and 36.5% were from Asia. The huge surge of Asians arriving in North America after 1970 can be partly explained by recognizable push factors, such as wars and the search for economic opportunities, as in other periods of migration growth. But the surge also coincided with and benefited from a transportation revolution that brought transcontinental wide-body jetliners into operation. The economy of travel dramatically changed as a result. First, the cost of traveling declined despite oil price increases in 1973-1974 and 1979, and later the steady rise in fuel prices during the last quarter of the twentieth century. Secondly, transcontinental and transoceanic travel time by airplanes took a fraction of the time spent travelling by sea before wide-body jetliners were introduced in the 1960s.

We have not yet worked out the implications of this revolutionary change in moving people and what it has meant for migration and the receiving host countries. We need to take into account these implications

---

1 For the purpose of this migration study, North America consists of Canada and the United States, and excludes Mexico. Europe includes the former communist countries of Eastern Europe and the former Soviet Union. Population movement has occurred from Eastern Europe and the former Soviet Union into Western Europe; consequently, the percentage of foreign-born people in the western half of Europe is much larger than that of Europe as a whole (Williamson, 2005: 2–3).

in order to determine whether the words "immigrant" and "immigration" carry the same meaning as they did before 1960, or whether we need to introduce new terms such as "migrant worker." In a global economy, such terms may provide a better understanding of why newcomers— in particular, those within Muslim communities in North America and Europe—are resisting integration or assimilation into the host country's political culture.

Immigrant Muslim communities in Canada and the United States

The number of Muslims in Canada and in the United States as a percentage of the total population is still very small but is showing the most rapid growth among religious groups in these countries. A recent Pew Research Center on Muslim Americans estimated that the number of Muslims in the United States, based on the Census Bureau data, is 2.35 million—about 0.8% of a total population of over 302 million (2007: 3). Two-thirds (65%) of adult Muslims in the United States are foreign-born, and 39% have immigrated to the States since 1990.

Similar to the United States, Canada's census data show a relative surge of Muslim newcomers in the 1990s. In 1991, there were 253,265 Muslim Canadians, making up 0.9% of the total population. Ten years later, the Muslim population had doubled. In 2001, there were 579,640 Muslim Canadian, accounting for 2.0% of the Canadian population (Statistics Canada, 2003: 8, 18). In 2006, there were an estimated 700,000 Muslim Canadians, making up 2.2% of the population. The median age of Muslim Canadians is 28 years—the youngest in the country based on religious affiliation—which means that they have the most rapid growth potential of all religious communities.

Immigrants or migrant workers

In the conventional or traditional sense, an immigrant is an individual who leaves his native country—for whatever combination of push or pull factors—for an intended host country with the commitment to permanently adopting it as his country in the fullest meaning, accepting its values, participating in its political culture, and giving it his unreserved loyalty. Before World War II and for sometime until the 1950s, traveling by way of trains or ships took many weeks and entailed considerable expense. This contributed to the psychological aspect of the decision-making involved in starting out as an immigrant. There are many poignant stories of these journeys—stories of leaving behind native lands with some certainty of never returning, and of anticipating the new lands as well the accompanying challenges of settlement and assimilation. Immigration involved cutting one's ties in order to enter a new world. An immigrant was, for the most part, brimming with gratitude for the opportunities open to him that did not exist or were denied him in his native country.

In contrast, a migrant worker remains situated in two countries: his native home and his place of his work. He does not have to make the same choices an immigrant makes, and he is not asked to make these choices by the host country, since his presence is acknowledged as temporary. A migrant worker is not a new phenomenon, although globalization has contributed to the increasing demand for and the supply of migrant workers. For example, this phenomenon is apparent in the oil-rich Persian Gulf states where the economy is sustained by migrant workers.

But what happens when the host country admits migrant workers and allows them to stay on as immigrants? This phenomenon of migrant workers becoming immigrants can be observed in the surge of migration to Europe in recent decades, and the dissonance between the expectations of the host country and the behaviour of newcomers. This surge occurred as push and pull factors coincided. Over the past 30 years, the phenomenon of failed and near-failed states has created a dramatic increase in push factors, resulting in a surge of migrants from states in Asia and North Africa that have a Muslim majority population. The impact of the revolution in transportation also occurred during this period. This revolution made it possible for an individual in Asia, for example, to have his breakfast in Karachi and look for dinner in New York City or Toronto on the same day.

Moreover, the new arrival process an immigrant faces in the host country often does not require him to submit himself to the sort of preparation immigrants of an earlier era did. The documents provided by the host country, which may include accelerated citizenship, can in some cases be papers of convenience that allow the immigrant to reside in his adopted country and earn income there, while still being able to be connected to his native country with which he did not cut his umbilical ties. Most host countries would not require him to do so.

Host country dilemma

Since the late 1960s, host countries—particularly, those in Western Europe—have been squeezed by changes in internal political-cultural debates, and by the arrival of newcomers who are mostly from parts of the world once ruled as colonies by some of these countries. By questioning their country's colonial-imperialist past, as well as racism, fascism, and wars, the 1960s generation in the West began chipping away at their respective national identities. When Deconstruction[2] came into vogue, deconstructing the legacy of the Enlightenment in modern Europe and North America deprived the West of its ability to face the cultural opposition from marginal groups and developing societies. In due course, the weakening of the Western identity left a space to be filled. Since Western liberal democratic societies became more averse to demanding that newcomers embrace any part or the whole of their identity, such identity being subjected to critical reexamination, these newcomers were increasingly left to their own resources to shape their views about themselves in foreign lands.

It has been said that there is a hole at the centre of liberalism, for it does not address the subject of group identity (Fukuyama, 2006). Classical liberalism was concerned with acquiring and defending individual liberty from the clutches of collectivism—that is, politics that are organized around the identity of tribes, nations, castes, class, church, or mosque. Classical liberalism was also a product of Christian Europe. As Europeans chiseled away their national identities in the post-Christian age, they were faced

---

2   Traced back to contemporary French philosopher, Jacques Derrida, Deconstruction began to be used in literary, historical, and cultural studies in the 1960s. The American Heritage Dictionary (2005) defines it as a philosophical movement and theory of literary criticism that questions traditional assumptions about certainty, identity, and truth.

with the problem of reconciling their liberalism and secularism with the group identity of newcomers—especially the group identity of Muslims, which is based on their religion.

The answer to the liberal problem came in the form of multiculturalism, an idea promoted most vigorously in Canada, despite the protests of Québec elitists who wanted the country to remain bicultural. Multiculturalism offered the tantalizing prospect of moving the post-Christian West into an openly pluralist society in which different cultures could coexist harmoniously on the basis of equality, without having to adopt the "melting pot" approach of the United States. This policy of multiculturalism was an invitation to newcomers to maintain their own respective religious-cultural values, while embracing cultural relativism—the belief that all cultures are equal. Western liberals concurred that, given the history of Europe and North America, the West did not possess the moral authority to demand that immigrants reform their cultural values in accordance with the values of the host country in order to be accepted as equal members in Western societies.

But liberalism's silence on group identity and group rights was not a matter of forgetfulness; it was a recognition that when the individual and collective collide, the freedom of the individual takes precedence. By promoting multiculturalism, Western liberals began undermining liberalism, since all groups do not embrace liberal values equally, and Muslims, in particular, remain resistant to the idea of individual rights and gender equality (Lewis, 2004; Meddeb, 2003; UNDP, 2002). In practice, multiculturalism has tended towards a plural "monoculturalism" that allows cultural groups to withdraw into their own spaces (Sen, 2006). The effort of Muslims in the West to secure host countries' recognition of their group rights in law—the rule of *shariah* (Islamic laws)—based on the premise of multiculturalism is not surprising. Denying the demands of the Muslims while subscribing to multiculturalism further complicates the liberal problem.

9/11 and homegrown terrorism

The recent Islamist terrorist attacks on New York City and Washington, DC, were followed by terrorist attacks in Madrid, Amsterdam (the killing of Theo van Gogh), London, and elsewhere, as well as riots in France. Since 9/11, there have also been a number of planned terrorist attacks in the United States, Britain, and Canada that have been foiled. All of these events have their roots in the politics and cultural-political upheavals within the Arab-Muslim world. When four British-born Muslim suicide-bombers attacked London on July 7, 2005, Tony Blair, Britain's Prime Minister, clearly expressed his view on the origin and spread of Islamism—the converting of Islam from a faith-tradition into a political ideology with an emphasis on *jihad* or holy war—in relation to the making of Muslim fanatics who are going to war against the West. Blair noted that "its roots are not superficial, but deep, in the Madrassas of Pakistan, in the extreme forms of Wahhabi doctrine in Saudi Arabia, in the former training camps of al-Qaeda in Afghanistan, in the cauldron of Chechnya, in parts of the politics of most countries in the Middle East and many in Asia; in the extremist minority that now in every European city preach hatred of the West and our way of life" (Blair, 2005).

How far the roots go back is beyond the scope of this chapter, but a number of observations can be made. Large-scale Muslim migration to Europe and North America after the 1970s and during the surge in the 1990s has coincided with the revival of a Muslim fundamentalism that changes into Islamist extremism, and with the retreat in the Arab-Muslim world from its hesitant opening to modern politics based on secular nationalism.

For secular-minded Arabs, the Arab-Israeli war of June 1967 brought a humiliating end to the Pan-Arabism of Egyptian dictator, Gamal Abdel Nasser, and this defeat spurred the revival of Islam as preached by the Muslim Brotherhood and financed by the Saudi Wahhabists. In 1971, Pakistan broke apart in the midst of a brutal civil war, mass killings by the military in East Pakistan (now Bangladesh), and a humiliating military defeat in its war with India. In Iran, the Shah's regime faced increasing opposition from anti-royalists who succeeded in driving the Shah into exile and making it possible for fundamentalist religious forces led by Ayatollah Khomeini to secure power. The former Soviet Union invaded Afghanistan, Iran and Iraq engaged in a long-running war in the 1980s, and many were dislocated as a result of Iraq's occupation of Kuwait. Political instability and violent attacks shook Algeria, and great bloodshed continues in the endless Palestinian-Israeli conflict. These events together created a push factor for Muslims to migrate to the West.

The arrival of Muslims from failed and failing states, which began in the 1970s, occurred as Europe and North America entered a new era of economic expansion in which the West opened doors to immigration from non-traditional areas of the developing world, including the Middle East and North Africa. The slow demographic shift caused by declining birth rates began in this era, as did the full-blown intellectual engagement in deconstructing liberalism. The Muslims who arrived in the West came into this environment and settled as immigrants, but had most of the characteristics of migrant workers.

The new arrivals founded their own institutions for meeting their religious-cultural needs. The most important institution that was built was the mosque, which provided day-care for children and religious education, and became a centre for social networking. Much of this was not entirely new for the West, which had already experienced cycles of earlier migrations of ethnic and religious groups within its own cultural boundaries. What was new about the most recent phase of migration was the new arrivals—in particular, Muslims from the Arab-Muslim countries of Asia and Africa—who came from outside of the West's cultural boundaries and were not prepared to fully accept the host country's culture. In time, Muslims constructed their own cultural wall between the host country and themselves, assisted with funds from oil-rich Arab countries—especially Saudi Arabia. This cultural wall was invisible at first, and no one in the host country paid much attention to what was taking place behind it. It is estimated that, between 1973 and 2003, about $70 billion US was distributed by the Saudi Wahhabi establishment for Islamist missionary work, and a portion of this money flowed into building mosques and related activities of Muslim communities in Europe and North America (Allen, 2006: 277; Alexiev, 2003; Ehrenfeld, 2005; Levitt, 2003).

The Muslim children of the new arrivals who came of age in the 1990s found themselves caught between two worlds—that of their parents, to which they could not return, and that of the West, which their parents did not fully accept. After 9/11, the West began to awaken to the story of these children who were growing into adulthood (Malik, 2007). This generation of youth has been inducted into the globalized version of an historical Islam that harkens back to an idealized and airbrushed seventh century of the Common Era (or the first century of the Islamic calendar), which emphasizes the collective Muslim identity of the *ummah*—the community of believers. This idealized conception is the version of Islam that dwells exclusively and obsessively on the idea of *jihad* (holy war), the religious obligation of Muslims that is preached by the Wahhabi imams or those associated with the politics of the Muslim Brotherhood in mosques that are funded by money solicited from Saudi Arabia, the Gulf states, and Libya, within the Shiite branch of Muslims with support from Khomeini's Iran. This brand of Islam has appealed to rootless young Muslims by providing them with a group identity that carries with it the romanticism of belonging to an international faith-community—the *ummah*—which transcends borders and ethnic markers.

This ideology (Islamism) has given that small segment of Muslims striving for political activism the ready-made cause of opposing the West as an imperial hegemon in its relations with the Muslim world. For the Islamists and their sympathizers, the Muslim world is a victim of the Western world, which has exploited its resources and occupied its lands in the Middle East (Palestine), South Asia (Kashmir), the Caucasus (Chechnya), and Southeast Asia (islands in the Indonesian and the Philippines archipelago). In the post-9/11 world, recruits known as "homegrown terrorists" have come out of the ranks of the Islamists.

Islamism, as an ideology and an organizing principle for religiously-based political parties, eventually supplanted secular-nationalist parties within the Muslim world during the 1990s. In the West, Islamism was imported into Muslim communities, and gradually acquired a presence in the media through organizations such as the Council on Islamic-American Relations in the United States and its branch in Canada, the Muslim Council of Britain, and similar organizations in France and elsewhere in Europe. Its presence was established in educational institutions through campus organizations such as the Muslim Student Association, and in the wider Muslim community through organizations such as the Islamic Society of North America. It was only a matter of time before these Muslim organizations would position themselves in the political arena of host countries, claim to represent Muslim communities as voting blocs, and receive excessive attention from mainstream, established political parties—particularly those on the left—seeking electoral support in return.

Islamism acquired respectability in the West during the last quarter of the twentieth century by escaping scrutiny. Muslim dissenters opposing Islamism remain ostracized within larger Muslim communities and, ironically, are marginalized by the mainstream Western media and political parties. Muslims who embrace liberal values and are at ease in the West are viewed with suspicion by Islamists, and are increasingly intimidated with threats of violence for being opponents of Islamism.

The "Rushdie affair" remains the most prominent cultural indicator of the rise and spread of Islamism in Europe and North America and its assault on the core values of the West. The Rushdie affair first took flight in 1988 in the Muslim communities of Britain, where people publicly burned Salman Rushdie's novel, *The Satanic Verses*, which they condemned as being blasphemous. In February 1989, it became an international affair after Ayatollah Khomeini issued his infamous *fatwa*—a legal opinion of a Muslim religious scholar—calling for Rushdie's murder (Ruthven, 1990).

Conclusion

The West significantly contributed to the increasing prominence of Islamism before 9/11 through its naivety, its ignorance, its openness to the movement of funds from the Middle East to Muslim immigrant communities, and its reluctance to publicly declare Islamism to be an ideology that is unacceptable in liberal democracies. The West also contributed by exhibiting a degree of willingness to accommodate the requirements of Muslim practices and entertaining the argument for permitting the use of *shariah* law.

Many in the West now face the urgent task of examining the extent to which harm caused by the rise of Islamism and homegrown terrorism is self-inflicted. This task will require a frank critical assessment of how multiculturalism has contributed to the erosion of the West's own universal values of individual rights, gender equality, democracy, and secularism. The Islamist war against the West is far from over, and the Islamists are not yet prepared to offer any terms for their surrender—i.e., to cease their waging a campaign against the West. This war has all the signs of generational conflict, similar to the Cold War between the West and the former Soviet Union. Its Cold War experience should be valuable to the West in its conflict with Islamism, for, not unlike Communism, Islamism is internationalist in its scope and agenda. If it confronts Islamism, the West does not face even a remote possibility of military defeat, as was the case with fascism and communism. But by failing to require Muslim immigrants to adapt and abide by Western values, on the same basis as all other immigrants, the West does face the insidious unraveling of the values and political culture that make a free society.

References

Alexiev, Alex (2003). Wahhabism: State-Sponsored Extremism World Wide. Testimony before the US Senate Subcommittee on Terrorism, Technology, and Homeland Security, June 26, 2003. <http://kyl.senate.gov/legis_center/subdocs/sc062603_alexiev.pdf>. Accessed January 15, 2008.

Allen, Charles (2006). *God's Terrorists: The Wahhabi Cult and the Hidden Roots of Modern Jihad*. Da Capo Press.

American Heritage Dictionary of the English Language (2005). *Deconstruction*. Bartleby. <http://www.bartleby.com/61/96/D0079 600.html>.

Blair, Tony (2005, July 16). Full text: Blair speech on terror. *BBC News*. <http://news.bbc.co.uk/2/hi/uk_news/4689363.stm>. Accessed December 19, 2007.

Ehrenfeld, Rachel (2005). *Funding Evil: How Terrorism is Financed and How to Stop It*. Bonus Books.

Fukuyama, Francis (2006). Identity, Immigration, and Liberal Democracy. *Journal of Democracy* 17, 2 (April): 5–20.

Levitt, Matthew (2003). Subversion from Within: Saudi Funding of Islamic Extremist Groups in the United States [Edited version]. Testimony before the US Senate Judiciary Subcommittee on Terrorism, Technology, and Homeland Security, September 10, 2003. Edited version dated October 2, 2003. <http://www.washingtoninstitute.org/templateC05.php?CID=1668>. Accessed January 15, 2008.

Lewis, Bernard (2004). *The Crisis of Islam*. Random House.

Malik, Shiv (2007). My Brother the Bomber. *Prospect* 135 (June): 1–16.

Meddeb, Abdelwahab (2003). *The Malady of Islam*. Basic Books.

Pew Research Center (2007). *Muslim Americans: Middle Class and Mostly Mainstream*. <http://pewresearch.org/assets/pdf/muslim-americans.pdf>. Accessed September 24, 2007.

Powell, Enoch J. (1991). *Reflections of a Statesman: The Writings and Speeches of Enoch Powell*. Bellew.

Ruthven, Malise (1990). *A Satanic Affair: Salman Rushdie and the Rage of Islam*. Chatoo & Windus.

Sen, Amartya (2006). *Identity and Violence: The Illusion of Destiny*. W. W. Norton and Company.

Statistics Canada (2003). *2001 Census: Analysis Series. Religions in Canada*. Statistics Canada. <http://www12.statcan.ca/english/census01/Products/Analytic/companion/rel/pdf/96F0030XIE2001015.pdf>.

United Nations Development Programme [UNDP] (2002). *Arab Human Development Report*. UN Publications.

Williamson, Jeffrey G. (2005). *The Political Economy of World Mass Migration: Comparing Two Global Centuries*. The AEI Press.

Chapter 3

Mass Immigration Defeats Homeland Security

Mark Krikorian

The security challenges posed by immigration are usually viewed as discrete problems that can be addressed through better watch lists, for example, or through additional resources for consular staff who conduct visa interviews. But this is a mistake. Under modern conditions, mass immigration itself is incompatible with security. This is true for two reasons: first, immigration overwhelms our efforts to screen out security threats; and, second, it creates large immigrant communities that shield and incubate terrorists.

In the past, references to the "home front" were metaphorical, intended to create among civilians at home a greater sense of solidarity with soldiers at the war fronts. But advances in communications, transportation, and weapons technology mean that today—and in the indefinite future—the home front is no longer a metaphor, but is an actual war front. As President George W. Bush has said, "Our country is a battlefield in the first war of the 21st century" (White House, 2003).

This new context makes immigration a central issue—perhaps the central issue—in considerations of national security. The staff report of the National Commission on Terrorist Attacks Upon the United States on "terrorist travel" opens by stating, "it is perhaps obvious to state that terrorists cannot plan and carry out attacks in the United States if they are unable to enter the country" (Eldridge et al., 2004). Enemy operatives not only need to enter the United States, or whatever country they are targeting, but also often need to remain under the radar, as it were, for an extended period of time. This means that keeping foreign terrorists out—and keeping them on the run or arresting them if they do get in—is a security imperative.

The fact that the home territories of the developed world are now, as they were in Europe during World War II, genuine theaters of war is a consequence of "asymmetric" or "Fourth-Generation" warfare, in which weaker countries or political forces use unconventional tactics against stronger opponents (Krikorian, 2004). These tactics are not new, but the success of the 9/11 attacks, and the subsequent bombings in London, Madrid, and elsewhere, have made high-casualty attacks on civilians in the homelands of Western nations the chief tactical goal of Islamic terrorists. Neither the United States nor Canada has experienced anything like this before, having long been protected by oceans serving "in the office of a wall," to borrow a phrase from Shakespeare's *Richard II*. But, as the Pentagon's *Quadrennial Defense Review* observed, "geographic insularity no longer confers security for the country" (United States Department of Defense, 2006).

It is important to note that this threat to our territory and our civilian population will not end when radical Islam is tamed or defeated. In all future wars, the enemy will at least consider using our immigration system as a means of attacking us, whether the enemy is North Korea, China, Colombia's Fuerzas Armadas Revolucionarias de Colombia–Ejército del Pueblo (FARC), or any other nation or force with whom we may go to war.

Excessive immigration overwhelms our ability to detect threats

One security problem created by excessive immigration is that it overwhelms a country's ability to detect and exclude malefactors. In the United States, the lead agencies in this task are not part of the military. Instead, they fall under the State Department's Bureau of Consular Affairs (which issues visas) and the immigration-related elements of the Department of Homeland Security (DHS). When we examine the immigration histories of prior terrorists, the need for these agencies to be effective becomes clear. One analysis of the 48 foreign-born al-Qaeda operatives who committed crimes in the United States between 1993 and 2001 (including the 9/11 hijackers) found that they had penetrated almost every part of the immigration system (Camarota, 2002). Of the 48, one-third were in the United States on various temporary visas, one-third were legal residents or naturalized citizens, one-fourth were illegal aliens, and the remainder were former illegal aliens with pending asylum applications. Nearly half of them had, at one point or another, violated ordinary immigration laws. Another examination of 94 foreign-born terrorists in the United States, who belonged to al-Qaeda, Hamas, Hezbollah, and other groups, found that about two-thirds (59) had committed immigration violations prior to or in conjunction with taking part in terrorist activity, and some had multiple violations (Kephart, 2005).

These statistics demonstrate that strict enforcement of regular immigration laws could yield significant security benefits by keeping terrorists out and making it harder for them to operate. Strict enforcement could also result in the arrest of terrorists who are already here, thus disrupting conspiracies and providing subjects for interrogation. This enforcement is related to but separate from security-specific tools such as watch lists.

The immigration-control network

The immigration-control network has three layers of defense: (1) overseas, where visas are issued; (2) at the border, including inspection points at air, sea, and land ports of entry, as well as the long stretches between such entry points; and (3) in the interior of the country. Each of these layers faces huge, unmanageable demand, which breeds pervasive fraud and leads overwhelmed administrators to wave people through without adequate scrutiny. In the nineteenth century, it did not matter as much how effectively aliens were screened—after all, how much damage could a gang of Bolsheviks or anarchists do, given the primitive communications, transportation, and weapons technologies of the time? But today's volume of immigration simply cannot be subjected to the level of scrutiny that is needed because of the modern security environment.

Security filters overseas

The first of the three security filters is the responsibility of visa officers working for the State Department, which has been described by one writer as "America's other Border Patrol" (Wenzel, 2000). This layer is particularly important because the closer a foreigner is to the United States, the greater the practical difficulty of keeping him out. Rejecting a visa applicant who lives abroad is much easier than turning away a foreigner who has already made his way to the border because the burden of proof for turning him away increases.

However, the most difficult task is finding and removing people who have already come into the United States. In 2005, about 800 visa officers issued around six million visas to foreigners, an average of about 7,500 visas per officer, or roughly one visa issued every 15 minutes. Because of the large number of permanent and temporary visas allowed by current legislation, officers seldom have more than a few minutes to decide a case, leading to staggering rates of failure on the part of the officer to keep terrorists from entering. To wit, at least four million people who entered the United States with "temporary" visas simply stayed as illegal aliens after their time ran out (United States Department of State, 2006). In addition, an unknown number of people simply lied to obtain permanent immigrant visas.

The claim that proper immigration scrutiny would yield security benefits is not merely a supposition. Investigative reporter Joel Mowbray acquired copies of 15 of the 19 visa applications made by the 9/11 hijackers, and found that every application should have been rejected on ordinary, non-security grounds (2002, Oct. 28). They were improperly completed, included obviously absurd answers to questions, and the applicants were all young, unattached men with no income—precisely the kind of people who are likely to become illegal aliens if permitted to enter the United States.

The State Department, like any government agency, complains that its resources are inadequate for the job, and it is certainly correct. But even massive increases in personnel—beyond anything that is actually feasible—would not ensure the proper vetting of applicants at the current level of admissions. The staff increases that have taken place since 9/11 are not what they seem, since many of the new officers are simply replacing locally hired foreign staff who never should have been part of the visa process in the first place.

The only way that the United States will ever be able to have a visa system that is appropriate, given modern security needs, is by reducing the number of immigrant and non-immigrant visas available. Even the State Department recognizes the trade-off between volume and quality. One staff report for the National Commission on Terrorist Attacks upon the United States noted that "quality decisions can make the process less efficient, and, in the context of declining staff, posts have often been forced to choose efficiency over quality" (Eldridge et al., 2004). The report suggested that efficiency could be increased by approving a larger portion of non-immigrant (temporary) visas without interviewing the applicant—the exact opposite of what security demands.

Security at the border

The second layer of the immigration security filter is at the border, where the overload is even worse than at the visa offices abroad. In 2004, about 180 million foreigners were admitted into the United States as non-immigrants—visitors of all kinds—and that is only an estimate because the overwhelming majority were Mexicans and Canadians whose entry was not recorded (Grieco, 2007; United States Customs and Border Protection, 2006; United States Department of Homeland Security, 2006). In addition, about 169 million Americans and 75 million permanent residents (green card holders) returned from abroad (US Department of Homeland Security, Office of Immigration Statistics, 2006).[1] Of the 32 million entries by foreigners that were actually recorded in 2005, about 24 million were tourists and nearly five million were business travelers. As well, in between

---

1   These figures do not represent the number of individuals who crossed the border because these numbers include people who travelled back and forth across the border and thus were counted more than once.

ports of entry, mostly along the Mexican border, more than 1.1 million foreigners were arrested by the Border Patrol while trying to sneak in.

This massive workload has led to the same response as that in the visa offices overseas—a collective shrug by a demoralized bureaucracy and the normalization of massive lawbreaking by both inspectors and Border Patrol agents. At ports of entry, inspectors are simply unable to do their jobs properly. Referring to the busiest crossing on the entire northern border, a 2006 report noted that "US and Canadian inspectors on the Ambassador Bridge [in Detroit] and elsewhere say they are routinely told by supervisors to wave vehicles through checkpoints without scrutiny to satisfy commercial interests" (Audi, 2006, Mar. 29). At airports, when the inspectors' computers are down, foreign visitors are admitted without being checked against the various watch lists because it would take too long and would lead to complaints from the airlines.

The overload is dealt with a little differently at ports of entry on the Mexican border. There, Mexicans are issued a "Border-Crossing Card"—colloquially known as a "laser visa"—for short local trips to shop or visit relatives. These are modern, high-tech cards with digitized fingerprints and the like, but they are almost never scanned because it would slow down traffic (United States Department of Homeland Security, 2005). The holders simply show the cards to the border inspectors as they pass through, which results in massive fraud, both through the use of fake cards and the use of genuine cards that belong to others. This is a major vulnerability because half of all non-immigrant entries by foreigners into the United States are Mexicans using a Border-Crossing Card.

The Border Patrol deals with its own massive workload by simply giving most Mexican border-jumpers what is called a "voluntary return"—i.e., the alien waives a hearing in exchange for not having a formal deportation on his record, which would make any subsequent penetration of the United States a felony. In other words, border policing is much like the old Soviet joke: "we pretend to work and they pretend to pay us." The Border Patrol goes through the motions of law enforcement but does not actually punish anyone.

Border failures caused by overload have already had security consequences. For instance, the immigration inspector in Miami—one of the nation's busiest international airports—who screened Mohammed Atta's return to the United States from Spain in January 2001 said "he knew that if he took more time than 45 seconds to determine a visitor's admissibility or if he made too many referrals to secondary inspection, he could receive a poor performance appraisal" (Eldridge et al., 2004: 17). Nonetheless, he referred Atta to "secondary inspection" for further scrutiny, after which Atta was eventually admitted, despite his lack of the proper documents and despite his having overstayed his visa during his previous visit. Steven Camarota (2002) notes that "the scale of illegal immigration creates a tacit acceptance by law enforcement, policy makers, and even the INS [Immigration and Naturalization Service] itself. For example, it was far easier for an immigration inspector to allow Mohammed Atta back into the country even though he overstayed his visa in January 2001 knowing that there have been millions of overstayed visas in the past decade and policy makers had done nothing about it."

Security at home

The third layer of immigration control is inside the country. Similar to the other two layers, the overload in this layer also results from a lack of enforcement. Because there so many illegal aliens already in the United States, the immigration enforcement bureaucracy simply goes through the motions of doing its job, but seldom attempts to actually reduce illegal immigration.

In addition to illegal immigration, this third layer of immigration control is also overloaded because of excessive legal immigration. While it may seem that terrorists would require only physical access to the United States—even as illegal aliens—this is not the case. As a former staff member of the 9/11 Commission has written, "once within US borders, terrorists seek to stay. Doing so with the appearance of legality helps ensure long-term operational stability" (Kephart, 2005).

Think of a foreigner's access to the United States as a ladder. At the bottom are those outside the United States, and at the top are immigrants who have become naturalized American citizens. Visas and border control are essential because they help keep malefactors from getting into the country in the first place. But once in, terrorists seek to climb up the ladder—from illegal alien to short-term visitor, long-term visitor, permanent resident, and finally American citizen—thereby gaining additional opportunities with each step. Every time a foreigner tries to take another step up the ladder, the authorities—in this case, United States Citizenship and Immigration Services (USCIS), a part of the Department of Homeland Security (DHS)—have another chance to screen him for security problems.

Unfortunately, massive overload makes proper screening impossible. In 2005, USCIS received 6.3 million applications for 50 different kinds of immigration benefits and adjudicated 7.5 million applications (United States Government Accountability Office, 2006). On any given day, USCIS processes 30,000 applications, conducts 135,000 national security background checks, and answers 82,000 telephone inquiries (United States Department of Homeland Security, US Citizenship and Immigration Services, 2005). The immigration bureaucracy is so utterly overwhelmed that even DHS Secretary Michael Chertoff was forced to concede that "parts of the system have nearly collapsed under the weight of numbers" (Chertoff, 2005).

A particularly outrageous example of what happens if a bureaucracy becomes overloaded occurred in 2003 when contract workers at an immigration processing center in California decided to cope with the ongoing tide of paperwork by simply shredding immigration documents in order to wipe out a 90,000-document backlog there. After two months of shredding, the backlog was cleared, and they kept shredding as new applications came in to prevent the backlog from recurring (Broder, 2003, Jan. 31).

We can shake our heads at the irresponsibility of the people who would do such a thing, but the real problem is systemic; it is the result of excessive immigration. According to one government report,

> It would be impossible for USCIS to verify all of the key information or interview all individuals related to the millions of applications it adjudicates each year—approximately 7.5 million applications in fiscal year 2005—without seriously compromising its service-related objectives. (United States Government Accountability Office, 2006)

Excessive immigration reinforces enclaves

The foregoing discussion examined how excessive immigration has clogged the plumbing of a modern immigration control system. Another reason why high immigration compromises security is that it creates and constantly reinforces communities of foreigners that unwittingly but unavoidably provide cover and incubation for attackers. In his address to Congress after the 9/11 attacks, President George W. Bush offered an apt analogy: "Al-Qaeda is to terror what the Mafia is to crime" (Bush, 2001). This comparison is instructive. During the great wave of immigration around the turn of the century, and for some time after immigration was stopped in the 1920s, law enforcement had very little luck with penetrating the Mafia. This was because Mafia-affiliated immigrants lived in enclaves, had limited knowledge of English, were suspicious of government institutions, and clung to Old World prejudices and attitudes such as *omerta*—the Sicilian code of silence. But with the end of mass immigration, the assimilation of Italian immigrants and their children accelerated, and the offspring of the immigrants developed a sense of genuine membership and ownership in America—what John Fonte (2003) of the Hudson Institute calls "patriotic assimilation." This process eliminated the enclaves in which the Mafia had been able to develop, allowing law enforcement to become more effective and eventually cripple the Mafia.

The relevance of this phenomenon to security concerns is clear. As the chief intelligence officer for the DHS has said, "As previous attacks indicate, overseas extremists do not operate in a vacuum and are often linked with criminal and smuggling networks—usually connected with resident populations from their countries of origin" (Allen, 2007).

Even worse than the role immigrant enclaves play in shielding terrorists is their role in recruiting and incubating new ones. One disturbing example is that of Lackawanna, New York, where six Yemeni Americans—five of them born in the United States to immigrant parents and raised in an immigrant community—were arrested in 2002 for operating an al-Qaeda terrorist sleeper cell. The six arrested men had traveled to Pakistan in 2001, ostensibly for religious training, but actually went to an al-Qaeda terrorist training camp in Afghanistan. All of them are serving prison terms for providing material support to terrorism. The seventh member of the cell—a naturalized American citizen—did not return after training in Afghanistan, was later jailed in Yemen, and escaped from prison in 2006. The ringleader of the cell, another American citizen, was killed in Yemen by the CIA in 2002.

The community that bred this cell has been shaped largely by immigration. As the local paper reported,

> This is a piece of ethnic America where the Arabic-speaking Al Jazeera television station is beamed in from Qatar through satellite dishes to Yemenite-American homes; where young children answer "Salaam" when the cell phone rings, while older children travel to the Middle East to meet their future husband or wife; where soccer moms don't seem to exist, and where girls don't get to play soccer—or, as some would say, football. (*The Buffalo News*, 2002, Sep. 23)

Between 1996 and 2005, more than 18,000 Yemenis immigrated legally to the United States. In Lackawanna, the Arab population ballooned by 175% during the 1990s. The median household income in the Yemeni neighbourhood is currently 20% lower than the median in Lackawanna as a whole (*The Buffalo News*, 2002, Sep. 18).

A report at the time of the Lackawanna arrests said it was likely that more such groups existed among undigested immigrant communities. "Federal officials say privately that there could be dozens of similar cells across the country, together posing a grave danger to national security. They believe that such cells tend to be concentrated in communities with large Arab populations, such as Detroit" (*The Buffalo News*, 2002, Sep. 18).

Of course, Muslim immigrant communities are not alone in exhibiting characteristics that may shield or even incubate criminality. For instance, as criminologist Ko-lin Chin has written, "the isolation of the Chinese community, the inability of American law enforcement authorities to penetrate the Chinese criminal underworld, and the reluctance of Chinese victims to come forward for help, all conspire to enable Chinese gangs to endure" (1996: 18). The solution for Muslim immigrant communities is the same for these other ethnic groups. William Kleinknecht, author of *The New Ethnic Mobs*, notes that "If the mass immigration of Chinese should come to a halt, the Chinese gangster may disappear in a blaze of assimilation after a couple of decades" (1996: 292).

Conclusion

The idea that there is a connection between immigration and terrorism has been dismissed by many policy makers and activists. For instance, then INS Commissioner James Ziglar piously observed shortly after 9/11, "We're not talking about immigration, we're talking about evil" (United States Department of State, 2001). Similarly, Cecilia Munoz of the National Council of La Raza said, "There's no relationship between immigration and terrorism" (Bunis, 2001, Sep. 13). Referring to 9/11, Jeanne Butterfield, executive director of the American Immigration Lawyers Association and former head of the Marxist Palestine Solidarity Committee, echoed this denial of reality: "I don't think the events of last week can be attributed to the failure of our immigration laws" (Martin, 2001, Sep. 19).

Indeed, to argue that a reduction in the level of immigration is necessary for homeland security may seem opportunistic, similar to how agricultural lobbyists used 9/11 to argue for farm subsidies by peddling the idea of "food security." After all, the only immigrants who pose a threat to the security of the United States are Muslim extremists. But it is clear that under modern conditions of asymmetric warfare, mass immigration itself represents a significant security threat, both by overwhelming the United States' ability to filter out undesirables and by constantly refreshing the immigrant communities that serve as havens for malefactors. While there is no question that other security measures are also needed—such as improved intelligence gathering overseas, greater cooperation with foreign governments, and continued military operations—if the United States does not reduce the levels of both permanent and temporary immigration, it leaves itself open to the enemy.

References

Allen, Charles E. (2007). Statement of Charles E. Allen, Assistant Secretary for Intelligence and Analysis, Chief Intelligence Officer, Department of Homeland Security, before the Select Committee on Intelligence, United States House of Representatives, January 18, 2007.

Audi, Tamara (2006, March 29). Inspectors: Security Lags When Traffic Jams. *Detroit Free Press.*

Broder, John M. (2003, January 31). Shredder Ended Work Backlog, US Says. *The New York Times.* <http://query.nytimes.com/gst/fullpage.html?res=9C0DE6DE1738F932A05752C0A9659C8B63>. Accessed December 13, 2007.

The Buffalo News (2002, September 18). On Call to Aid al-Qaida from Unlikely Places. A1.

The Buffalo News (2002, September 23). A Separate World. A1.

Bunis, Dena (2001, September 13). Amnesty May Lose Support: Backers Fear Concerns about Border Security will Hurt Their Cause. *The Orange County Register.*

Bush, George W. (2001). Address to a Joint Session of Congress and the American People, the White House, September 20, 2001. <http://www.whitehouse.gov/news/releases/2001/09/20010920-8.html>. Accessed December 13, 2007.

Camarota, Steven A. (2002). *The Open Door: How Militant Islamic Terrorists Entered and Remained in the United States, 1993-2001.* Center for Immigration Studies Paper No. 21. <http://www.cis.org/articles/2002/theopendoor.pdf>. Accessed December 13, 2007.

Chertoff, Michael (2005). Statement of Secretary Michael Chertoff, US Department of Homeland Security, before the United States Senate Judiciary Committee, Washington, DC, October 18, 2005. <http://judiciary.senate.gov/testimony.cfm?id=1634&wit_id=66>. Accessed December 13, 2007.

Chin, Ko-lin (1996). *Chinatown Gangs*. Oxford University Press.

Eldridge, Thomas R., Susan Ginsburg, Walter T. Hempel II, Janice L. Kephart, and Kelly Moore (2004). *9/11 and Terrorist Travel: Staff Report of the National Commission on Terrorist Attacks Upon the United States*. National Commission on Terrorist Attacks upon the United States. <http://www.9-11commission.gov/staff_statements/911_TerrTrav_Monograph.pdf>. Accessed December 13, 2007.

Fonte, John (2003). *We Need a Patriotic Assimilation Policy*. Hudson Institute. <http://www.hudson.org/index.cfm?fuseaction=publication_details&id=2770>.

Grieco, Elizabeth M. (2007). *Temporary Admissions of Non-immigrants to the United States: 2005*. United States Department of Homeland Security, Office of Immigration Statistics. <http://www.dhs.gov/xlibrary/assets/statistics/publications/NI_FR_2006_508_final.pdf>. Accessed December 13, 2007.

Kephart, Janice L. (2005). *Immigration and Terrorism: Moving Beyond the 9/11 Staff Report on Terrorist Travel*. Center for Immigration Studies Paper No. 24. <http://www.cis.org/articles/2005/kephart.pdf>. Accessed December 13, 2007.

Kleinknecht, William (1996). *The New Ethnic Mobs: The Changing Face of Organized Crime in America*. The Free Press.

Krikorian, Mark (2002, July 3). Eternal Vigilance: Handing Out Green Cards is a Security Matter. *National Review Online*. <http://

www.nationalreview.com/comment/comment-krikorian072302.asp>.
Accessed December 13, 2007.

Krikorian, Mark (2004). Keeping Terror Out: Immigration Policy and
Asymmetric Warfare. *The National Interest* 75 (Spring): 1–9.

Martin, Gary (2001, September 19). Lawmakers Want Tighter Border.
The San Antonio Express-News. A8.

Mowbray, Joel (2002, October 28). Visas for Terrorists: They were Ill-
prepared. They were Laughable. They were Approved. *National Review*.
<http://findarticles.com/p/articles/mi_m1282/is_20_54/ai_92712403>.

United States Customs and Border Protection (2006). *National
Workload Statistics*. <http://www.cbp.gov/xp/cgov/toolbox/about/
accomplish/national_workload_stats.xml>. Last updated May 25, 2006.

United States Department of Defense (2006). *Quadrennial Defense
Review Report*. Office of the Under Secretary of Defense (Policy).
<http://www.defenselink.mil/qdr/report/Report20060203.pdf>.

United States Department of Homeland Security [DHS] (2006).
FY04 Crossing Volume. Fax received by author from United States
Department of Homeland Security official, August 17, 2006.

United States Department of Homeland Security, Office of Inspector
General (2005). *Implementation of the United States Visitor and
Immigrant Status Indicator Technology Program at Land Border
Ports of Entry*. Department of Homeland Security, Office of Inspector
General, OIG-05-11. <http://www.dhs.gov/xoig/assets/mgmtrpts/
OIG_05-11_Feb05.pdf>.

United States Department of Homeland Security, Office of Immigration
Statistics (2006). *2005 Yearbook of Immigration Statistics*. <http://www.dhs.
gov/xlibrary/assets/statistics/yearbook/2005/OIS_2005_Yearbook.pdf>.

United States Department of Homeland Security, US Citizenship and Immigration Services (2005). *Fact Sheet: A Day in the Life of USCIS.* <http://www.uscis.gov/files/nativedocuments/dayinlife_050629.pdf>.

United States Department of State (2001). *Attorney General Ashcroft Briefing on New Anti-Terrorism Immigration Policies.* Last updated October 31, 2001.

United States Department of State (2006). *Report of the Visa Office 2006.* United States Department of State, Bureau of Consular Affairs. <http://travel.state.gov/visa/frvi/statistics/statistics_1476.html>.

United States Government Accountability Office (2006). *Immigration Benefits: Additional Controls and a Sanctions Strategy Could Enhance DHS's Ability to Control Benefit Fraud.* Government Accountability Office, GAO-06-259. <http://www.gao.gov/new.items/d06259.pdf>. Accessed December 13, 2007.

Wenzel, Nikolai (2000). *America's Other Border Patrol: The State Department's Consular Corps and its Role in US Immigration.* Center for Immigration Studies Backgrounder. <http://www.cis.org/articles/2000/back800.pdf>. Accessed December 13, 2007.

White House (2003). President Discusses the Future of Iraq. News release (February 26). White House, Office of the Press Secretary. <http://www.whitehouse.gov/news/releases/2003/02/20030226-11.html>. Accessed December 10, 2007.

Chapter 4

Canada's Broken Refugee Policy System

Stephen Gallagher

Compared to other countries in the developed world, Canada is soft on illegal immigration. It is easier for an irregular migrant to secure permanent resident status in Canada than in any other developed country. In Canada, the primary policy system that accomplishes the transition from irregular migrant to resident status is the extended refugee policy system. An irregular migrant is "a person without legal status in a transit or host country owing to illegal entry or the expiry of his/her visa" (International Labour Organization, 2005), and the extended refugee system is the web of entry, determination, appeal, and removal institutions tasked with processing those who make a refugee claim in Canada. Aside from infrequent migrant amnesties, refugee systems are the primary gateway through which irregular migrants gain entrance to the developed world. Compared to other countries, the unparalleled generosity of the Canadian extended refugee system, along with the absence of disincentives to abuse, makes it undeniably attractive to status-seeking irregular migrants, and clearly stimulates what is described in other countries as abuse and illegal immigration.

However, in Canada, there is an absence of political and partisan debate on the issue of abuse of the refugee system. In fact, there is an absence of political and partisan debate on immigration policy in general. The reason for this lack of debate is connected to Canada's self-image of multiculturalism, openness, and tolerance, which is used by partisan actors to gain electoral advantage. In this way, political actors can avoid the migration debate and remain unwilling to implement and sustain effective migration management instruments. Meanwhile, well-funded and well-organized advocacy and special interest groups connected to the immigration field work tirelessly to ensure that the government lives up to its pro-immigration rhetoric. The result is a maze of migration policies that merely regularizes the bulk of the irregular migrant influx. This has the political benefit of avoiding the contentious and difficult process of deporting large numbers of illegal immigrants.

The problems with Canada's extended refugee policy system are well-known to the Canadian government. All of the recent Ministers of Citizenship and Immigration have stated a desire to more effectively "balance" Canada's international obligations towards those fleeing persecution with Canada's interest in controlling irregular migration. To follow through on any significant reform initiative, however, would be controversial and difficult in the current context because the current government, led by the Conservative Party, holds a minority in the House of Commons, and is actively pursuing the support of voters who have recently become Canadians (Ivison and Hanes, 2007, Jan. 6). In the recent past, members of the federal Liberal Party have had success labeling the Conservative Party and its predecessors as racist and anti-immigration because of their criticisms of refugee policy. Given a new opportunity, these Liberals would likely renew their attacks (Ivison, 2007, Feb. 23).

The federal government's Safe Third Country Agreement (STCA) has been Canada's primary response to an influx of approximately 300,000 refugee claimants received in the last decade (UNHCR-PDU, 2004: table 2). This agreement with the United States, which is intended to allocate to the first country entered the responsibility to hear a refugee claim, came into force in December 2004 (Canada, 2004, Nov. 3). But the STCA system has structural flaws and is failing to protect Canada's refugee claimant reception and determination processes from excessive cost, abuse, and overload.

In the absence of an effective entry management mechanism, such as a *functional* safe third country policy, the Canadian government may wish to consider adopting a manifestly unfounded policy or a safe country of origin policy. A manifestly unfounded policy involves asking a claimant upon arrival whether he or she has any claim whatsoever. If not, the individual is quickly deported. Such a system is widespread in Europe, including the United Kingdom where it is called a "clearly unfounded policy." A safe country of origin policy allows for the expedited review of claimants from countries that are not normally associated with persecution. Reforming Canada's refugee determination system by adopting both of these policies would involve changes to Canada's Immigration and Refugee Board (IRB), the administrative tribunal that reviews refugee claims. The objective of such reform would be to make the determination process "faster, fairer, and firmer," in the words of the United Kingdom's reform mantra.

However, fundamental reform of the refugee system is not likely to take place in the near future because it would not be politically expedient. The attitude generally held by the media, most society-based commentators, and the advocacy community is that the main problem with the refugee system relates to "first instance" determination—the first examination of a refugee's claim—inconsistencies and errors. According to them, rejected claimants do not have an opportunity to appeal on the merits of their claim. The rise and success of the "church sanctuary movement" provides evidence of the difficulties the government would likely face if it pursues a migration control agenda. To make matters more difficult, the process of removing rejected claimants is very complex, attracts significant societal criticism, and the government appears very willing to address individual and group cases with special immigration deals.

Reform of the refugee system is also unlikely because the number of refugee claims in Canada in 2004-2006 was relatively low compared to 1999-2003, as has been the case in most of the developed world. As a result, political pressure to reform the system has lessoned, and the government has become more willing to seek ad hoc solutions to irregular migration problems.

In all, Canada presents a good example of the workings of "client politics"—the benefits of Canada's open door system are highly concentrated in new-Canadian communities and the immigration and rights activist industries, while the costs are diffused broadly across the entire political and social system (Freeman, 2003: 5). This means that a defense of the public's interest in having an effectively managed migration system is, for the most part, left up to partisan actors who are constrained by the electoral and expediency concerns noted above. To a great extent, this explains why the existing Parliamentary, special interest, and electoral situation does not provide decision makers with an environment conducive to reform, regardless of both the cost and dysfunctionality of the existing system and the common understanding that reform is needed to address the incentives in the existing system that "pull" irregular migrants. Consequently, in the foreseeable future, Canada's costly extended refugee policy system will continue to attract significant numbers of irregular migrants and will be vulnerable to overload. Moreover, if efforts to reform the immigration system in the United States fail, Canada may see a major influx of status-seeking migrants in the near future. In fact, there are already signs that such an influx is beginning to take shape as large numbers of irregular migrants in the United States are reportedly considering traveling to Canada to make a refugee claim (Davey and Goodnough, 2007, Sep. 21).

The asylum migration issue and the politics of entry

A large part of the difficulty that the government faces with respect to irregular migration control measures results from the fact that the media and the general public view immigration positively, and they generally fail to distinguish between selected immigrants or resettlement refugees, and self-selected in-country refugee claimants or asylum seekers. In fact, refugee claimants are often simply referred to as "refugees" by the media; the term "asylum seeker" is not in popular usage. Even failed asylum seekers, such as those who have been given church sanctuary, are often referred to either as "refugees" (*Montreal Gazette*, 2004, Dec. 15) or "rejected refugees." Both of these terms imply that the migrant possesses a legitimate residency claim. Because of these biases, a defence of migration management efforts is difficult. Even clear cases of abuse may be framed and vilified as anti-refugee, anti-immigrant, and "un-Canadian" by advocacy groups and those who profit from gaining status for foreigners in Canada.

Canada is out of step with other countries that have "high volume" refugee determination systems because it does not fully utilize the available range of migration management instruments, such as safe country of origin, application time limits, and "last in-first out" policies (Legomsky, 1996). These entry controls include a mix of three types of policies: (1) a detention policy; (2) a manifestly unfounded policy; and (3) a safe third country policy.

A willingness to detain

In Australia, illegally arriving refugee claimants are detained until their claim is fully processed. In the United States, the law states that illegal arrivals must be detained and removed. If they make an asylum claim, they should be detained until the process is complete (although many if not most refugee claimants are paroled). In Canada, an illegal entrant who makes a refugee claim at a point of entry is usually not detained. While there is little doubt that other countries use detention and reception centers as both a deterrent to entry and a means by which to avoid claimant integration prior to determination, this is simply not practical in Canada because the extended refugee process takes so long to complete. In addition, detention initiatives attract criticism, even in the national security arena. For example, in February 2005, Canada's Federal Court forced the government to release Adil Charkaoui, an asylum seeker, on $50,000 bail. Charkaoui was being held under a "security certificate," which allows the government to detain non-Canadian citizens who are considered to be threats to national security. Since 2001, certificates have been issued for only six people, and not one of them has been unwillingly deported.

A manifestly unfounded policy

Unlike other refugee-hosting countries in the developed world, Canada has no manifestly unfounded policy. In the United States, this policy requires those who arrive illegally and make a refugee claim to have a "credible fear" of persecution in order to be granted a full assessment of their claim. If they cannot convince an asylum officer or an immigration judge that they have a credible fear, they can be deported within a matter of days. In August 2004, this "expedited removal" policy was first applied to illegal entrants seeking entrance to the United States at the Canadian land border. In Canada, however, almost anyone from anywhere can make a refugee claim for almost any reason, even if it is a transparent attempt to slow a removal process. For example, a man who argued that if he remained in Poland he would relapse into alcoholism could not be denied access to a full refugee determination hearing, including a federal court review (Freeze, 2005, Sep. 23). Although Canada does not have a manifestly unfounded policy, claimants face, at the very outset, a security screening to determine if they are eligible to enter the refugee process. But if they are found to be ineligible, that does not mean a speedy removal, or, as the Charkaoui case shows, detention until a decision is made. It is not surprising that when the government sought to quickly deport a well-known holocaust-denier, Ernst Zundel, after he was deported from the United States and made a refugee claim on entry to Canada, they chose to use the security certificate route. This proved unsuccessful when the process became bogged down in court. In the end, after two years in detention, Zundel agreed to be deported (*The Globe and Mail*, 2005, Mar. 2). In practice, there is simply no mechanism in Canadian law that allows the government to quickly deport a reluctant foreign national who has made a refugee claim.

A safe third country policy

A country may also regulate entry by establishing a safe third country policy. Having such a policy means, for example, that if a refugee claimant entered one of the 27 European Union countries from another EU country, only the first country entered has the responsibility to hear the claim. In the absence of such a policy, the majority of asylum seekers in Europe would likely end up in Germany or the United Kingdom, where jobs, family, and friends are likely to be found.

In 2001, Canada signed a safe third country agreement with the United States, expecting that it would become operational by the end of 2002. The agreement finally came into force in December 2004. The agreement matters little to the United States because there are so few people passing through Canada to make a refugee claim in the United States. In fact, in 2005, the first year of operation, only 66 claims were made (Citizenship and Immigration Canada, 2006: 44). In addition, relatively few of the refugee claimants who pass through the United States to reach Canada would have much chance of being recognized in the United States or in any other country for that matter. For example, in 2004, Canada's top two refugee claimant source countries were Columbia and Mexico, which together lodged more claims in Canada than in the United States (UNHCR-PGDS, 2005: table 8). Their recognition rates in Canada were 86% and 33% respectively compared to 44.6% and 2.8% in the United States. That same year, Canada's recognition rate of claimants from China, one of Canada's top source countries in 2004, was roughly double the recognition rate in the United States. These figures illustrate the need for Canada to legislate a manifestly unfounded policy. In 2005 and 2006, this pattern persisted with one change: Columbia fell to third place as a source country after China (UNHCR-DS, 2007a).

Clearly, the absence of a functional safe third country policy is a fundamental problem with Canada's refugee system. However, it is a problem that will be very difficult to address because refugee lawyers and advocates can rightly claim that no country, and certainly not the United States, is as generous to refugee claimants in terms of reception conditions and recognition rates. For example, Amnesty International's 2005 report claims that the United States is not a "safe protection partner" (*Ottawa Citizen*, 2005, May 25).

Of course, much of this concern about the impact of the agreement is propagandistic. As I have argued elsewhere, the current agreement with the United States is fundamentally flawed as an instrument of migration management and will not have much of an impact on the flow of refugee claims, except possibly as a psychological deterrent (Gallagher, 2003). In a recent report, the Canadian government reported that, in 2005, only 303 claims out of a total of 19,735 claims, 4,033 of which were made at the border, were declared "ineligible" to make a refugee claim in Canada because of the agreement. In 3,254 cases, claimants at the border were able to invoke an exception in the agreement, such as the presence of a family member residing in Canada (Citizenship and Immigration Canada, 2006: 31).

There are many reasons why a refugee claimant would want to pass through the United States or Europe to come to Canada. The claimant may have family or friends in Canada, which is why more than half of the refugee claims in Canada are made inland by claimants who may have originally obtained a legal visitor's visa. The visa screening mechanism makes every effort to block potential "overstayers," but the government is often criticized for excesses in this effort.

Another benefit of making a refugee claim in Canada is that a claimant can apply to work in Canada while awaiting a decision. To obtain a work permit, the claimant must not be self-supporting. The reason behind this policy is the idea that allowing a claimant to work will reduce support costs for the government. Nevertheless, support costs are high in any case because refugee claimants often lack language or technical skills. For this reason, governments often provide language training, as well as a range of educational opportunities to claimants. Another attractive benefit of making a claim in Canada is that, unlike the United States, refugee claimants often have access to free legal assistance in order to prepare their cases.

Ultimately, the most important attraction of Canada, which will be discussed further below, is that for many migrants from the developing world, making a refugee claim is an effective conduit for securing residence status in Canada. Put simply, Canada's existing extended refugee policy system guarantees a few years stay in Canada and holds the promise of a prosperous new life in a wealthy, developed country.

The Immigration and Refugee Board

The core weakness in Canada's migration management regime is the Immigration and Refugee Board (IRB). This board makes the first assessment as to whether an individual is a legitimate refugee. The process of making this decision requires an independent decision maker—an IRB board member—to hold a formal hearing on whether a claimant should be recognized as a United Nations' "convention" refugee. No other country implements this type of "first instance" refugee determination process. Close to 20 years of the author's experience with the IRB shows that, regardless of the presence of so many hardworking and professional individuals, this system produces inconsistent decisions, is administratively unwieldy, overly legalistic, open to abuse, and slow. Much effort has gone into addressing these concerns and some improvement can be observed. However, there remains a number problems associated with the independent first instance approach. Some of these issues could be remedied if public officials conducted the first instance determination process. The decision making of an IRB board member is much less likely to be consistent than that of a public official. Unlike an IRB board member, a public official can be rigorously trained and carefully monitored to ensure that his decisions accurately reflect government policy. Examples of decision making inconsistency within the current independent process are numerous and well documented (Jimenez, 2004, July 24).

Moreover, unlike the independent decision maker, a public official can be required to meet targets. Backlogs are a fact of life at the IRB. Although refugee determination work is challenging and requires a high level of diligence, the patronage appointment system has been a focus of criticism since the creation of the IRB. The presence of such concerns suggests that the workload requirements and remuneration likely do not match norms found elsewhere, such as the United States, where a high turnover rate is identified as a concern among its corps of asylum officers (Ewing and Johnson, 2005).

Another problem with Canada's first instance determination approach stems from the fact that all claimants appear before a tribunal. This approach requires a structured and formal process which leads to administrative and procedural complexity. In other countries such as Australia, France, the United Kingdom, and the United States, the claimant is interviewed by administrative officials. The formalities and procedural guarantees of a tribunal setting are reserved for appeal stages.

In addition, other countries manage first instance determination directly to ensure that only legitimate cases of persecution are recognized. This is done to avoid the development of a self-selected parallel immigration system which may stimulate people-smuggling and abuse. Even the most cursory review of recognition statistics shows that Canada suffers from such a parallel system. Canada's aggregate convention refugee recognition rate is usually above 50%, which is higher than that of any other country in the world. In addition, when country of origin statistics are examined, Canada's determination record is simply extraordinary. For example, in 2005, Canada was the only country to recognize convention refugees from Brazil, Costa Rica, Granada, Guyana, Israel, Jamaica, Philippines, Republic of Korea, Saint Lucia, Saint Vincent, and Trinidad and Tobago. Canada recognized more convention refugees from Cuba, Lebanon, Mexico, Pakistan, Peru, and Romania than all the other countries in the world did put together. Canada also recognized the most refugees from Columbia, Iran, Nigeria, and Ukraine, in terms of absolute numbers (UNHCR-DS, 2006: table 9). Such anomalous decision making has been characteristic of the IRB since its establishment.

Ultimately, however, one problem with Canada's current approach is intractable. The "independent" process of first instance refugee determination through a hearing process is too slow and no reform of the IRB is likely to change this. Moreover, the time required for an IRB determination to occur may soon lengthen by 50%. A private member's bill (Bill C-280), which was passed by the House of Commons on May 30, 2007, and received first reading in the Senate on October 17, 2007, will, if passed, implement an IRB internal appeal mechanism—the Refugee Appeal Division. This additional level of appeal was an element of the 2001 *Immigration and Refugee Protection Act* (IRPA), which was not implemented because of the large number of refugee claims that were made while the legislation was working its way through Parliament (House of Commons Standing Committee on Citizenship and Immigration, 2007b: 9–13). If Bill C-280 is implemented, this reform will add an estimated five months to the nearly year-long IRB decision making process (House of Commons Standing Committee on Citizenship and Immigration, 2007a: 11–13).

During this slow process of determination, provision must be made for claimant needs. Given the prevailing political climate in Canada, such support must be comprehensive and generous, as noted above. As a result, asylum seekers are given an opportunity to put down deep roots in Canada, and this makes the removal of failed claimants problematic in a large number of cases. Canada's solution to this problem has been to provide numerous and relatively easy mechanisms for failed claimants to secure Permanent Resident Status (PRS).

Other countries in the developed world are unwilling to regularize the granting of a residence status to "mixed" and self-selected migrants, unless the individual in question is a legitimate refugee (Straw, 2000). Consequently, refugee determination in these countries is structured so as to quickly differentiate refugees from unqualified migrants. In Australia, Germany, the United Kingdom, and the United States, the initial decision on whether a person is a legitimate refugee is made by specially trained public officials who are carefully scrutinized by the government to ensure that the decisions reached in an interview setting come swiftly and meet international obligations. In the United States, the entire determination process, including appeals, must be completed within 180 days, while in the United Kingdom, 60% of cases are fully completed, including appeals, in six months (United Kingdom Home Office Immigration and Nationality Directorate, 2006: 8). In addition, the United Kingdom is aiming to reach a 90% "grant or remove" rate in the same time frame by 2011. In other countries, the refugee system is structured to provide for a short and stingy period of support and residence while the first instance determination takes place. This period is followed by aid to those who are granted asylum, and, by contrast, an array of disincentives and discomforts for those who fall short and must appeal or leave. Canada is the only country in the world that makes the determination period both long and comfortable for the claimant. It is also the most generous country with respect to the outcome of the determination process.

Given all these facts, one would expect that fundamental IRB reform would be at the top of the agenda. However, the proponents of reform in the policy-knowledgeable government bureaucracy lack significant support in the policy-knowledgeable public, let alone the general public. Given the nature of the policy field described above—the patron-client politics model coupled with partisan political expediency—it is not surprising that there is little in the way of an organized public defence of aggregate national interests. As a result, society-government stakeholder meetings are dominated by rights, humanitarian, and immigration-industry advocates who condemn—unopposed—the public official "interview" model that is employed in first instance determination elsewhere. They argue that Canada's IRB system is a superior approach because it is "independent" and it retains the procedural safeguards consistent with a "hearing model." For example, this kind of defence was made at a 2004 roundtable of experts brought together at the University of Ottawa to discuss reforms to the refugee determination process. Government officials who participated in the roundtable were faced with society-based participants who were of one mind on this issue. The conclusion of the discussion on the "institutional setting of refugee determination" was that "there was strong support for an independent, quasi-judicial process with full due process safeguards in view of the sensitive nature of refugee status determination and the high stakes involved" (Kumin and Showler, 2004: 14). The processes used in the United States and elsewhere were discussed very little by the roundtable.

The politics of regularization or removal

Although the IRB is very liberal in its decision making, it does reject a large number of claimants. However, obtaining recognition as a convention refugee is not the only way by which an irregular migrant may secure PRS, and being rejected by the IRB does not signal quick removal or a withdrawal of social benefits, although, some changes have been made recently to pressure failed claimants to leave on their own. Before removal, the law stipulates that there has to be a "risk assessment" known as a Pre-Removal Risk Assessment (PRRA). This process is undertaken by Canadian Border Services Agency (CBSA) officials, and, due to current staffing and resources, this review can take a very long time. While this process is going on, a failed claimant can make a humanitarian and compassionate review application to a branch of Citizenship and Immigration Canada. The number of people appealing to this immigration category has ballooned, and now as many as 60% of those who apply gain PRS in this way (*The Globe and Mail*, 2005, Apr. 16).

Generally, the cases presented in these humanitarian reviews are the same as those that were heard by the IRB, except "new evidence or changed circumstance" is required. Similar to the determination process, an appeal to the Federal Court is possible at the completion of each of these stages. Although the focus of an appeal should be on legal errors, in practice, the substance of the case is presented once again. If an individual is willing to foot the expense, this process can go on for many years.

In contrast, the United States has no equivalent "humanitarian" process at the end of its refugee determination process. Most failed claimants simply become part of its illegal alien population, which has reached approximately 11 million people (United States Government Accountability Office, 2006: 17). This population is relatively free to earn a living and participate in society, but there are many drawbacks to not having legal status. One such drawback has led to a raging battle over whether illegal aliens should be issued drivers' licenses.

At the end of Canada's extended refugee process, there are still some claimants who have not gained PRS or secured some means of accessing the regular immigration system to gain PRS. Special deals at an individual level are possible at this time. A deal may allow failed asylum seekers to leave Canada (officially, these claimants are "removed"), but, simultaneously, this allows an expedition of their immigration application (*Montreal Gazette*, 2004, Aug. 6). Eventually, however, failed claimants who have resided in Canada for many years are scheduled for removal. To the advocacy community, the solution to the clogged refugee determination system is simple enough: grant them all PRS (Goldman, 2004, July 6).

In fact, such a solution has always been attractive to the government, given the general failings attributed to the IRB and the criticism the government faces each time it attempts to deport failed claimants who often have Canadian children. Consequently, when high profile cases arise, the government attempts to naturalize the individual or group in an ad hoc manner. When a moratorium on removals to Algeria was lifted in 2002, those who were affected—mostly failed asylum seekers—organized and staged protests. The federal government responded by working out a deal with the province of Québec to naturalize the bulk of them (*Montreal Gazette*, 2004, Sep. 8). When the media began to focus on failed asylum seekers who had been given sanctuary in churches, the government offered to allow churches to select 12 people annually for "special reconsideration," essentially granting them PRS. But when this proposal was rejected by the churches, the New Democratic Party protested. The government reacted by creating a new offer for churches, which would give them the opportunity to select cases for "re-examination" by the IRB (*The Globe and Mail*, 2004, Nov. 3).

Arguably, the greatest mystery surrounding Canada's refugee system is not the lack of reforms which would bring the system in line with international norms; instead, it is the relatively small number of claimants, given the fact that the system guarantees a benefit-rich legal status for at least two years, and, if all the opportunities and side entrances are taken into consideration, the system is obviously capable of granting PRS to large numbers of illegal arrivals and overstayers.

The reason why there are few claimants is likely the result of three factors. First, although the people-smuggling industry recognizes the benefits of Canada as a destination country, Canada is very difficult to reach from the developing world (*Montreal Gazette*, 2005, May 2). Furthermore, since 9/11, the United States and European countries have become much more vigilant in their screening of migrants who are passing through these areas in order to reach Canada. In the absence of this tightened screen, it is likely that the trend in Canadian refugee claims, which rose from 23,500 in 1997-1998 to 45,000 in 2001-2002, would have continued (Consulting and Audit Canada, 2005). Secondly, the Canadian government has made greater efforts to screen visitor visas granted to foreign nationals of less developed countries, and to interdict potential claimants prior to embarkation (*Montreal Gazette*, 2004, Dec. 28).

The third reason why there are few claimants relates to the attractiveness of the United States and the possibility that the American government may regularize its population of illegal immigrants. Political and electoral forces make this possibility very controversial. Consequently, American policies have vacillated between a softening stance, such as President George W. Bush's recent support for Comprehensive Immigration Reform, and a hardening stance, such the *REAL ID Act* which was passed in May 2005. The migratory pressure on Canada, in terms of the arrival of a large number of irregular migrants, is related to what the Americans decide to do with their undocumented population. A clear example of this relationship occurred in 2002, when the United States government implemented a domestic call-in registration—National Security Entry-Exit Registration System (NSEERS)—for foreign nationals who were living in the United

States but were originally from countries where al-Qaeda was thought to be active. Soon afterwards, Canada began to receive a significant stream of Pakistani refugee claimants who had been living illegally in the United States (Jimenez, 2003, Mar. 1).

With a safe third country policy now in place, such migrants would be likely to seek entry to Canada by clandestine means. Mexicans, however, who are now by far Canada's largest claimant source country, are an exception. Unlike the United States, Canada does not require Mexicans to obtain a visa to visit and thus they can bypass border controls. It is easy to see the potential for a major migratory influx, considering that Canada's refugee recognition rate for several Latin American countries is high, and all of these countries have large undocumented populations in the United States. The countries with the highest undocumented populations in the United States are Mexico, El Salvador, and Guatemala. The United States government estimates that, in 2006, there were almost 7.5 million undocumented foreign nationals from these countries living in the United States (Hoefer et al., 2006: 4). However, in terms of their success with gaining access to the Canadian refugee system, in 2006, Mexico had the lowest rate of success of the three countries (23.4%), while El Salvador and Guatemala had success rates of 37.6% and 39.4%, respectively. Columbia, which is estimated to have well over 150,000 undocumented residents in the United States, had a determination success rate of 82% (UNHCR-DS, 2007b: table 9). In addition, there are number of countries for which Canada has a moratorium on removals. For example, irregular Haitian migrants in the United States are able to gain status in Canada if they can avoid the application of the safe third country policy. This possibility is currently being publicized in the Haitian community in the United States, and may trigger a northward migration (Davey and Goodnough, 2007, Sep. 21).

Should a mass influx of migrants from any of these countries occur, the IRB, which is already backlogged, will become overloaded and the wait time for determination may lengthen greatly. Given that Canada's enforcement resources are already woefully inadequate, the government may be forced to consider an amnesty. Eventually, the government will have to consider employing migration management instruments that are currently in use elsewhere in the developed world, such as a manifestly unfounded policy.

Conclusion

Canada's national interest requires an effectively managed migration policy. Despite the importance of this policy and the clear shortcomings in the Canadian process, there does not seem to be substantive political debate on the subject. The reason for this is simple. Multiculturalism, openness, and tolerance have become so central to Canadian identity that speaking about Canada's "interests" in terms of immigration is verboten.

To make matters worse, Canada may be the only country in the world where its citizens cannot expect guidance on these issues from their Parliament. In the past, the federal Liberal Party has successfully used the issue of immigration to damage the political aspirations of the Conservative Party and its predecessors (Wattie, 2005, May 5; Ivison, 2007, Feb. 23). Because of electoral considerations, it is likely that the Liberals will be careful not to lose their edge on this issue, and the Conservative party is not likely to challenge them.

But now, more than ever, Canada must take a hard look at the issues surrounding both immigration in general, and asylum migration in particular. Over the course of only four years, Canada receives one million new residents. Since 1950, Canada has received nine million immigrants. Soon, the majority of Canadians will not be able to trace their primary roots back to Canadians of the World War II era.[1]

The immigration process is vast and costly. According to the Auditor General of Canada, the government does not have anywhere near the resources necessary to effectively screen this influx (2000: 3.5). Although there is immobilism and avoidance in partisan circles, hardly a day goes by without a newspaper making at least one reference to a migration policy shortcoming.

---

1   The technical term for this phenomenon is "rootedness." Over time, a high immigration rate coupled with a low indigenous birth rate lowers the rootedness of the resident population (Statistics Canada, 2003).

Canada needs to analyze the effects of this constant, large influx of immigrants on existing social and economic structures. In this regard, Canada's immigration-rich history will not provide much guidance. Today, new Canadians are not filling empty land, nor are they all from the same general region of the world, and, therefore, relatively easy to assimilate. They generally move to the largest cities, transforming Toronto, for example, into the most multicultural city in the world. Assimilation can no longer be viewed in the way it once was, now that globalization provides so many communication and travel opportunities through which migrants can maintain close connections with their regions of origin.

In addition to these basic immigration-related problems, there are also humanitarian, enforcement, and security issues. Canada's Immigration and Refugee Board has a long history of controversy, and all recent ministers have tried to fix it. No other country in the world emulates Canada's approach to refugee policy, especially when it comes to the regularization opportunities afforded to failed claimants.

In order to address the many problems with Canada's refugee system, a number of questions must be answered: what kind of system will meet Canada's international refugee obligations most effectively, and realistically curtail abuse? What can be done to address the concerns of the Auditor General, whose reports consistently document weaknesses across a range of refugee migration related policies? In terms of enforcement, what can Canada do to ensure that its immigration laws are respected? And finally, how can such an important and contentious discussion be provided for, so that it engages more than just those representing special interests and does not degenerate into a partisan slugfest?

References

Auditor General of Canada (2000). *The Economic Component of the Canadian Immigration Program*. Government of Canada.

Canada (2004, November 3). Regulations Amending the Immigration and Refugee Protection Regulations. *Canada Gazette* 138, 22. <http://canadagazette.gc.ca/partII/2004/20041103/html/sor217-e.html>. Accessed December 19, 2007.

Caplan, Elinor, Minister of Citizenship and Immigration (2000). Address by the Minister of Citizenship and Immigration to the Canada China Business Council, Beijing, China, April 25, 2000.

Citizenship and Immigration Canada (2006). *A Partnership for Protection: Year One Review*. Government of Canada. <http://www.cic.gc.ca/english/about/laws-policy/partnership/index.asp>. Accessed December 19, 2007.

Consulting and Audit Canada (2005). *Formative Evaluation of the IRB's Streamlining Initiative*. Prepared for the Immigration and Refugee Board of Canada. <http://www.irb-cisr.gc.ca/en/about/transparency/evaluations/streamlining/stream02_e.htm>.

Davey, Monica, and Abby Goodnough (2007, September 21). Illegal Immigrants Chase False Hope to Canada. *The New York Times*. A1.

Ewing, Walter A., and Benjamin Johnson (2005). *Asylum Essentials: The US Asylum Program Needs More Resources, Not Restrictions*. American Immigration Law Foundation.

Freeman, Gary P. (2003). *Political Science and Immigration: Policy Types and Modes of Politics*. Unpublished paper, presented at the R.F. Harney Lecture Series, University of Toronto, March 21, 2003.

Freeze, Colin (2005, September 23). Polish Man Seeks Refuge in Canada from Bar Buddies. *The Globe and Mail*. A6.

Gallagher, Stephen (2003). *Canada's Dysfunctional Refugee Determination System: Canadian Asylum Policy from a Comparative Perspective*. Public Policy Sources 78. Fraser Institute.

The Globe and Mail (2004, November 3). Church Groups Reject Sgro's Proposal on Refugee Claimants. A13.

The Globe and Mail (2005, March 2). Holocaust Denier is Returned to Germany. A7.

The Globe and Mail (2005, April 16). Canada's Welcome Mat Frayed and Unraveling. A8.

Goldman, Richard (2004, July 6). Hardening Attitudes toward Refugees. *Montreal Gazette*. A19.

Hoefer, M., N. Rytina, and C. Campbell (2006). *Estimates of the Unauthorized Immigrant Population Residing in the United States*. United States Department of Homeland Security, Office of Immigration Statistics.

House of Commons Standing Committee on Citizenship and Immigration (2007a). Evidence Presented to the House of Commons Standing Committee on Citizenship and Immigration, March 29, 2007. Canada, House of Commons.

House of Commons Standing Committee on Citizenship and Immigration (2007b). *Safeguarding Asylum – Sustaining Canada's Commitments to Refugees*. Canada, House of Commons. <http://cmte.parl.gc.ca/cmte/CommitteePublication.aspx?COM=10469&SourceId=209847&SwitchLanguage=1>. Accessed December 19, 2007.

International Labour Organization (2005). Irregular migrant. In *International Labour Organization Thesaurus 2005*. International Labour Organization. <http://www.ilo.org/public/libdoc/ILO-Thesaurus/english/tr1747.htm>. Accessed January 17, 2007.

Ivison, John (2007, February 23). Liberals Playing Immigration Card. *National Post*. A5.

Ivison, John, and Allison Hanes (2007, January 6). Turncoat MP has "Passion of Canada." *National Post*. A4.

Jimenez, Marina (2003, March 1). America's Refugees. *National Post*. B1, B4–5.

Jimenez, Marina (2004, July 24). Refugee Approval Rates Vary Widely. *The Globe and Mail*. A1.

Kumin, Judith, and Peter Showler (2004). *Roundtable on Canada's Refugee System: Summary Report*. University of Ottawa. <http://www.cdp-hrc.uottawa.ca/eng/project/refugee-forum/projects/showler_report.pdf>.

Legomsky, Stephen H. (1996). The New Techniques for Managing High-Volume Asylum Systems. *Iowa Law Review* 671. Reprinted in Peter McNab (ed.), *Retreating from the Refugee Convention* (Charles Darwin University). <http://www.cdu.edu.au/law/apl/Retreating/legomsky.htm>.

Montreal Gazette (2004, August 6). Ordeal is Over as Colombian Family Reunited at Border. A7.

Montreal Gazette (2004, September 8). Algerians Seek Sponsors in Quest for Legal Status. A8.

Montreal Gazette (2004, December 15). Refugees Free to Leave Church. A8.

Montreal Gazette (2004, December 28). More Travelers Turned Back for Using Fake Passports. A28.

Montreal Gazette (2005, May 2). Canada "Preferred Destination" for Immigrant Smuggles: Report. A1.

Ottawa Citizen (2005, May 25). US Undermining Human Rights in the Name of Security. A10.

Statistics Canada (2003). *Generation Status (4A) and Sex (3) for Population 15 Years and Over, for Canada, Provinces and Territories, 1971 and 2001 Censuses - 20% Sample Data*. Catalogue number 97F0009XCB2001006. Statistics Canada.

Straw, Jack, Home Secretary of the United Kingdom (2000). Towards a Common Asylum Procedure. Address by the Home Secretary of the United Kingdom to the European Conference on Asylum, Lisbon, Spain, June 16, 2000.

United Kingdom Home Office Immigration and Nationality Directorate (2006). *Fair, Effective, Transparent and Trusted: Rebuilding Confidence in Our Immigration System*. Government of the United Kingdom. <http://www.homeoffice.gov.uk/documents/ind-review-250706/ind-review-eng?view=Binary>. Accessed December 19, 2007.

United Nations High Commissioner for Refugees, Division of Operational Services, Field Information and Coordination Support Section [UNHCR-DS] (2006). *2005 Global Refugee Trends: Statistical Overview of Populations of Refugees, Asylum Seekers, Internally Displaced Persons, Stateless Persons, and Other Persons of Concern to the UNHCR*. United Nations High Commissioner for Refugees.

United Nations High Commissioner for Refugees, Division of Operational Services, Field Information and Coordination Support Section [UNHCR-DS] (2007a). *Asylum Levels and Trends in*

Industrialized Countries: 2006 Overview of Asylum Applications Lodged in European and non-European Industrialized Countries in 2006, Tables 17 and 18. United Nations High Commission for Refugees.

United Nations High Commissioner for Refugees, Division of Operational Services, Field Information and Coordination Support Section [UNHCR-DS] (2007b). *2006 Global Trends: Refugees, Asylum Seekers, Returnees, Internally Displaced and Stateless Persons.* United Nations High Commissioner for Refugees.

United Nations High Commissioner for Refugees, Population and Geographical Data Section, Division of Operational Support [UNHCR-PGDS] (2005). *2004 Global Refugee Trends: Overview of Refugee Populations, New Arrivals, Durable Solutions, Asylum Seekers, Stateless Persons, and Other Persons of Concern to UNHCR.* United Nations High Commissioner for Refugees.

United Nations High Commissioner for Refugees, Population Data Unit/PGDS Division of Operational Support [UNHCR-PDU] (2004). *Asylum Levels and Trends: Europe and non-European Industrialized Countries, 2003.* United Nations High Commissioner for Refugees.

United States Government Accountability Office (2006). *Estimating the Undocumented Population: A "Grouped Answers" Approach to Surveying Foreign-Born Respondents.* Report to the Subcommittee on Terrorism, Technology and Homeland Security, Committee on the Judiciary, US Senate. <http://www.gao.gov/new.items/d06775.pdf>.

The Washington Times (2003, December 2). Registration of Muslims, Arabs Halted.

Wattie, Chris (2005, May 5). Volpe Refuses to Apologize for Klan Remark. *National Post.* A9.

Chapter 5

Security Threats in Immigration and Refugee Policies

James Bissett

It seems self-evident that Canada's immigration and refugee policies have a direct bearing on our nation's security concerns. But despite the horrific Air India bombing by Sikh terrorists in 1985 that killed 329 Canadians, despite the common knowledge that the Liberation Tigers of Tamil Eelam (LTTE) have been operating actively in Canada for years, and despite numerous examples of Muslim extremists planning terrorist strikes or using Canada as a safe haven for fund-raising and other terrorist operations, many of our political leaders seem unwilling to accept that Canada's immigration and refugee policies present security concerns.

Their refusal to accept this reality while determining Canada's security strategy has weakened our efforts to play an effective role in the war against Islamist extremists. Moreover, this failure has led senior political leaders and bureaucrats in the United States to look upon Canada as the weak link in North American security concerns. They see us as an uncertain and uncommitted ally. This perception persists despite evidence that the anti-terrorist measures taken by Canada in the wake of 9/11 closely matched those taken by the United States.

Unfortunately, these impressive first steps were neutralized by hesitation and ambivalence on the part of Canada's political leaders.

Furthermore, these measures did not include any review of or changes to our immigration and refugee policies. Consequently, it may be argued that Canada is more vulnerable to a terrorist attack today than it was in the months following 9/11. To understand how this has come about, it is necessary to understand the nature of Canada's immigration and refugee policies.

Background

Political parties have always solicited support from ethnic or religious groups and have offered rewards of one sort or another in return for votes. Block voting by new immigrant groups is an old phenomenon—these groups tend to vote for the party that promises them the most benefits. This tradition of "pork barrel" politics lives on, but the modern version has become far more ominous than the old practice of exchanging votes for free beer, a new road, or a turkey at Christmas. The new "spoils" system, which has now become institutionalized, is the direct result of multiculturalism and a sustained high volume of new immigrants.

In the 1970s, political parties discovered that they could gain and maintain the allegiance of ethnic voters by formalizing the concept of multiculturalism. Multiculturalism became a formal policy of the government, and multicultural institutions were created within the framework and structure of the bureaucracy. This was a revolutionary step and it transformed Canadian politics. It was no longer necessary to use party funds to entice ethnic voters. Once in power, a party was able to expend large sums of the taxpayers' money in support of ethnic organizations, including newspapers and media outlets, and ethnic or religious celebrations and related events. All of this was done in the name of multiculturalism—and with the expectation of block voting from ethnic groups.

After multiculturalism was implemented, all of the political parties realized that more immigrants meant more votes, and frequently, these votes could be manipulated. Consequently, it was in their interest to increase and maintain a high level of immigration. Canada's former policy of adjusting immigration levels to accommodate the ups and downs of the labour force was ended. It was decided that one percent of the Canadian population should become the annual target.[1] The decision to implement this policy had no rationale, apart from the notion that more immigrants meant more potential voters for the party in power.

In 1977, the *Citizenship Act* was passed, reducing the waiting time for citizenship eligibility from five to three years. Voting patterns show that new immigrants often vote for the party that was in power at the time the immigrant was admitted to the country. In return for the immigrants' votes, the party in power will usually become a powerful advocate for large scale immigration.

Immigration policy is no longer about the costs or benefits of immigration, or whether immigration is needed to sustain our economy. Now, it is only about maintaining high levels of immigration, and it seems that all political parties in Canada do their best to ensure that there is no open or public debate about this important issue of public policy. Immigration is seldom, if ever, discussed in Parliament, and all parties ensure that their members who sit on the House of Commons Standing Committee on Citizenship and Immigration are frequently those who come from strongly ethnic ridings and who are in favour of immigration. In addition, witnesses who are called before the Committee often represent organizations or groups that support high immigration levels.

In Canada, it has become politically incorrect to suggest that immigration may have negative aspects. To question the wisdom of adding 250,000 newcomers each year (Singer, 2002, Dec. 6) to the already swelling populations of Canada's three major cities—Toronto, Montréal, and Vancouver—is to risk the accusation of being racist or xenophobic. Immigration has been accepted, automatically, as being essential for nation building and for strengthening two recently created pillars of the new Canadian society: diversity and multiculturalism. For many Canadians, immigration has

---

1   The notion that one percent of the Canadian population should become the annual target for immigration intake came out of the Liberal Party's "Red Book" in 1993. The "Red Book" stated, "we should continue to target immigration levels of approximately one percent of the population each year, as has been the case for more than a decade." The fact was, however, that annual immigration intake reached one percent only once in the four decades prior to 1993. This happened in 1967, when it was 1.1 percent.

acquired an almost mythical status. Given the current state of popular opinion in Canada, it is not surprising that many Canadians and politicians do not want to recognize that there may be an adverse security dimension to immigration and refugee policies.

Tough anti–terrorist measures passed

In the weeks following the tragic events of 9/11, the Canadian government responded immediately with a series of tough anti-terrorist measures which gave the impression that Canada was serious in its determination to combat the terrorist threat. Canadian troops were sent to Afghanistan to help fight Taliban insurgents. Bill C-36, a controversial anti-terrorist bill similar to the *USA PATRIOT Act*, was rushed through Parliament, giving police and intelligence forces extraordinary powers normally used only in a time of war.

The government created a new Department of Public Safety and Emergency Preparedness closely resembling the United States Department of Homeland Security. It possessed the similar aim of achieving better coordination of security agencies and improved information sharing. The government quickly set up a National Security Plan, a Threat Assessment Centre, and four Integrated National Security Teams, which were designed to identify and prevent terrorist attacks. Only two months after 9/11, Canada signed a Smart Border Declaration with the United States, which was aimed at making the border more secure while facilitating cross-border traffic and trade.

The rapid and vigorous response following the attacks in New York and Washington signaled to Canadians and our allies in the war against Islamist extremists that Canadian political leaders understood that Canada was a potential target. This response also suggested that the government had a strategic plan to ensure the safety and security of its citizens.

Essential measures not enacted

However, these impressive first steps soon came to an inexplicable halt. Some of the key elements necessary to implement and give life to the anti-terrorist legislation were not enacted. Bill C-36 called for the prosecution of people identified as active terrorists, and provided for the "listing" of organizations that the government identified as "terrorist." However, months passed before the government placed any of the most obvious terrorist groups on the list. It was only after pressure from the media and Jewish organizations that terrorist organizations such as Hamas, Hezbollah, the Al Aqsa Martyrs' Brigade, and the Armed Islamic Front were finally listed as terrorist organizations. The government offered no explanation as to why the implementation of this provision of the bill had been delayed. The fact that the Canadian Security Intelligence Service (CSIS) had reported that there were 50 terrorist groups operating in Canada—as early as 1998—suggests a curious disinclination to place such groups on the terrorist list (Duff-Brown, 2005, July 15).

One of the more obvious terrorist groups not placed on the list was a Sikh terrorist group known as Babar Khalsa. This organization was held responsible for the 1985 Air India bombing. The reason for this omission is easy to understand, but difficult to excuse. There are thousands of Sikh Canadians residing in British Columbia and Ontario, and they are known to be supporters of the federal Liberal Party. It is likely that the Liberal Party did not wish to alienate Sikh supporters by placing one of their organizations on the terrorist list. Eventually, in June 2003—18 years after the Air India bombing—Babar Khalsa was designated as a terrorist organization, but only because it became publicly known that CSIS had named the group as one of the 50 terrorist organizations operating in Canada. Because of this revelation, it was impossible to keep it off the terrorist list.

Another obvious terrorist organization that was not immediately put on the list was the Liberation Tigers of Tamil Eelam. The Tamil Tigers were acknowledged to be one of the most notorious terrorist groups in the world and yet they were operating openly in Canada, raising millions of dollars for the organization each year (Collacott, 2006). Again, the notorious Tigers were not listed because the government feared it would lose the support of the more than 250,000 Tamil Canadians residing in Canada. The Tamil Tigers were finally designated a terrorist organization in April 2006 (*CBC News*, 2006, Apr. 10).

This reluctance to designate internationally recognized terrorist organizations for fear of losing ethnic votes reveals a frightening degree of irresponsibility and cynicism on the part of Canadian political leaders. On the one hand, these politicians are prepared to send Canadian troops to risk their lives fighting Taliban and al-Qaeda terrorists in Afghanistan, but on the other hand, they are prepared to permit terrorist organizations to operate freely in Canada. There is something seriously wrong with this tolerance of terrorist groups. Either our elected representatives are not taking the terrorist threat seriously, or they are willing to trade the safety and security of their fellow citizens in exchange for voting support from those who may be sympathetic to the terrorist cause.

Immigration security concerns

As noted above, for the past 17 years, Canada has received approximately 250,000 immigrants each year. Many thousands of these newcomers have come from Muslim countries whose populations are known to contain significant numbers of Islamist radicals. For example, between 1996 and 2005, Canada accepted over 118,000 immigrants from Pakistan, 62,000 from Iran, and 25,000 from Algeria (Citizenship and Immigration Canada, 2006). It would be foolish to suggest that the majority of these immigrants or their families represent a security threat, but it would be equally wrong to assume that there are no potential radicals among them, who would be willing to support or engage in terrorist activities.

The experience of other countries that receive a high volume of Muslim immigrants has shown that some of these migrants or their children— even those born in the new country—are susceptible to the radical Islamist cause. The bombings in London and Madrid, the rioting of young Muslims in France, and the murder of Theo Van Gogh in Amsterdam have clearly demonstrated that there is a connection between Islamic immigration and security. Although, so far, Canada has been fortunate enough not to have experienced an Islamist terrorist strike, our security service has warned us that it may only be a question of time before an attack occurs.

In March 2004, a Canadian Muslim was charged in connection with a planned bomb attack in England (*CBC News*, 2006, Oct. 24). He has been in custody since that time, but because of numerous appeals and a constitutional challenge, his case has not yet come to trial. There have been a number of instances of Canadian Muslims fighting for or supporting al-Qaeda activities outside Canada. It is obvious that the terrorist threat is real and that it involves Muslims in Canada, whether they immigrated to Canada or were born here.

In June 2006, 18 Canadian-born Muslims were arrested and charged with planning a series of terrorist attacks against selected targets, including the Canadian Parliament buildings and Prime Minister Stephen Harper. It has recently been disclosed that these suspects were part of a larger group of almost 50 Muslims who were under investigation (Bell, 2006, June 2). Some of the members of the group were known to have received training overseas. Security officials have explained that only those with a reasonable chance of being convicted were charged, and the remaining suspects are still under investigation.

In April 2007, an Environics Poll showed that over 80% of the approximately 700,000 Muslims living in Canada "were satisfied with their lives here" (Corbella, 2007, Feb. 18). Alarmingly, however, the poll also indicated that 12% of Muslims polled thought that the terrorist plot for which 18 Canadian Muslims were arrested was justified. In other words, the poll showed that approximately 84,000 Canadian Muslims believed that blowing up the Parliament buildings and beheading the Canadian Prime Minister was justified. Not surprisingly, this portion of the poll received little publicity in the Canadian media and the issue was not raised in Parliament.

Considering that the evidence available suggests that Canada is on Osama bin Laden's hit list (Bell, 2006, June 3) and that there are Muslim terrorists operating here—including people born and raised among their fellow Canadian citizens—it would be prudent, from a security point of view, for Canada to review its immigration policy in relation to the admission of immigrants from Muslim countries that are known to produce terrorists. But such a review has not happened. Immigrants from these countries are admitted under the same criteria and selection systems as any other immigrants. Many of those who are issued visas never meet a Canadian visa officer. They are not asked questions about whether they will be comfortable living in a secular society, whether they can accept the principle of equality for women and homosexuals, whether they will be tolerant of other religions, and whether they will be willing to accept the principle of free speech, even if it may be considered offensive to Islam. These types of questions are not raised. If these migrants meet the normal economic or sponsorship admission requirements, they are issued visas.

The priority of immigration officers is to issue visas and to do so as quickly as possible. Positive decisions are never challenged, but a rejection frequently ends up in Canadian courts, where the officer is required to defend the negative decision. The emphasis on numbers and the litigious nature of the immigration process make it difficult for visa officers to refuse applicants. At one time, officers were able to use their discretion to override the selection system if they believed an applicant possessed negative personality traits or attitudinal problems that demonstrated it was likely that he would not be able to become integrated satisfactorily into Canadian society. Unfortunately, visa officers no longer have this discretionary power.

The Netherlands and France have adopted a more realistic approach to the security problems associated with Muslim immigrants. Both countries recognized the connection between immigration and security, and were concerned that multiculturalism was not working with many of their Muslim newcomers. The Netherlands has changed course from its formerly tolerant approach to the Muslim population. Citizenship classes for Imams in charge of Mosques are now mandatory (Pereira, 2002, Nov. 28). Before being accepted for entry, Muslim immigrants are tested about their knowledge and familiarity with Dutch society and values (*Fox News*, 2006, Mar. 16). As well, the Prime Minister has proposed a law that would outlaw the wearing of the burka in some public places. Moreover, they have instituted a "zero tolerance" policy towards those who preach violence and hatred.

In 2007, Brice Hortefeux, the head of France's Ministry of Immigration and National Identity, announced a policy of controlling the inflow of immigrants and protecting French values and cohesion. He reiterated President Nicolas Sarkozy's goal of expelling 25,000 illegal entrants by the end of 2007, and expanding the system through which illegal immigrants are paid to return home voluntarily (Gangley, 2007).

However, the realization that millions of Muslims in France have not been willing to integrate into French society may have come too late. Now that Muslims account for an estimated 10% of France's population (United States Department of State, 2008), there are more Muslim voters added to the electoral roll each election. Since 2005, three million new voters have been qualified to vote in France, and at least-one third of these voters are Muslims (Trifkovic, 2007). Only 1% of Muslim voters voted for Sarkozy in the recent election, while 90% cast ballots for his left-wing competitors who are not nearly as forceful on immigration and security issues (Trifkovic, 2007).

Nevertheless, too late or not, France and some other European countries have now accepted that immigration is a legitimate topic for public debate for mainline political parties. They have accepted the reality that, in a very short amount of time, high volumes of immigrants of a different culture, who hold strongly to a different value system, can not only change the demographic landscape of a host country, but can also present a threat to many of its traditional beliefs and principles. This is the challenge of large-scale Muslim migration into Western societies. The challenge becomes more complicated when even a tiny proportion of the Muslim population is sympathetic to the mission of al-Qaeda and other extremist groups because this creates a security problem of major proportions.

Canada's asylum system

Countries that have experienced a terrorist attack have been forced to acknowledge that immigration has a bearing on security. In Canada, that realization has not occurred. Nothing illustrates this more than our refusal to reform our refugee asylum system. Few Canadians know the difference between a "refugee" and an "asylum seeker" and, as a result, there is a great deal of confusion and misunderstanding regarding refugee issues. Frequently, the media will describe someone who is seeking asylum in Canada as a refugee. By doing so, they elicit, whether deliberately or not, sympathy and compassion for the individual concerned.

An asylum seeker is a person who claims to have been persecuted in his own country and asks a host country for protection. A refugee is a person who has been accepted by an authorized body—in Canada, the Immigration and Refugee Board (IRB)—as meeting the definition of a refugee set forth by the United Nations Refugee Convention. A refugee is given the protection from persecution that is needed and a guarantee that he will not be sent back to the country to which he fears to return. Most refugees can be found in refugee camps in developing countries. They are cared for and protected by the United Nations High Commissioner for Refugees (UNHCR). In the past, Canada has selected many thousands of refugees for permanent resettlement: Hungarians, Czechs and Slovaks, Poles, Ugandan Asians, Vietnamese, Chileans, and others. In 1986, Canada was awarded the prestigious Nansen Medal by the United Nations for its contribution to helping to resolve global refugee problems. Canada is the only country that has received this honour (Citizenship and Immigration Canada, 2007).

But since that time, Canada has not been able to accept large numbers of genuine refugees or to contribute significantly to world refugee problems because of the large number of asylum seekers entering the country and claiming to have been persecuted. The numbers are large—more than 600,000 asylum seekers have entered in the past 20 years (Citizenship and Immigration Canada, 2006). And Canada continues to receive many asylum seekers each year—28,300 in 2007 alone (*BBC News*, 2008, Mar. 18).

Though anyone can claim to be a refugee, not all claims are genuine. Thousands of asylum seekers who claim to have been persecuted are refused refugee status because their claims are found to be unfounded or fraudulent. Many deliberately claim to be persecuted in order to avoid having to meet normal immigration requirements. Seeking asylum is the primary method of gaining entry into Western countries by those who have little chance of legal admission. Those coming to Canada are no exception.

Canada's asylum system is recognized as the most generous in the world. The IRB's acceptance rate is quite high by international standards. In 2004, citizens of 152 different countries applied for asylum in Canada, including citizens from the United States, Costa Rica, Brazil, Portugal,

Pakistan, India, Hungary, Mexico, Turkey, Barbados, Germany, Sweden, Switzerland, France, Spain, and the Netherlands. Many of those who seek asylum in Canada come from terrorist producing countries such as Iran, Iraq, Afghanistan, Pakistan, Algeria, and Morocco.

Because most people who come to Canada require visas, with the exception of those coming from the United States and Western Europe, many asylum seekers arrive in Canada without documents or with fraudulent documents. Asylum seekers who are unable or unwilling to apply for a visa at a Canadian Embassy pay to be smuggled into the country by international criminal gangs who sell them documents that enable them to board aircraft destined for Canada. Afterwards, these documents are usually picked up by a member of the gang who is aboard the aircraft to be recycled and resold later.

Upon their arrival in Canada, these smuggled individuals claim asylum. After being fingerprinted and photographed, they are released and asked to show up at a refugee hearing which may be scheduled months after their arrival. Few asylum seekers are detained, even if very little is known about their background. None of them are initially screened for health, criminality, or security. There is no system for keeping track of them and they are free to travel anywhere in Canada. Many asylum seekers do not attend their refugee hearing. Those who do appear and are found not to be genuine refugees are asked to leave, but many do not go home. In 2003, the Auditor General found that a "large gap" of 36,000 existed between the number of removal orders issued and the number of departures confirmed (Jimenez, 2005, Apr. 16). Today, insiders estimate that that figure is likely to be close to 50,000 or more. Yet our government does little to address this problem.

In December 2004, a Safe Third Country Agreement was put into place as part of the Smart Border Declaration signed by Canada and the United States. The agreement prevents certain categories of people in the United States from applying for asylum in Canada at the land border. The agreement also prevents people in Canada from applying at the border for asylum in the United States (Canada, 2004). Those entering either country by sea or air are still able to submit asylum claims, but this discrepancy has never been explained.

But after signing the agreement, Canadian officials feared that it would prevent individuals in the United States who had been charged or convicted of an offense that might result in the death penalty from finding refuge in Canada. To ensure that such individuals could find refuge in Canada, the government—quietly and without publicity—passed a law in December 2004 which exempted those individuals from the terms of the agreement (Canada, 2004). Consequently, any person in the United States who has been charged or convicted of a capital offense and applies for asylum at the border must be permitted entry by our officers. Essentially, such a policy "lays out the welcome mat" for murderers. This policy also indicates that our government is not taking the terrorist threat seriously.

Almost all of the known or alleged terrorists who have been apprehended in Canada have entered as asylum seekers. Ahmed Ressam, the Algerian who tried, unsuccessfully, to blow up the Los Angeles airport, entered Canada in this fashion. Six of the eight alleged terrorists who were held in custody under security certificates until recently entered the country as asylum seekers. Since Canada cannot prevent the entry of anyone who claims asylum, and is obliged to give anyone who is physically in the country Charter of Rights protection (*Singh* v. *Minister of Employment and Immigration*), it is, in effect, impossible to keep undesirables out. Moreover, once these people enter the country, it is almost impossible to remove them.

Since Canada is a signatory to the United Nations Convention Against Torture, it cannot deport anyone to a country where they may be mistreated or tortured. Most suspected or known terrorists come from countries that are known to mistreat prisoners and, consequently, Canada cannot deport them. Among the members of the United Nations committee that is responsible for overseeing the Torture Convention are Egypt, Morocco, Russia, China, and Senegal. Canada would be unlikely to deport anyone to any of these are countries. Thus, Canada now finds itself in a position where it cannot keep terrorists from getting into the country, and it cannot remove them once they get in.

Other countries that are signatories to the United Nations Convention Against Torture have taken a proactive approach to this problem. For example, Britain will deport failed asylum seekers to countries known to practice torture after it has signed an agreement with the country concerned that permits British consular officers to have access to prisons where persons deported from Britain are held. Consular officers ensure that the individuals are not being mistreated or tortured. Germany follows a similar practice. This would appear to be a suitable compromise, but it requires forceful political direction which, sadly, has been lacking in Canada's approach to the war on terror.

Canada's wide open asylum system was made even more generous only two months after the tragic events of 9/11 when the government passed the new *Immigration and Refugee Protection Act*. The asylum provisions of the new legislation made it easier for people to apply for asylum and even more difficult to remove those who do not qualify as refugees. A small group of former diplomats and retired senior public servants tried to persuade the Senate to send the bill back to the House of Commons, but these attempts were summarily dismissed.

The motivation of our political leaders to maintain a dysfunctional and dangerous asylum system cannot be a desire to act in a humane and compassionate manner towards potential refugees because the current system does not effectively aid genuine refugees. The asylum system prevents Canada from donating any substantial funding to help the UNHCR aid millions of genuine refugees who live in sordid and unhealthy camps around the world. At all levels of government, there are enormous financial costs associated with the current asylum system. These costs prevent our government from providing the UNHCR with anything other than a token annual contribution.

The government continues to support the present system, not to aid those in need, but to placate and meet the vociferous demands of special interest groups. In Canada, there is a powerful refugee lobby, consisting of immigration lawyers, consultants, religious denominations, academics, activists, and subsidized non-governmental organizations that are entrusted with caring for and looking after the thousands of asylum seekers who enter Canada each month.

The asylum system is a multi-million dollar industry. The groups that profit from it are highly organized and influential. In fact, the immigration department and some Members of Parliament consider them "stakeholders" rather than lobbyists, and they are treated accordingly. These groups also receive favourable media coverage of their attempts to help asylum seekers.

No other country allows universal access to their asylum system. European Union countries will not accept refugee claims from people who come from countries that are signatories to the United Nations Refugee Convention, are democratic, and follow the rule of law. They also screen out obvious, unfounded claims, and detain claimants who enter with false documents until they have verified the claimant's identity and that the claimant does not present a security threat. There is nothing to prevent the government of Canada from adopting a similar policy except the risk that such a policy would alienate special interest groups.

Canada's asylum system is a threat to North American security. It undermines every other measure that has been taken by Canada and the United States to strengthen and bolster our respective defences against a terrorist strike by al-Qaeda or other Islamist radicals. Canada's is no longer able to control its borders, and this inability presents a threat to our southern neighbour. When a nation gives up its right to decide who may or may not enter its territory, and compounds this folly by forfeiting its right to remove dangerous criminals and terrorists, it has effectively abandoned its sovereignty. In an age of terrorist attacks, there is no excuse for such a dereliction of duty and a loss of common sense.

Conclusion

There is a strong argument to be made that Canada and the United States should form a common security shield against the threat of a terrorist attack. While both sides should strengthen their common border, it is folly to believe that a stronger border will stop determined terrorists from striking either country. The terrorist attacks in Madrid, London, and the United States were carried out by native-born Muslims or by Muslims who had entered the country legally. Today, radical Islamism can be found among Muslim communities in every Western country.

A fortified border and a tough border crossing policy between Canada and the United States is the wrong way to combat terrorism. Such actions may be expedient for political leaders, by serving as evidence that something tangible is being done, but this will not prevent terrorists from entering the United States or Canada. Few terrorists have criminal records and suicide bombers are seldom on the watch lists of our security forces. Consequently, it is easy for them to enter Canada or the United States as legal visitors, students, or temporary workers.

Furthermore, there are enormous costs associated with a fortified border. These costs are not just the cost of electronic surveillance, drone aircraft, "smart cards," and hundreds of additional border guards. The real costs are the obstacles a fortified border creates, which prevent the swift and easy flow of tourists and commercial trade. As well, a more serious long-term cost may be the deterioration of the "good neighbour policy" that has been the hallmark of Canada-United States relations. When we consider that almost all border traffic between Canada and the United States is clean and does not present any real threat, it is clear that the benefits of a fortified border do not outweigh the costs.

A much more effective approach to the terrorist threat for Canada and the United States would be to enter into an agreement to establish a common security shield for the protection of both countries. Such an idea has been proposed before. In October 2000, the former United States Ambassador to Canada, Gordon Giffen, made such a proposal, arguing that it was a sensible and logical move to coordinate and improve the efficacy of the security of both countries. This concept has also been endorsed by the Canadian Council of Chief Executives, which represents 150 of Canada's leading corporations.

A common security perimeter would not entail dismantling the Canada-United States border. Instead, it would make border crossing between the two countries easier. The possible structure of such a perimeter can already be found in the Smart Border Declaration, which was signed by both countries in December 2001. That declaration provides for a number of common security measures including: the removal of people who were ordered deported from either country; the designation of terrorist groups; the sharing of intelligence and advanced travel information; freezing the assets of organizations suspected of financing terrorist groups; and, joint training of personnel from both countries. The United States already has its customs officers located in Canada to conduct pre-screening of United States-bound passengers and inspection of sea going containers.

A common security border already exists in Europe where a number of European Union countries in the Schengen Accord have effectively done away with internal borders, allowing free movement of people between member states. This was done by creating an external perimeter that provides immigration control for all member countries. This has allowed them to devote more funding to internal security and to anti-terrorist operations in their own countries.

From an operational point of view, expanding the Smart Border Declaration into an effective security perimeter would not require very much. Canada and the United States would need to have a common policy for designating countries visa-free for visitors and other temporary entrants. Common guidelines regarding the types of questions to ask visa applicants would be necessary, as would a common agreement on reasons to refuse admission. Canada would have to reform its current asylum system by denying access to people who come from countries considered "safe" by the United Nations High Commissioner for Refugees. Canada would also have to enforce a policy of detaining people who arrive without documents until their identities are verified and they are believed not to be dangerous. Canada would also have to improve its capacity to apprehend and remove people who are in the country illegally. Though it would be possible to meet these requirements and establish such a perimeter, both Canada and the United States lack the political will to seriously consider the idea. In the meantime, both countries will have to deal with the terrorist threat in their own fashion.

Since 9/11, Canada has dismantled two of the most effective anti-terrorist clauses of Bill C-36, which related to preventative arrest and investigative hearings, and the courts have neutralized the one remaining useful instrument for detaining and removing foreign terrorists: the immigration security certificate. The anti-terrorist measures that are still in place are constantly being attacked by lawyers, the courts, civil rights activists, and privacy advocates.

Canada's security forces have not been given the financial and personnel resources needed to conduct adequate counterterrorist activities. The

British security agency MI5 estimates it takes 50 intelligence operatives to trail one suspect (Nelson, 2007, May 2). Moreover, following the Maher Arrar affair,[2] the reputation and status of the police and CSIS have been badly tarnished. If Canada suffers a terrorist attack, these organizations will be blamed rather than their political heads.

None of Canada's political parties are willing to admit that our immigration and refugee policies are in any way a security concern. However, in Canada, there is little attempt to screen prospective immigrants from terrorist producing countries. Our asylum system presents a clear and present danger to both Canada and the United States, but it is not likely to change. Canadian citizenship is easy for anyone to obtain and little effort is made to stress that citizenship entails obligations and duties as well as benefits. We fail to keep criminals and terrorists out of Canada, and when they do get in, we cannot remove them.

Considering the state of Canada's policies, it would appear that the prospect of dealing with the threat of Muslim terrorism in Canada is pretty grim. Perhaps Canada will be lucky and will not experience a catastrophic event. If so, our political leaders should not take credit for this good fortune.

---

2   In 2002, Maher Arar, a Syrian-born immigrant who came to Canada in 1987 and became a Canadian citizen, was detained by US officials who claimed that he had links to al-Qaeda. They deported him to Syria, even though he was carrying a Canadian passport. When Arar returned to Canada a year later, he claimed he had been tortured while in Syria. After a long investigation, in 2007, the Canadian government issued an apology to Arar and offered him a multi-million dollar settlement.

References

Anti-terrorism Act, R.S.C. 2001. c. 41.

BBC News (2008, March 18). Iraqi Asylum Seeker Numbers Jump. <http://news.bbc.co.uk/2/hi/middle_east/7301985.stm>.

Bell, Stewart (2006, June 2). 17 Part of Bigger Plot: Officer. *National Post*.

Bell, Stewart (2006, June 3). Never Mind Foreign Terrorists, Why is Canada Growing its Own Extremists? *National Post*.

Canada (2004). Regulations Amending the Immigration and Refugee Protection Regulations. *Canada Gazette* 138, 22. <http://canadagazette. gc.ca/partII/20041103/html/sor217-e.html>. Accessed December 18, 2007.

CBC News (2006, April 10). Canada Adds Tamil Tigers to List of Terrorist Groups. <http://www.cbc.ca/story/canada/ national/2006/04/10/tamils-terror-designation.html>.

CBC News (2006, October 24). In Depth: Canadian Security.

Citizenship and Immigration Canada (2006). *Facts and Figures 2005: Immigration Overview – Permanent and Temporary Residents*. <http:// www.cic.gc.ca/english/pdf/pub/facts2005.pdf>.

Citizenship and Immigration Canada (2007). *Citizenship: A Canadian Story*. <http://www.cic.gc.ca/english/about/citizenship/60/retro.asp>. Accessed December 18, 2007.

Collacott, Martin (2006). *Canada's Inadequate Response to Terrorism: The Need for Policy Reform*. Fraser Institute Digital Publication. Fraser Institute. <http://www.fraserinstitute.org/COMMERCE.WEB/product_ files/Terrorism%20Response5.pdf>.

Corbella, Licia (2007, February 18). Disturbing Reality Buried. *Calgary Sun.*

Dube, Rebecca Cook (2006, May 3). Canada Pinches Tamil Tigers' Pocketbooks. *Christian Science Monitor.* <http://www.csmonitor.com/2006/0503/p07s02-woam.html>.

Duff-Brown, Beth (2005, July 15). Officials Believe 50 Terror Groups Reside in Canada. *USA Today.* <http://www.usatoday.com/news/nation/2005-07-05-border-canada-terror_x.htm>. Updated July 26, 2005.

Fox News (2006, March 16). Dutch Immigrants Must Watch Racy Film. <http://www.foxnews.com/story/0,2933,188079,00.html>.

Gangley, Elaine (2007, June 4). France Sets Quotas for Immigrant Arrests. *American Renaissance.* <http://www.amren.com/mtnews/archives/2007/06/france_sets_quo.php>. Accessed December 18, 2007.

Jimenez, Marina (2005, April 16). Broken Gates: Canada's Welcome Mat Frayed and Unravelling. *The Globe and Mail.* <http://migration.ucdavis.edu/rs/more.php?id=158_0_2_0>.

Nelson, Fraser (2007, May 2). MI5 is Much Enhanced Since Crevice: But It Still Can't Make Guarantees. *The Spectator.* <http://www.spectator.co.uk/the-magazine/the-week/29392/mi5-is-much-enhanced-since-crevice-but-it-still-cant-make-guarantees.thtml>.

Pereira, Clarisse (2002, November 28). Imams on Dutch Culture Course. *BBC News.* <http://news.bbc.co.uk/1/hi/world/europe/2525407.stm>.

Singer, Colin (2002, December 6). The Facts about Immigration. *National Post.* <http://www.immigration.ca/permres-nationalpost.asp>.

Singh v. *Minister of Employment and Immigration*, [1985] 1 S.C.R. 177.

Trifkovic, Srdja (2007, June 5). A French Lesson for George W. Bush. *Chronicles*. <http://www.chroniclesmagazine.org/?p=108>. Accessed December 18, 2007.

United States Department of State (2008). *Background Note: France.* <http://www.state.gov/r/pa/ei/bgn/3842.htm>.

Chapter 6

Security Threats on America's Borders

Glynn Custred

There are probably no two countries in the world that are as much alike as the United States and Canada. Each is proud of its legal system derived from Anglo-Saxon law and, with the exception of Québec, both share a common language and a common cultural heritage. Canadians and Americans are "children of a common mother," as the Peace Arch on the border at Blaine, Washington, proclaims. Indeed, immigration and settlement patterns explain this commonality. The core of English-speaking Canada emigrated from the newly independent United States after the American Revolution and, during the settlement of western North America, the populations of the two countries crossed their mutual border, mingling along the way in response to changing opportunities (Hanson, 1940).

The great transatlantic migration from Europe in the nineteenth century brought the same kinds of immigrants to both the United States and Canada. The Second Great Migration, which is now in full-swing, is bringing similar kinds of people from other continents into both countries. This new wave of immigration is creating immigrant populations on both sides of the border who are similar in composition and dynamics.

Canada and the United States also have interdependent economies. Trade is one of the most important relationships between the two countries.

An enormous volume of trade passes across the border each way every day. Trade contributes to the prosperity of Canada to a great extent, and to the prosperity of the United States to a lesser extent.

Despite increasing economic interdependence and the commonality of language, cultural heritage, and population, the border that separates the two countries, "the continental divide" as Seymour Martin Lipset (1990) has described it, is a significant element, not only in their relationship with one another, but also in their separate identities. Historian Benedict Anderson (1991) has described modern nation states as "imagined communities" because nations are collectively imagined by their members as communities. In other words, nations are thought of by their members as definable cohesive entities, imagined as sovereign and limited by the special rights and privileges of citizenship that mark the distinction with other polities and by borders that define the territorial limits of sovereign states. They are imagined thusly, despite the necessary heterogeneity of their large populations. From this definition, we can infer that borders are important to the definition and the constitution of the modern nation and state.

In this broad sense, the Canada-United States border is like all others. It differs from other borders, however, because of the unique history of the two countries and because of the different roles the border plays in how Americans and Canadians imagine their distinctive identities. Roger Gibbins writes that the border has "a mythic significance, at least in Canada," both due to its great length and because of its reputation as the longest undefended border in the world. Two factors account for the symbolic importance of the border in Canada: the overshadowing presence of its powerful neighbour to the south, and the fact that four-fifths of the Canadian population lives within 150 kilometres of the international boundary, making Canada a "borderland society" where the border "penetrates the Canadian consciousness, national identity, economy and polity to a degree unknown and unimaginable in the United States" (1997: 316–317).

American vulnerability on the northern border

Since 9/11, the border has assumed a more prominent place in American consciousness, not as a defining element in its collective identity, but rather as a zone of vulnerability along its entire northern rim. The danger comes not from a hostile country to the north, but from an immigration policy that makes it easier for aliens hostile to the United States to enter Canada, disappear within the country, and connect with networks submerged in its large immigrant communities. Indeed, lax immigration laws in Canada concern both American and Canadian authorities.

This situation is graphically illustrated by the case of Ahmed Ressam, the "millennium bomber," who was caught trying to enter the United States from Canada with material for a bomb that was designed to blow up the Los Angeles International airport during the millennium celebration. Ressam entered Canada with no documents at all. Though he was not given refugee status, Ressam did not appear at a scheduled government hearing on his case. He was arrested several times but was never expelled from Canada, and was eventually caught by an alert United States customs agent while coming into the United States from Canada at the Port Angeles crossing in Washington. The customs agent suspected Ressam possessed drugs, but found materials for bombs instead.

The Ressam case illustrates what Canadian experts have described as parallel systems of immigration: one with formal regulations and procedures, and the other—the one that Ressam and thousands of others take advantage of every day, which operates as an end-run around the formal system, creating in Canada an entryway for foreigners, some of whom are hostile to both the United States and Canada—which operates outside the boundaries of security. As a result, the border has taken on a greater significance in the United States as Americans contemplate national security.

The incoherence of American homeland security

The problem with American border security, however, does not lie solely with Canada, despite the clear and present danger indicated by a number of incidents before 9/11. The American government's incoherent policies reflect a mix of inattention, incompetence, and the tug-of-war between the security needs of the nation and powerful economic and ideological interests.

The case of the millennium bomber illustrates the problem of incompetence under the Clinton administration. The National Security Advisor at that time, Sandy Berger, ordered Richard Clarke, then Chief of Counterterrorism, to prepare an "after action" report on the incident. The report is classified and has been described as "highly secret." However, speaking to journalists on the condition of anonymity, one federal official who has seen the report said that it was actually "a scathing indictment" of the administration's anti-terrorism policies (Gerstein, 2006, Dec. 21). There must be some truth to this statement because after 9/11, when security policies were under close scrutiny, Berger was caught stealing multiple copies of the document from the National Archives with the intent of destroying them. Berger avoided prison with a plea bargain that gave him probation, community service, and a $50,000 fine (York, 2004, July 21).

American laxity regarding its borders has existed since long before the Clinton administration. In 2005, Mark Reed, a former Immigration and Naturalization Service commissioner with authority over both the Mexican and Canadian borders, told a joint meeting of the Subcommittee on Immigration, Border Security, and Citizenship, and the Subcommittee on Terrorism, Technology, and Homeland Security of the Senate Committee on the Judiciary about a high level meeting he attended 20 years prior. In attendance were representatives from federal law enforcement, as well as the Departments of Defense, Justice, and State. They had met to decide how the agencies would coordinate their efforts on the war on drugs that the president had just declared.

One topic was the urgency of sealing the Mexican border so as to stop drug smuggling into the United States. Members of the Department of Defense (DOD) said that they were capable of detecting and interdicting any intrusion across the border. They were unable, however, to distinguish between groups of migrants and drug smugglers until the individuals detected had been interdicted. At that point, said Reed, "the dialogue became difficult. When DOD refused to entertain the idea that they should only detain drug smugglers upon interdiction, the meeting was abruptly terminated. The safety valve that illegal immigration provided toward the stability of Mexico seemed to be a more compelling national security priority than drug smuggling" (Reed, 2005).

Reed told the committee that almost 10 years later, the Border Patrol launched a highly visible project, Operation Gatekeeper, "to stop an invasion of thousands of illegal border-crossers from Mexico" who were coming across the border every night between the ports of entry just south of San Diego (Reed, 2005). Gatekeeper was part of a larger border strategy known as the Southwest Border Initiative, designed to gain control of the border one sector at a time, "marching," as Reed put it, from the Pacific to the Gulf of Mexico until the entire border was secured. The initiative also included plans to concentrate resources on corridors of human and drug smuggling and on aggressive work site enforcement in order to attack the "magnet" that draws illegal immigrants into the country. "It seemed to be a very measured, balanced approach to border enforcement", he told the committees, "and still does" because entries were actually deterred. The project, however, turned out to be a piecemeal effort. "Resources to attack the corridors never materialized and work site enforcement resources actually dwindled." Eventually the "marching strategy" was abandoned (Reed, 2005).

Purposely porous borders

Under the administration of George W. Bush, the situation became even worse. Border control and interior enforcement came to a halt. The pursuit of fleeing aliens was prohibited, check points along corridors leading from the border into the interior were greatly curtailed and thus made ineffective, and agents were assigned to fixed positions. Line agents and supervisors have said that illegal entrants simply go around these fixed positions.

The 9/11 Commission highlighted the role that illegal immigration plays in the threat to American security, and recommended, among other things, that additional manpower be devoted to the Border Patrol (National Commission on Terrorist Attacks Upon the United States, 2004). The Bush administration, however, immediately began a campaign to remove any measures that would have an impact on the immigration status quo. In 2005, when Congress authorized the hiring of 2,000 new Border Patrol agents as recommended by the commission, the Bush administration only allocated enough money for 210 agents—not even enough to cover attrition. When asked about this funding reduction, current Homeland Security Chief Tom Ridge called the money "fools gold." In fact, for the 2006 fiscal year, the budget for the Border Patrol was only $80 million, an indication that the function the Patrol serves has fallen out of favour with the present administration.

In 2006, Congress authorized a 700 mile-long fence along the Mexican border. However, by the end of the year, only 150 miles had been built (Nuñez-Neto and Garcia, 2007). Even along the most modernized section of the border in San Diego County, which before Operation Gatekeeper was a place of massive illegal entry, there is still a gap, known as Smuggler's Gulch, through which illegal migration still flows. Congress made provisions in the 2006 legislation to secure this gap. However, it remains open (Nuñez-Neto and Garcia, 2007).

In his testimony before the Senate Judiciary Committee, Reed observed, "the DOD stated that they could provide the technology and resources to detect any intrusion along the Mexican border." But, he added, "almost two decades later the Border Patrol still cannot 'see' most of the border." He told the committee that "detection is a fundamental enabler of any border security strategy. Acquisition of that ability cannot languish any longer" (Reed, 2005).

In 2007, the Border Patrol was still lacking adequate detection capabilities, even though an effective system has been developed for that purpose. The system, produced by the Raytheon Corporation, is known as Project Athena and is similar to the North American Aerospace Defense Command (NORAD), which routinely monitors a large number of targets for North American air defense. The system consists of a secure wireless network, integrated ground-air surveillance, and enhanced communications and computer data processing. Although Project Athena is able to detect low flying aircraft and terrestrial movement, its ability to detect maritime targets is especially effective. The advantage of the system is that it focuses on enforcement rather than arbitrary patrolling and tracking, thus making border control far more efficacious. The system was field tested by multiple enforcement agencies in Operation Gulfview along 120 miles of land border, 160 miles of coastline, and nine ports of entry between the United States and Mexico. That test showed that the system is effective and ready for deployment (Raytheon, 2006).

The Department of Homeland Security, however, has indicated that it has no intention of deploying the system. In the meantime, the vehicles and communication equipment used by the Border Patrol are inadequate. Moreover, the bulletproof vests and armaments issued to agents are no match for the mercenaries hired by the smugglers to guard their illicit trade (Carter, 2006, June 7).

In the absence of better surveillance or a physical barrier, putting troops along the border offers the best enhancement through which to curb mass migration and the crime that it causes. Under pressure, the Bush administration did assign soldiers to the border, but this move appeared to be more of a public relations tactic than a real effort to secure the border, as the troops have not been allowed to perform effectively. For example, in 2006, when a unit was confronted by heavily armed intruders from Mexico, the American soldiers were told to fall back. Most of them were veterans of Iraq and Afghanistan, where their orders had been much different. This situation did not go over well with the troops (Associated Press, 2007, May 1).

Going north after dark

As thousands of migrants pass uncontrolled across the border each year, the situation is becoming chaotic. For example, in the winter of 2007, an organization (of which the author is a member) called Friends of the Border Patrol took a visiting congressman, Ted Poe, a Republican from Texas, on a tour of the border in San Diego County. Just after sunset, while standing on a hilltop above Smuggler's Gulch, we heard gunfire on the other side of the border. We did not know the cause, but the former United States Army Corps of Engineers officer who had built the infrastructure that we were inspecting—and who was guiding us on our trip—quietly told us that it was time to leave. Indeed, such precautions must be taken in many other places along that often perilous border—sometimes even before dark.

The sheer mass of migrants flowing across the border is disruptive to small borderland communities and rural dwellers, and brings the danger of criminals, individuals, and organizations who enter unrestricted with this flow. In this regard, Congressman Poe said, in a speech in the House of Representatives in 2007, that small communities on the border "live in fear of their lives because our borders are open"—a fact that seems to carry little weight with the United States government (Poe, 2007).

The situation is even worse in Mexico. Organized drug cartels, together with weak institutions and a long tradition of corruption, have neutralized the sovereignty of the Mexico state in certain areas such that the government in those areas can be regarded as equivalent to a failed state. For example, in areas where some military units act as mercenaries for the drug cartels, the government cannot exercise control over its own military. These mercenary units enter the United States at will and sometimes fire at outgunned American authorities (*KFOX*, 2006, Mar. 21).

The United States government is well aware of these incidents. In fact, the Border Patrol in the Tucson area—one of the most traveled corridors of illegal entry—has issued a wallet-sized plastic card to its agents that states, "REMEMBER, Mexican Military are trained to escape, evade, and counter-ambush if it will affect their escape." The card also gives directions regarding how agents should react if Mexican army units are encountered on the American side of the border, advising agents to stay out of their way, as a last resort (Carter, 2005, Dec. 19). In an internal document that was leaked to journalists, the Department of Homeland Security (DHS) noted that 200 such incursions had occurred between 1996 and 2006, and included a map showing the points of entry (Carter, 2006, Jan. 15; *Inland Valley Daily Bulletin*, 2006, Jan. 20). The United States government, however, has downplayed these incidents repeatedly. The Sheriff of Hudspeth County has called attention to this problem (West, 2006), as has Congressman Poe. In a speech on the House floor in September 2007, Poe argued, "Our federal government has the duty to keep the Mexican military out of our Nation," adding that "it has no business being here for any purpose." Yet the government refuses to do anything about it (Poe, 2007).

The volume of illegal entry, as well as the fact that the ability of the Border Patrol to do its job has been hindered, has resulted in a rising level of attacks on agents, some involving shots fired across the border and some involving assaults by armed intruders into the United States. For example, in 2005, two agents were ambushed on the American side of the border near Nogales, Arizona. Both agents were wounded and had to be evacuated by helicopter (Seper, 2005, July 6).

In Mexico, the problem is even worse. Mexican police who obstruct drug trafficking, or have accepted a bribe from the wrong side of a struggle between the cartels, are assassinated. This problem is not restricted to border cities, but is found in the interior as well. In several instances, officers have been found decapitated, their heads left in one place and their bodies in another. This brutal act serves as a warning to authorities to keep out of the traffickers' business.

This problem is particularly well illustrated by a spectacular series of events that took place in Nuevo Laredo, a borderland community, on June 8, 2005. On this day, Alejandro Dominquez was murdered only hours after taking office as the city's police chief. Federal police were dispatched to the city after the assassination. When they arrived, a gunfight broke out between the federal police and the local police, causing several casualties. Troops from the Mexican army were dispatched to the city in an effort to get control. The entire 750 man local police force was suspended until drug tests and background checks could be completed. Two hundred policemen resigned or were fired. One suspended policeman committed suicide, and 41 others were flown to Mexico City for further investigation (Associated Press, 2005, Oct. 6). To make matters worse, Dominquez's successor, Omar Pimentel was also attacked on his first day in office in a drive-by shooting. Pimentel escaped with his life, but one of his bodyguards was killed (Associated Press, 2005, Oct. 6). As of August 2005, it was estimated that Nuevo Laredo was experiencing three execution-style murders per week, totaling 109 to date for that year (Thompson, 2005, Dec. 4).

The international bridge between Nuevo Laredo and Laredo, usually one of the busiest corridors between Mexico and the United States, was nearly empty on the Monday following the shoot-out in Nuevo Laredo. On the following Friday, the head of the city council's public security committee and a police commander were ambushed and murdered only blocks from city hall. A policeman and an unidentified passerby were wounded in the incident. A total of 170 deaths resulting from drug-related violence in Nuevo Laredo were reported in 2005 (Jordan and Sullivan, 2005, June 16).

These incidents are not isolated. On July 28, 2005, a middle-class neighbourhood two miles south of the border was rocked by automatic rifle fire, bazookas, and grenades. For 30 minutes, the battle raged with sounds of explosions echoing through the city. Residents later told reporters that they heard nothing. The police did not immediately provide a version of what happened. Eye witnesses, who asked to remain anonymous, said that armed men wearing what appeared to be the uniform of the Mexican Federal Agency of Investigation descended upon a house in the district when the firing began. Afterwards, 300 well-armed troops from the Mexican army used tanks to cordon off the devastated area for inspection (Associated Press, 2005, Oct. 6). The United States Embassy in Mexico issued an announcement describing the battle as an "alarming incident" in which "unusually advanced weaponry" was used (Associated Press, 2005, Oct. 6).

Before and since those events, gunfire has erupted in the borderlands of Mexico and people have been killed. One of the most recent reported incidents took place in May 2007, in the town of Cananea, which is 20 miles south of the Arizona border. The incident occurred after police and soldiers confronted a band of "Zetas"—former Mexican army elite troops who now work as mercenaries for the cartels. A total of 23 died as a result of the incident, five of whom were policemen (McCombs, 2007, May 20; Nevarez, 2007, May 17). In March 2008, the police chief of another Mexican border town, Palomas, showed up at the port of entry at Columbus, New Mexico, seeking asylum, saying that his two deputies had left him and that he feared for his life and needed protection (Associated Press, 2008, Mar. 21). At a recent conference of Mexican and American law enforcement agents, one official with the Sonora State Attorney General's office said that the drug war situation is "a constant battle, because the monster is so very powerful" (Associated Press, 2007, June 6).

The connection between terrorism and drug trafficking

Terrorists seek power vacuums in which to operate and chaotic situations in order to move about. The United States-Mexico border provides such conditions. It shouldn't seem unimaginable that terrorists with lots of money and drug cartels that have no scruples may eventually cooperate with one another. In fact, this state of affairs is confirmed by documents from the Department of Defense and the Drug Enforcement Agency (DEA) that were leaked to journalists. The DEA documents, dated 2005, report that terrorist cells inside the United States are cooperating with drug smuggling cartels in order to fund terrorist activities abroad. The document also reports that Islamic radicals who speak Spanish, Arabic, and Hebrew fluently are camouflaging themselves as Hispanics. The report even contains photographs of such individuals "who appear to be Hispanics" but are "in fact, all Spanish-speaking Arabic drug traffickers supporting Middle Eastern terrorism from their base of operations" in the Southwest. The report notes that some of these individuals have ties to the radical Muslim Brotherhood. In addition, a Department of Defense document dated 2006 reports that al-Qaeda has attempted and is planning to use the United States-Mexico border as an entry point into the United States (Carter 2007, Aug. 8; 2007, Aug. 9).

Asa Hutchinson, who began his three-year term as director of the DEA one month before the 9/11 attacks, emphasizes the link between trafficking and terrorist activity. Hutchinson notes that extremists everywhere around the world are "benefiting from drug trafficking," and—in reference to the Mexican border—that "it should be no surprise to anyone that terrorists should exploit our weakness" (Carter, 2007, Aug. 14). In 2001, he told federal authorities that terrorists would exploit weaknesses in the system if the United States did not create and maintain a foolproof immigration system and enhance security on the border.

Mark Juergensmeyer, director of the Ortalen Center for Global and International Studies at the University of California, Santa Barbara, notes that links between terrorist organizations are well established around the world. Speaking specifically about the 2005 DEA documents, he said that the information reported there reveals a new evolution in terrorist tactics that poses serious security concerns. "In some ways," he said, "that's even more frightening to think that drug trafficking organizations in Mexico may adopt some jihadist's ideology. If it's an ideology being adopted by a drug culture then that makes the situation very dangerous" (Carter, 2007, Aug. 8).

Mike McConnell, a retired Vice Admiral, director of the National Security Agency from 1992 to 1996, and current director of National Intelligence, serves as the principal advisor to President George W. Bush on matters of national security. Regarding the possibility of terrorists using the southwest border as a means of entry into the United States, McConnell has said, "There are some [terrorists]. And would they use it as a path given that it was available to them? In time they will." He cited the easing of visa restrictions in Latin America, which has facilitated the movement of people within the Western Hemisphere, as a contributing factor. A passport from a Middle Eastern country will allow an individual to enter one of the South or Central American countries. McConnell noted that "there are a significant number of Iraqis that came across [the southwest border] last year" (Roberts, 2007, Aug. 23).

In a speech before the North Texas Crime Commission in September 2007, Texas Homeland Security Director Steve McGraw echoed those concerns, reporting that individuals who have connections to Hamas, Hezbollah, and al-Qaeda have been arrested on the Texas-Mexico border. "A porous border," he said, "without question is a national security threat" (Carlton, 2007, Sep. 12). When the Associated Press queried federal officials regarding the threat described by McGraw, the possibility of this threat was downplayed by the officials (Carlton, 2007, Sep. 12).

Secure trade, corruption, and visions of a New North America

Despite the military effort against terrorist organizations currently underway in the Middle East in the name of national security, the Bush administration still refuses to face the security consequences of its de facto partial open border policy with Mexico. One can only speculate as to why, but it seems that there are a number of factors contributing to the government's unwillingness to acknowledge these security concerns. A major factor is the constant tug-of-war between commercial interests and security—a struggle that commerce seems to be winning.

Certain ideologies also contribute. The no-borders libertarianism of, for example, *The Wall Street Journal*, supports open markets at any cost. There is also a new transnational vision of North America that has been articulated among an elite group of business leaders, government officials, and intellectuals. This vision follows the example of the European Union, and was often articulated by former Mexican President Vicente Fox. Such plans have been presented in a report titled *Building a North American Community*, sponsored by the Council on Foreign Relations, along with the Canadian Council of Chief Executives and the Consejo Mexicano de Asuntos Internacionales (Pastor et al., 2005). The architect of the plan was American university professor Robert Pastor who has testified in support of the plan before the United States Congress and the Canadian Parliament.

Progress towards the creation of an European Union-like single market for North America has gone beyond the initial stages and is now under consideration for practical application by work groups made up of officials and bureaucrats from all three countries. This initiative is known as the Security and Prosperity Partnership of North America (SPP), and was launched by President George Bush, President Vicente Fox, and Prime Minister Paul Martin at a meeting held in Waco, Texas, in March 2005 (United States Department of State, 2005).

An ideological commitment to furthering North American economic integration—what may be called a "New North America"—constitutes the context in which markets and commerce trump national sovereignty and security. The problem is not with commerce and security. We have both all the time. In fact, we need security in order to have productive commerce. The problem is the way in which the elite in the United States are mismanaging the kinds of changes that are now under way. Because of this, commerce is being favoured over security in a way that is detrimental to almost everyone concerned.

Another factor contributing to the government's unwillingness to acknowledge border-related security concerns is corruption. More commerce and closer relationships between countries do not mean that negative features from one country will necessarily flow to another. However, it is naïve to think that a New North America will result in a one way diffusion of positive public behaviour from the United States to Mexico. With the reduction in border enforcement and the amount of money involved in the illegal drug trade, the kind of corruption that has plagued

Mexico since colonial times is spilling over the border and seeping into the United States.

This trend is developing as a result of what is, in essence, a partial open border policy with Mexico, as well as a failure on the part of the American elite to recognize that there are great differences between the United States-Canada border and the United States-Mexico border. The European Union is not a good model for North America because, unlike anywhere else in the world, the United States-Mexico border is the only place where a common land border separates the first and the third worlds. This fact should be recognized and dealt with when considering border policy.

Under these conditions, a North American defense perimeter to guard against the international terrorist threat is either disingenuous or wishful thinking. To the north, the Canadian elite are too committed to a politically correct immigration policy in which security plays a minor part. To the south, Mexico cannot even defend itself against powerful and dangerous domestic enemies that threaten the Mexican state. The only prudent move that the United States can make under such conditions is to reinforce its own borders.

References

Anderson, Benedict (1991). *Imagined Communities*. Verso.

Associated Press (2005, October 6). Mexican Border Struggles with Lawlessness.

Associated Press (2007, May 1). Gunmen Attack National Guard Border Patrol Site in Arizona. *Fox News*. <http://www.foxnews.com/story/0,2933,241783,00.html>. Accessed December 20, 2007.

Associated Press (2007, June 6). Mexican US Law Agents Worried about Drug Cartel Violence. *KTAR*. <http://ktar.com/?nid=6&sid=503766>. Accessed December 20, 2007.

Associated Press (2008, March 21). Mexican Police Chief Requests Asylum.

Carlton, Jeff (2007, September 12). Security Chief Says Terrorists Have Been Arrested on Texas Border. Associated Press.

Carter, Sara (2005, December 19). Border Patrol Fears Run-Ins with Mexican Military. *Inland Valley Daily Bulletin*. <http://lang.dailybulletin.com/socal/beyondborders/part_4/p4_day2_military.asp>. Accessed December 20, 2007.

Carter, Sara (2006, January 15). Mexican Soldiers Defy Border. *Inland Valley Daily Bulletin*.

Carter, Sara (2006, June 7). Smuggling, Drug-Running, Violence Define Mexican Border: Testimony. *Inland Valley Daily Bulletin*. <http://www.dailybulletin.com/search/ci_4016983?IADID=Search-www.dailybulletin.com-www.dailybulletin.com>.

Carter, Sara (2007, August 8). Hearings Urged on DEA Report. *Washington Times.* <http://washingtontimes.com/article/20070808/ NATION/108080102/1002>. Accessed December 20, 2007.

Carter, Sara (2007, August 9). Hearings Sought on Islamic, Mexican Ties. *Washington Times.*

Carter, Sara (2007, August 14). Drug Cartel-Terrorist Ties Known in 2001. *Washington Times.* <http://www.washingtontimes.com/apps/ pbcs.dll/article?AID=/20070814/NATION/108140073/1001>. Accessed December 20, 2007.

Gerstein, Josh (2006, December 21). How an Ex-Aide to President Clinton Stashed Classified Documents. *New York Sun.* <http://www. nysun.com/article/45551>. Accessed December 20, 2007.

Gibbins, Roger (1997). The Meaning and Significance of the American-Canadian Border. In Paul Ganster, Alan Sweedler, James Scott, and Wolf-Deiter Eberwein (eds.), *Borders and Border Regions of Europe and North America.* San Diego State University Press.

Hanson, Marcus (1940). *The Mingling of the Canadian and American Peoples.* Yale University Press.

Inland Valley Daily Bulletin (2006, January 20). Congress Must Probe Reports of Border Incursions. <http://dreier.house.gov/inthepress/ ap051605.htm>. Accessed December 20, 2007.

Jordan, Mary, and Kevin Sullivan (2005, June 16). Border Police Chief Only Latest Casualty in Mexico Drug War. *Washington Post.* <http:// www.washingtonpost.com/wp-dyn/content/article/2005/06/15/ AR2005061502553_pf.html>. Accessed December 20, 2007.

KFOX (2006, March 21). Hudspeth County Incursion Latest. <http:// www.kfoxtv.com/bordersecurity/8174431/detail.html>.

Lipset, Seymour Martin (1990). *Continental Divide: The Values and Institutions of the United States and Canada.* Routledge.

McCombs, Brady (2007, May 20). In Cananea Residents Still on Edge. *Arizona Daily Star.*

National Commission on Terrorist Attacks Upon the United States (2004). *The 9/11 Commission Report.* W.W. Norton & Company.

Nevarez, Oman (2007, May 17). Body Found Invokes Attacks by Cartels. Associated Press.

Nuñez-Neto, Blas, and Michael John Garcia (2007). *Border Security: The San Diego Fence.* Congressional Research Service, The Library of Congress. <http://opencrs.cdt.org/document/RS22026>. Accessed December 20, 2007.

Pastor, Robert, John P. Manley, Pedro Aspe, William F. Weld, Thomas P. d'Aquino, and Andreas Rozental (2005). *Building a North American Community.* Council on Foreign Relations Press. <http://www.cfr.org/publication/8102/>. Accessed December 20, 2007.

Poe, Ted (2007). The Texas/Mexico Border. Speech delivered in United States House of Representatives, September 7, 2007. <http://poe.house.gov/News/DocumentSingle.aspx?DocumentID=73482>. Accessed October 1, 2007.

Raytheon (2006). Project Athena Multi-Domain Awareness System. <http://www.raytheon.com/media/pas07/pdf/athena.pdf>. Accessed October 1, 2007.

Reed, Mark (2005). The Need for Comprehensive Immigration Reform and Strengthening Our National Security. Testimony before the Subcommittee on Immigration, Border Security, and Citizenship, and the Subcommittee on Terrorism, Technology, and Homeland Security

of the United States Senate Committee on the Judiciary, United
States Congress, May 17, 2005. <http://judiciary.senate.gov/testimony.
cfm?id=1502&wit_id=4281>. Accessed December 20, 2007.

Roberts, Chris (2007, August 22). Transcript: Debate on the Foreign
Intelligence Surveillance Act. *El Paso Times*. <http://www.elpasotimes.
com/news/ci_6685679>. Accessed December 20, 2007.

Roberts, Chris (2007, August 23). Intelligence Chief Sees Border as
Terrorist Entryway. *El Paso Times*. <http://www.elpasotimes.com/news/
ci_6683672>. Accessed December 20, 2007.

Seper, Jerry (2005, July 6). Injured Border Agents Likely Were
Ambushed. *Washington Times*. A3.

Thompson, Ginger (2005, December 4). Rival Drug Gangs Turn the
Streets of Nuevo Laredo into a War Zone. *The New York Times*. <http://
www.nytimes.com/2005/12/04/international/americas/04barbie.html>.
Accessed December 20, 2007.

United States Department of State (2005). North American Leaders
Unveil Security and Prosperity Partnership. News release (March 23).
<http://usinfo.state.gov/is/Archive/2005/Mar/23-209281.html>.
Accessed December 20, 2007.

West, Arvin (2006). Armed and Dangerous: Confronting the
Problem of Border Incursions. Statement before the Subcommittee
on Investigations, of the Committee on Homeland Security,
United States House of Representatives, February 7, 2006. <http://
frwebgate.access.gpo.gov/cgi-bin/getdoc.cgi?dbname=109_house_
hearings&docid=f:35965.pdf>. Accessed December 20, 2007.

York, Byron (2004, July 21). Sandy Berger's Heavy Lifting. *National
Review*. <http://www.nationalreview.com/york/york200407210837.asp>.
December 20, 2007.

Chapter 7

The Need to Balance Liberty and Security

Jan C. Ting

Since the terrible attacks of September 11, 2001, democratic governments in North America and Europe have tried to respond to the threat of Islamic terrorism by adopting new security procedures intended to prevent a repetition of that day's events. In doing so, these governments have been admonished—sometimes, through the words of Benjamin Franklin—to find the right balance between liberty and security. But how exactly do we do that? What methods and measures can or should we employ to evaluate our new security procedures?

One way to balance liberty and security is to subject the new security procedures to political and judicial scrutiny. In the United States, for example, there has been a protracted debate over the *USA PATRIOT Act*, which was enacted overwhelmingly by both Houses of Congress in the wake of the terrorist attacks and signed into law by President George W. Bush on October 26, 2001.[1] This Act was a catchall for many new initia-

---

1   The Congressional vote in favour of the Act was 356 to 66 in the House of Representatives, and 98 to 1 in the Senate.

tives, most of which were non-controversial,[2] but a few of which drew public attention and controversy.

The Act authorized the sharing of foreign intelligence information among federal enforcement, intelligence, and national defense agencies (2001: s. 203; Ting, 2002). It expanded surveillance authority involving foreign powers or agents, and authorized roaming wiretap warrants specific to a target, rather than a device or carrier (*USA PATRIOT Act*, s. 206). It also authorized government inspection of business records (s. 215). As well, it extended to the internet the government's existing authority to record incoming and outgoing addressing and routing information (ss. 216–17).

In response to objections and controversy over these provisions, Congress added a "sunset clause" by which these parts of the Act would automatically expire in four years unless reauthorized by Congress (*USA PATRIOT Act*, s. 224). This provision ensured that the entire Act would be subject to review by the Congress. After extensive debate, during which the "sunset" deadline was extended by one year, reauthorizing legislation was enacted by Congress and signed by President Bush on March 9, 2006. This legislation made permanent 14 of 16 expiring parts of the 2001 Act (Yeh and Doyle, 2006). New four-year sunset extensions were enacted for two of the expiring provisions: section 206, which authorizes surveillance of foreign powers or agents, and section 215, which authorizes inspection of business records (Yeh and Doyle, 2006).

Does the overwhelming bipartisan support[3] for reauthorizing this legislation, as well as judicial oversight,[4] resolve the liberty versus security

---

2   The *USA PATRIOT Act* increased funding for counterterrorism activities, particularly for increased border protection. It also condemned discrimination against Arab and Muslim Americans, extended expiring immigration benefits for 9/11 victims, and provided direct assistance for victims and their families (ss. 101–103, 402–427, and 611–624). The Act also included new initiatives to prevent and disrupt the financing of terrorist organizations, strengthen criminal laws against terrorism, and improve intelligence gathering (ss. 301–377, 801–817, and 901–908).

3   The final vote on reauthorization was 251 to 174 in the House of Representatives, and 89 to 10 in the Senate (Congresspedia, 2007).

4   Legal challenges to some provisions of the *USA PATRIOT Act* have not been sustained by United States courts. For examples, see *American Civil Liberties Union* v.

debate, or are there other factors to be considered? This chapter will consider some other factors. But before considering these factors, I will examine another example of extensive Congressional and judicial oversight with respect to balancing liberty and security—namely, the subject of military tribunals and the detention of enemy combatants.

Balancing liberty and security: military tribunals and the detention of enemy combatants

Yasir Hamdi was a United States citizen who was captured in Afghanistan as an enemy combatant, fighting on behalf of hostile forces there. In the 2004 *Hamdi* v. *Rumsfeld* decision, the United States Supreme Court found that the Congressional Authorization for Use of Military Force authorized the detention of such enemy combatants for the duration of hostilities without criminal trial. But the Supreme Court also held that a United States citizen-detainee, such as Hamdi, who was seeking to challenge classification as an enemy combatant, was entitled to notice of the basis for classification and a fair opportunity to rebut before a neutral decision maker, which could be a military tribunal.

The United States government's attempts to conform to the Hamdi ruling by instituting Combatant Status Review Tribunals for alien enemy combatants detained in Guantanamo Bay, Cuba, were alternately approved and rejected by the courts in the United States.[5] To clarify the law and end litigation, Congress enacted the *Detainee Treatment Act* of 2005, which provided in part that, except as provided therein,

> no court, justice, or judge shall have jurisdiction to hear or consider—

United States Department of Justice, and *Doe* v. *Ashcroft*, which struck the non-disclosure provision of the national security letter subpoena power. On review, the US Court of Review for the Second Circuit vacated the ruling because changes made in the 2006 reauthorization made the issue moot (see *Bush* v. *Gonzales*).

5   Compare *Khalid* v. *Bush* with In Re Guantanamo Detainee Cases.

(1) an application for a writ of habeas corpus filed by or on behalf of an alien detained by the Department of Defense at Guantanamo Bay, Cuba; or

(2) any other action against the United States or its agents relating to any aspect of the detention by the Department of Defense of an alien at Guantanamo Bay, Cuba. (Jurist, 2005: s. 1005)

The case of *Hamdan* v. *Rumsfeld* provides another example of Congressional and judicial oversight. Hamdan was a Yemeni national taken into custody by United States forces in Afghanistan in 2002. Upon his transfer to Guantanamo Bay and classification as an enemy combatant, the United States military prepared to try Hamdan for conspiracy "to commit .... offenses triable by military commission." A federal district court granted habeas corpus and stayed the military commission proceedings. The District of Columbia Circuit Court reversed this decision. In its 2006 opinion, the United States Supreme Court reversed the District of Columbia Circuit Court's decision and remanded the case to the district court. With respect to the Hamdan case, the United States Supreme Court interpreted the *Detainee Treatment Act* as applying only prospectively and not to pending cases. Putting that statute aside, it found that Congress had, by a different statute, authorized courts to exercise jurisdiction over military proceedings, that the military commission at issue was not authorized by Congress, and that the commission violated the Uniform Code of Military Justice enacted by Congress, and the Geneva Conventions of 1949.

In response to this holding, Congress enacted the *Military Commissions Act* of 2006, which reinforced and broadened the language of the *Detainee Treatment Act*, denying courts jurisdiction over habeas claims of detained alien enemy combatants, and specifying its applicability "to all cases, without exception, pending on or after the date of enactment" (s. 7.b).

On February 20, 2007, the United States Circuit Court for the District of Columbia, in the *Boumediene* v. *Bush* case, dismissed the petitions for habeas corpus of alien enemy combatants detained at Guantanamo Bay, Cuba, ruling that the *Military Commissions Act* removed jurisdiction from the courts, except as specified in the *Detainee Treatment Act*.

On April 2, 2007, the Supreme Court of the United States declined to hear an appeal from the lower court holding in Boumediene. On June 27, 2007, the Supreme Court reversed itself and granted certiorari[6] to hear an appeal from the lower court holding in Boumediene. We await with interest the pending Supreme Court ruling on whether and to what extent laws enacted by Congress and signed by the President can limit the access of alien enemy combatants detained outside the United States to United States courts.

The so-called "Terrorist Surveillance Program" provides another example of the three branches of the United States government grappling with the balance between liberty and security. Under this program, communications to and from the United States were intercepted by the National Security Agency without judicial warrant or oversight (Eggen, 2007, Jan. 18). The American Civil Liberties Union and others expressed concern that the communications of people in the United States may be intercepted under this program without judicial oversight. In response, the Executive Branch agreed to continue the program only with warrants and the oversight of the federal judges who serve in the special court created under the *Foreign Intelligence Surveillance Act* (Eggen, 2007, Jan. 18; Gonzales, 2007), while continuing to assert authority whenever it is necessary to act unilaterally under the United States Constitution (Risen, 2007, May 2).

Balancing liberty and security: five factors to consider

It would certainly seem that the three branches of the United States government are actively engaged in trying to find the right balance between liberty and security. But does the close involvement of Congress and the courts provide the necessary checks and balances against executive power? Can we conclude that, because all three branches of government are directly involved, the national security initiatives of the government appropriately consider both liberty and security interests?

---

6   Certiorari is a writ (order) of a higher court to a lower court to send all the documents in a case to it so that the higher court can review the lower court's decision (Hill and Hill, 2008).

Even if that were true, we still might want some basis from which to evaluate the justifications for new security initiatives proposed or otherwise not yet subjected to Congressional oversight or to judicial challenge and scrutiny. Thus, in addition to legal and constitutional sufficiency, I would like to suggest five additional factors which could be considered while seeking the appropriate balance between liberty and security. In a democratic society, it may be sufficient to rely on the legal and political process to find the right balance between liberty and security, whether during a time of peace or war. But specific factors can also be considered. As a starting point for discussion, I suggest that the following factors be included:

- *Historical precedent.* We should examine what was done in the past and determine whether it was justifiable.
- *Revocability of the initiative.* We should consider whether security initiatives can be changed or withdrawn when the threat recedes or when mistakes are recognized.
- *Location.* We should recognize that initiatives may be justified in some contexts, but not in others.
- *The nature of the threat.* We must understand, and neither trivialize nor exaggerate, the nature of the external and internal threat.
- *The likelihood of success.* We must be forthright about what works in terms of applying our moral and ethical sensibilities to the struggle to defend our nation and preserve liberty.

Historical precedent

In the first place, we will consider historical precedent. In the case of some national security initiatives, the historical precedent is fairly clear. For example, American history is replete with examples of the use of military tribunals during wartime, and the Supreme Court stated in 1952 that,

> Since our nation's earliest days, such [military] commissions have been constitutionally recognized agencies for meeting many urgent governmental responsibilities related to war. They have been called our common-law war courts. They have taken many forms and borne many names. Neither their procedure nor their jurisdiction

has been prescribed by statute. It has been adapted in each instance to the need that called it forth. (*Madsen* v. *Kinsella*)

In other cases where security initiatives depend on technological advances, historical precedents, if any, are weaker and of less certain meaning. Consider, for example, the government's expanded use of national security letters, as authorized by the *USA PATRIOT Act*, to acquire communication, banking, and credit data which might be surveyed for revealing patterns (cf. Gellman, 2005; Leahy, 2007). This practice cannot be measured against historical precedent because no such precedent exists.

Sometimes historical precedent is cited as an example of the wrong balance between liberty and security. The "internment" of Japanese-Americans during World War II, for example, is cited as a warning against the use of race, ethnicity, appearance, or similar factors as part of security screening. But should governments be limited in the current war on Islamic terrorism by such a negative historical precedent?

At minimum, the use of historical precedent should require some understanding of the precedential facts. For example, the three United States Supreme Court rulings related to the "internment" do not use that term. In the first case, *Hirabayashi* v. *United States*, the Supreme Court unanimously upheld a military curfew order applying only to persons of Japanese ancestry within a designated war zone. The Supreme Court, while noting that "distinctions between citizens solely because of their ancestry are by their very nature odious to a free people whose institutions are founded upon the doctrine of equality," nonetheless concluded, "we decide only that the curfew order as applied, and at the time it was applied, was within the boundaries of the war power."

In the second and most famous ruling, *Korematsu* v. *United States*, the United States Supreme Court, by a six to three vote, upheld the military order excluding persons of Japanese ancestry from a designated war zone. The Supreme Court stated that "nothing short of apprehension by the proper military authorities of the gravest imminent danger to the public safety can constitutionally justify either [curfew or exclusion]," but concluded that, in wartime, "the power to protect must be commensurate with the threatened danger."

In the *Korematsu* decision, the Supreme Court distinguished exclusion from the issue of detention, which was at issue in the third and least known case, *Ex Parte Endo*, which was decided the same day as *Korematsu*. Mitsuye Endo was a United States citizen of Japanese ancestry who was excluded from her original place of residence by the order upheld in *Korematsu*. Residing temporarily in a relocation camp operated by the United States government, she sought release from the camp, but, without compliance with regulations requiring either confirmation of employment, adequate financial resources, or living arrangements, she was denied release. After citing facts that showed that the relocation camps were an afterthought of the evacuation order, the Supreme Court concluded that "whatever power the War Relocation Authority may have to detain other classes of citizens, it has no authority to subject citizens who are concededly loyal to its leave procedure," and unanimously ordered Endo's unconditional release (cf. Malkin, 2004).

The Supreme Court's allowance of the use of ethnic ancestry in national security measures was limited to the facts of the military emergency following the 1941 Japanese attack on Pearl Harbor, and did not include involuntary detention of United States citizens whose loyalty was unquestioned. Post-war declassification of intercepts of Japanese diplomatic communications has also been cited as previously undisclosed justification for the military curfew and exclusion orders (Lowman, 2000).

Revocability of the initiative

A second and related factor we may consider while contemplating new national security measures is whether such measures are revocable, or will have a lasting impact on the liberty of a democratic society. Returning to our previous example, the question we may ask is, Have wartime measures such as the emergency curfew and evacuation of Japanese-Americans in fact resulted in less civil liberties after the war and today? Considering the current situation in the United States, we may ask, Is it likely that national security measures invoked since 9/11, such as military tribunals, detention of enemy combatants, surveillance, and information gathering regarding terrorist suspects, will impact civil liberties after the current war is over and the terrorist threat recedes?

Suspending civil liberties will not necessarily have a long-term impact. President Abraham Lincoln defended his suspension of the writ and right of habeas corpus during the United States Civil War, saying that he could no more believe that the necessary curtailment of civil liberties in wartime would establish precedents fatal to liberty in peacetime "than I am able to believe that a man could contract so strong an appetite for emetics during temporary illness, as to persist in feeding upon them through the remainder of his healthful life" (quoted in McPherson, 1988: 599).

It is sometimes argued that the current war on Islamic terrorism is different because of its already long and still indefinite duration. In response, it may be argued that it is not clear why duration should make any difference, that every war is of indefinite duration until the prospect of imminent victory or defeat appears on the horizon, and that defeat in the current war will mean a much greater loss of civil liberties than is contemplated in the discussion of current national security measures. It should be noted that whether the United States is actually at war, even without a formal declaration, and is, therefore, properly exercising war powers, is well-settled. The Supreme Court, in *Hamdi* v. *Rumsfeld*, cited the Congressional Authorization for the Use of Military Force adopted after 9/11 as authority for the detention of lawful and unlawful enemy combatants, which by "universal agreement and practice" are "important incident[s] of war." Earlier Supreme Court cases—such as The Amy Warwick (The Prize Cases) and *Bas* v. *Tingy*—held that other undeclared conflicts, including the United States Civil War, were legally wars, despite being undeclared.

Location

A third factor for consideration while weighing national security against civil liberties is location. For example, stopping and questioning drivers of a certain ethnicity on the New Jersey Turnpike with the hope of identifying a threat to national security should not be permitted because of the imposition on civil liberty and the low prospect for a positive "hit," notwithstanding the recent immigrant plots uncovered against Fort Dix and the Kennedy International Airport. However, performing the same action at a border port of entry creates a different and more defensible scenario. On the turnpike, ordinary citizens who are commuting or running errands would be adversely impacted. But at the border, different considerations and expectations apply. Additional questioning by United States immigration inspectors on the basis of ethnicity, if officially authorized, would be legal and constitutional. Similarly, at an airport, subjecting boarding passengers to closer inspection because of ethnicity, if officially authorized, should not be rejected automatically as a violation of civil liberties. Even excluding immigrant passengers from flying at all because of religious provocations, as United States Airways did recently at Minneapolis airport (Von Sternberg and Miller, 2006, Nov. 21), can be an appropriate balancing of enormous public security risks against the liberty of individuals.

The nature of the threat

A fourth factor that could be taken into consideration while trying to balance liberty and national security is the nature and seriousness of the threat. According to the Pew Research Center survey of Muslim Americans released May 22, 2007, 47% of Muslim Americans think of themselves as Muslim first, rather than American. Eight percent of Muslim Americans think suicide bombing can often or sometimes be justified, and another 9% declined to answer this question. In addition, 5% have a favourable view of al-Qaeda, and 27% declined to answer. Finally, 28% do not believe Arabs carried out the 9/11 attacks, and another 32% declined to answer (Pew Research Center, 2007: 3, 5).

Higher percentages were reported for Muslim Americans aged 18 to 29 years. Of this group, 60% think of themselves as Muslim first, rather than American, and another 5% declined to answer this question. Of this group, 15% think suicide bombing is often or sometimes justified, and another 5% declined to answer. Moreover, 7% have a favourable view of al-Qaeda, while 19% refused to answer (Pew Research Center, 2007: 6).

The likelihood of success

A fifth factor to consider while weighing civil liberties against national security concerns is the likelihood that national security initiatives will succeed. I will offer just one observation regarding this factor, and although my observation is related to torture, it is by no means an endorsement of torture, which I condemn, as does the United States government.

My observation is that most Americans believe that torture works, and this is not necessarily because they have been watching television dramas such as *24*, a show about a fictional counterterrorist unit. Rather, the torture imposed upon American airmen who were captured by the Vietnamese during the Vietnam War suggests than anyone, even our best and most courageous warriors, can be forced to make involuntary disclosures by determined torturers.

United States Navy Captain (later Admiral) Jim Stockdale was the senior officer among the prisoners of war held in North Vietnam. In his memoir, he reports that American prisoners subjected to interrogation under torture were unable to limit their answers to name, rank, and serial number. Rather than leaving his troops feeling that they had betrayed their country, he issued new orders to his fellow prisoners to "communicate, level with your American neighbors on just what-all you compromised, what information you had to give up in the torture room," and that "you were required to take torture, forcing the Vietnamese to impose significant pain on you before acceding to these specific demands" (Stockdale et al., 1990: 252). For his leadership in the most difficult circumstances imaginable, Stockdale received the highest decoration in the United States: the Medal of Honor (Stockdale et al., 1990: 451–52).

The American belief that torture works is also reflected in Professor Alan Dershowitz's much-discussed proposal that warrants be required for torture when necessary, to prevent the "slippery slope" phenomenon which may make torture unnecessarily common (2002, Jan. 22: A19; cf. Dershowitz, 2006). His work suggests that our natural condemnation and rejection of torture in nearly every circumstance should be informed by the reality that it can be made to work, and the recognition that someday the alternative to torture could be the loss of innocent lives.

In a democratic society, it may be sufficient to rely on the legal and political process to find the right balance between liberty and security, whether during a time of peace or war. But specific factors can also be considered. And as a starting point for discussion, I suggest that these factors include historical precedent, revocability of the initiative, relativity or location, the nature of the threat, and the likelihood of success.

References

Congresspedia (2007). *USA PATRIOT Improvement and Reauthorization Act of 2005*. Congresspedia. <http://www. sourcewatch.org/index.php?title=USA_PATRIOT_Improvement_and_ Reauthorization_Act_of_2005>. Last updated June 7, 2007. Accessed December 11, 2007.

Dershowitz, Alan M. (2002, January 22). Want to Torture? Get a Warrant. *San Francisco Chronicle*: A19. <http://sfgate.com/cgi-bin/ article.cgi?file=/chronicle/archive/2002/01/22/ED5329.DTL>. Accessed December 12, 2007.

Dershowitz, Alan M. (2006, October 17). Warming Up to Torture. *Los Angeles Times*. <http://www.latimes.com/news/opinion/la-oe-dershowitz17oct17,0,7881821.story?coll=la-opinion-rightrail>. Accessed December 12, 2007.

Eggen, Dan (2007, January 18). Court Will Oversee Wiretap Program. *Washington Post*: A1. <http://www.washingtonpost.com/wp-dyn/ content/article/2007/01/17/AR2007011701256.html>. Accessed December 12, 2007.

Gellman, Barton (2005, November 6). The FBI's Secret Scrutiny. *Washington Post*. <http://www.washingtonpost.com/wp-dyn/ content/article/2005/11/05/AR2005110501366.html>. Accessed December 12, 2007.

Gonzales, Alberto R., United States Attorney General (2007). Letter to the Honorable Patrick Leahy and the Honorable Arlen Specter. <http:// media.washingtonpost.com/wp-srv/politics/documents/Leahy_Specter_ Letter.pdf>. Accessed December 12, 2007.

Hill, Gerald, and Kathleen Hill (2008). Certiorari. *The People's Law Dictionary*. <http://dictionary.law.com/default2.asp?typed=certiorari>.

Jurist (2005). *Detainee Treatment Act of 2005* [White House]. <http://jurist.law.pitt.edu/gazette/2005/12/detainee-treatment-act-of-2005-white.php>. Accessed December 11, 2007.

Leahy, Patrick, United States Senator for Vermont (2007). *Uniting and Strengthening America by Providing Appropriate Tools Required to Intercept and Obstruct Terrorism (USA PATRIOT) Act of 2001, H.R. 3162: Section by Section Analysis.* Office of Senator Patrick Leahy. <http://leahy.senate.gov/press/200110/102401a.html>. Accessed December 12, 2007.

Lowman, David D. (2000). *MAGIC—The Untold Story of US Intelligence and the Evacuation of Japanese Residents from the West Coast During WWII.* Athena Press.

Malkin, Michelle (2004). *In Defense of Internment.* Regnery Publishing.

McPherson, James M. (1988). *Battle Cry of Freedom.* Oxford University Press.

Pew Research Center (2007). *Muslim Americans: Middle Class and Mostly Mainstream.* <http://pewresearch.org/assets/pdf/muslim-americans.pdf>. Accessed December 12, 2007.

Risen, James (2007, May 2). Administration Pulls Back on Surveillance Agreement. *Common Dreams News Center.* <http://www.commondreams.org/archive/2007/05/02/906/>. Accessed December 12, 2007.

Stockdale, Jim, and Sybil Stockdale (1990). *In Love and War.* Revised edition. Naval Institute Press.

Ting, Jan C. (2002). Unobjectionable But Insufficient—Federal Initiatives in Response to the September 11 Terrorist Attacks. *Connecticut Law Review* 34, 1145 (Summer).

Von Sternberg, Bob, and Pamela Miller (2006, November 21). Uproar Follows Imams' Detention. *Minneapolis Star Tribune.* <http://www.startribune.com/local/11585901.html>. Accessed December 12, 2007.

Yeh, Brian T., and Charles Doyle (2006). *USA PATRIOT Improvement and Reauthorization Act of 2005: A Legal Analysis.* Congressional Research Service. <http://www.fas.org/sgp/crs/intel/RL33332.pdf>. Accessed December 11, 2007.

Cases

American Civil Liberties Union v. *United States Department of Justice,* 321 F.Supp.2d 24 (D.D.C. 2004).

Bas v. *Tingy,* 4 U.S. (4 Dell) 37 (1800).

Boumediene v. *Bush 476 F.3d 981 (D.C. Cir. 2007).*

Boumediene v. *Bush, 549 U. S. (2007)*

Boumediene v. *Bush, 551 U.S. (2007).*

Doe v. *Ashcroft,* 334 F.Supp.2d 471 (S.D.N.Y. 2004).

Ex parte Endo, 323 U.S. 283 (1944).

Khalid v. *Bush,* 355 F.Supp.2d 311 (D.D.C. 2005).

Korematsu v. *United States,* 323 U.S. 214 (1944).

Hamdan v. *Rumsfeld,* 126 S.Ct. 2749 (2006).

Hamdi v. *Rumsfeld,* 124 S.Ct. 2633 (2004).

Hirabayashi v. *United States*, 320 U.S. 81 (1943).

In Re Guantanamo Detainee Cases, 355 F.Supp.2d 443 (D.D.C. 2005).

Madsen v. *Kinsella*, 343 U.S. 341 (1952).

The Amy Warwick (The Prize Cases), 67 U.S. (2 Black) 635 (1862).

Statutes

Authorization for Use of Military Force, S.J. Res. 23, 107th Cong., 115 Stat. 224 (2001).

Military Commissions Act, Pub. L. No. 109-366, 120 Stat. 2600 (2006). Available at http://www.loc.gov/rr/frd/Military_Law/pdf/PL-109-366.pdf.

Uniting and Strengthening America by Providing Appropriate Tools Required to Intercept and Obstruct Terrorism (USA PATRIOT) Act, Pub. L. No. 107-56, 115 Stat. 272 (2001).

Chapter 8

Is Canada Losing the Balance Between Liberty and Security?

David B. Harris

Balancing liberty and national security is a task that involves resolving competing tensions, weighing evidence regarding risk, and making realistic and informed public policy choices and decisions. Conventional wisdom dictates that rights and freedoms would be limited as security restrictions increase. Although this is true in many respects, balancing liberty and national security involves much more than this. If we fail to appreciate the larger picture, then we also fail to understand the issue of proportion. Understanding proportion, in turn, requires an understanding of the threats and risks that determine how liberty and national security should be balanced.

As we try to determine how rights and restrictions should be balanced, it is important to begin by recognizing how vulnerable the Western world—as a community and a civilization—has made itself by ignoring or underestimating threats. The challenge with which we are presented when faced with complex, unpalatable, and anxiety-inducing phenomena has been partly captured by Anna Freud. She, like her father, wrote about denial, a defence mechanism (Juan, 2006, Sep. 29). There is much in the age of mass casualty terrorism that invites denial. An aid to short-term mental function, denial may help explain why, despite mounting evidence, our intellectual elite and others choose to observe our current crisis the way they do.[1] As anthropologist Dr. Stephen Juan has written, "denial is the path of psychological and moral least resistance" (Juan, 2006, Sep. 29).

Canada's academic and intellectual elite illustrate the difficulty of dealing with these painful issues. In Canada, gifted and well-meaning leaders, especially in certain arts and social science fields, have been far removed from the realities of terrorism and national security. Prior to 9/11, they had little interest in these areas. Those who warned the elite of what was to come faced an absence of interest, outright denial, and, not infrequently, hostility.

This reaction was, in many ways, natural. Most of us have trouble picturing life at the wrong end of a knife or gun, let alone an A-bomb. Having known mainly creature comforts for the past two generations, few people in Canada wanted their pre-9/11 reverie to end. Even ostensible specialists seem to have found the new reality difficult to grasp. Former American security official Larry C. Johnson, for example, asserted conclusively in *The New York Times* that international terrorism was of marginal significance, and that fears of terrorism were greatly exaggerated. According to Johnson, the American homeland faced no measurable threat:

> The greatest risk is clear: if you are drilling for oil in Colombia—or in nations like Ecuador, Nigeria or Indonesia—you should take appropriate precautions; otherwise Americans have little to fear. (Johnson, 2001, July 10)

Johnson's article was rendered unwise, if not self-immolating, however, by the fact that it appeared a scant two months before the 9/11 catastrophe.[2]

---

1   The author recognizes that rationalization and other psychological elements and mechanisms contribute to people's assessment of and reaction to terrorist threats.

2   Johnson's faulty methodology was at the heart of his inability to anticipate anything in the nature of 9/11. Relying on straight-line extrapolations of past experience into an uncertain future, Johnson could not foresee attacks whose combined magnitude and locale were unprecedented and, thus, unavailable in the historical record. The post-9/11

Canada's elite

Having taken little professional interest during the lengthy build up of the terrorist threat, some of Canada's most distinguished, influential academics—most notoriously, those in human rights studies, legal studies, and law schools—suddenly threw themselves into post-9/11 philosophizing about national security. With little noticeable understanding of risk assessment and conditions, and with the most tentative and highly skeptical grasp of the threat, they launched into criticizing security organizations, declared themselves experts on intelligence law and practice, and scribbled out counterterrorism policy prescriptions with abandon. They even became members of government security committees and other official bodies. Often thorough and frequently exhaustive in their criticism of security measures and initiatives, many of these academics unearthed manifold weaknesses in "the system," but did not recognize their own, most devastating frailty. Their criticism skipped over any serious assessment of the nature, scope, and extent of the threats that security law and policy were to be constructed to deal with. Thus, many of the academic prescriptions were made without any serious appraisal of the size or shape of the thing for which the prescription was being written.

An example of this academic approach can be found in *September 11: Consequences for Canada*, a book by Canadian legal academic and University of Toronto law professor Kent Roach. This book covers many issues, often very thoughtfully. To be sure, Roach's examination of post-9/11 approaches to security makes a certain appeal to the Canadian impulse that favours self-congratulation, and reminds us how realistic, sensitive, and generous we tend to be, compared to so many of our benighted American cousins. Roach helpfully discloses that his participation in a United States panel discussion on American and Canadian responses to 9/11 "affirmed my faith that the Canadian response to September 11, while

---

persistence of this weakness is illustrated in the unimaginative past-bound analytics of *Fear's Empire* by Benjamin Barber. Consistent with Johnson's approach, Barber finds little to worry about with respect to mass casualty and mass destruction terrorism, for the historical record is not replete with examples of such attacks (2003: 26–29).

far from perfect, was in many ways more civil, productive, and inclusive than the American approach" (Roach, 2003: 262).

But Roach notes that Canada's superiority is not without serious blemishes. *September 11* strains to condemn as overblown and exaggerated various aspects of Canadian security law, management, and attitude. As with many other similar books, the book's fatal flaw is that it does not make a serious attempt to evaluate the nature and scope of the terrorist threat against which the balance of any liberty-national security solution can be measured. The result of such an omission is something akin to studying physics without mathematics.

It appears that this approach to security may prevail among the denizens of many law schools and other faculties in Canada. After 9/11, the University of Toronto rushed into the fray, hosting a conference involving a large number of "security skeptic" academics, and produced an unbalanced book that, for a time, seemed to be a staple of human rights and national security university teaching (Daniels et al., 2001). Others were at least realistic enough to experience the shock of realizing that large-scale terrorism wasn't a myth after all.

In a temporary awakening from denial, some of Canada's intellectuals and opinion makers began to assert that the September 11 attackers "got through" because of a "failure of imagination." However useful this was as a phrase, it was, unfortunately, given the wrong spin. The failure was exclusively that of the national and local security authorities and their machinery, we were told, not a failure of national communities finally to realize the truth—that twenty-first century technology was being harnessed by religious ideologues in support of an upgraded seventh century world war that had been declared on the liberal-pluralist West many years before.

Fortunately, a few academic voices still struggle to challenge the academic orthodoxy with realistic appraisal. It has become the task of researchers such as Dr. Salim Mansur, a Sunni Muslim Canadian and professor of political science—who has twice had fatwas (religious edicts) issued against him, calling for his death—to compensate for some of the intellectual elite's shortcomings. Mansur recognizes 9/11 as merely another event in a series of thrusts in Islamo-fascism's long-standing and escalating, ideology-driven war against liberal democracy. "On September 11,

2001," he wrote, "Americans awoke to a war in progress" (Mansur, 2007, Sep. 8). Mansur has written extensively, warning Westerners about the virtually unprecedented nature and scale of the violence and subversion faced by liberal societies such as Canada.

As people such as Mansur have pointed out, the absence of an inclination to understand and quantify the threat means the menace will continue to be underplayed and our attitudes and preparedness will lag dangerously behind the reality of the situation. Thus, the want of reality-based thinking will worsen our plight. It will continue to invite into the vacuum of good sense a host of appealing, if lopsidedly facile, formulae, such as the bald assertion that "the terrorists will have won if we restrict our freedoms." Ironists who are aware of the hard reality of terrorism and its prospects should find much to consider in the near-bravado with which some of the elite pronounce such unhelpful, absolutist formulae. As Shapiro (2006) has pointed out, in an admittedly harsh retort, such arguments are "pure sophistry":

> If our enemies affect our freedoms, they affect our freedoms. We may not like our freedoms being affected. Nonetheless, that has no impact on whether the "terrorists have won" .... If the terrorists achieve global sharia, then they will have won. If they erect a mosque on the ruins of the World Trade Center, then they will have won. They will not stop until they achieve their goals. We must not stop until we have shattered their dreams forever.

Yet, as a whole, the message from Canada's elite has tended to be that threats are certainly exaggerated and possibly nonexistent. Where political correctness rules, it is difficult to open meaningful discussion about the problem and its solution, particularly if the discussion covers sensitive areas such as immigration.

Assessing threats

Certainly, classic terrorist strategy seeks to trigger a hostile governmental overreaction, but overemphasis on possible reaction has at times led to extravagant claims that terrorists will have "won" if citizens give up any freedoms in the course of the struggle. Such claims ignore the fact that modern martyrdom-bent religious terrorists will be satisfied with butchering every single nonbeliever. From their illiberal perspective, achieving this end is a more than acceptable form of "winning." The evidence of radical jihadists' passion for self-destruction and mass casualties makes the "liberty-though-the-heavens-may-fall" view look like the kind of thing George Orwell had in mind when he wrote, with endearing unfairness, that only "the intelligentsia [could] believe things like that: no ordinary man could be such a fool" (Orwell, 1945).

Let us look at a more concrete example of the importance of grasping the threat and risk of terrorism. Afterwards, let us determine the appropriateness of the balance between rights and restrictions. This exercise should enable analysts to reframe the issue properly, and ultimately ask the abiding question: what is liberty without national security?

Canada's leading terrorist threat has repeatedly been identified as Islamic extremism (see, for example, Commission of Inquiry into the Actions of Canadian Officials in Relation to Maher Arar, 2005, 6315, l. 21–25). This threat may be operationalized in any number of forms: chemical, biological, and so on. To simplify our discussion, let us focus on nuclear considerations, which are becoming insistent and point to our stake in understanding the dangers of terrorism before leaping into resolutions affecting the liberty and national security balance. Though there are various Islamic terror groups and state sponsors, this chapter will focus only on Iran as an example. However, the threat picture that is described in this chapter can, in certain dimensions, be multiplied several times over if one takes into account other countries, terrorist groups, and elements.

A précis of this particular threat must begin with Iranian President Mahmoud Ahmadinejad's September 2005 address to the United Nations General Assembly. In recorded conversations after the event, Mr. Ahmadinejad noted that, throughout his speech, his head was orbited by a green halo, and his divinely-inspired words paralyzed attending diplomats (Melman and Javedanfar, 2007: 41–42). For guidance, Ahmadinejad corresponds with a number of sources, including a deceased imam in a well, whom he is confident can be brought back to life as the Mahdi, the

Twelfth Imam, bringing with him an age of paradise. According to Mr. Ahmadinejad and his key associates, mankind is in the happy position of being able, through its own intervention, to accelerate this momentous development. All that is required is Armageddon (Melman and Javedanfar, 2007: 41–57). This violent eschatology encourages dyspeptic feelings abroad where many find it difficult to digest the regime's theology, which is routinely expressed in repeated Iranian threats to destroy selected countries and civilizations. In the meantime, discomfort deepens with the knowledge that Ahmadinejad is running crash nuclear weapons programs. Although Ahmadinejad claims Iran's nuclear program is peaceful, the United States and key European nations believe the program is a cover for an Iranian attempt to produce nuclear weapons. President Ahmadinejad is joined in his convictions by Iran's constitutional leader, the Supreme Guide Ali Khamenei, and by those whom the two leaders have inserted into influential government decision making positions— including military and security.[3]

In light of these facts, it seems that, for all practical purposes, Iran's national command authority is essentially of the same mind as the men who crashed 767s into the World Trade Center and Pentagon on September 11, 2001. Iran's leaders have associates among us. The country's aggressive foreign intelligence service has a documented record of assassinations and bombings throughout the world. In North America, their sleeper agents are called "submarines."

Also disturbing is that fact that the rabid, Iranian-controlled terrorist organization, Hezbollah, lives among us, too,[4] and has committed some of

---

3   Although reportedly variable in quality, the relationship between Supreme Guide and Ahmadinejad seems considerably more constructive than the Guide's dealings with former President Muhammad Khatami (for example, see Melman and Javedanfar, 2007: 36–40, 65, 149). As Yossi Melman and Meir Jafarzadeh report, based on a 2000 media assessment, "Contrary to some media reports, Ahmadinejad is fully devoted to Supreme Leader Ali Khamenei" (2007: 20).

4   Hezbollah's Canadian presence has been well documented in court proceedings and the press. Levitt, for example, notes that they have a "Canadian network ... under the direct command of Hajj Hassan Hilu Lakis, Hezbollah's chief military procurement officer who is also known to procure material for Iran" (2003).

its worldwide acts of bloodshed in close cooperation with Iran's VEVAK (Vezarat-e Etelaat va Amniat-e Keshvar) intelligence service, among other groups.[5] During the Israel-Hezbollah war in the summer of 2006, demonstrations in Toronto, Montreal, and other Canadian cities showed that Hezbollah supporters and operatives were prepared to brazenly advertise themselves, despite Parliament's having banned the organization in Canada.

In the face of martyrdom-fixated Iranian leaders, some would argue that the deterrence doctrine[6]—which guaranteed 40 years of Cold War nuclear peace—would be meaningless. "Meaningless" doesn't quite capture the situation, because, consistent with the 9/11 attackers' sensibility, the promise of paradise would actually be a positive incentive to trigger a nuclear cataclysm. Only in a secular, Westernized context could this logic seem controversial at a time when Mr. Ahmadinejad promises the "wiping out" of the United States, the West, Israel, and so forth. If Iran obtains nuclear weapons, the only questions remaining will be narrow ones: when? Where? And how often?

In light of this situation, it is possible that Hezbollah suicide squads could be used to smuggle multiple weapons into the cities of the "Great Satan"—the United States—or into Canada and other Western nations. Indeed, the prodigious number of actual and prospective Canadian al-Qaeda sympathizers may be sufficient to allow this to happen. Rough estimates based on an Environics poll suggest that there are thousands of these sympathizers (Corbella, 2007, Feb. 18). The polling data suggest that between 49,000 and 119,000 Canadian Muslims could justify an alleged

---

5   A classic example of cooperation between the two groups was the Mikonos operation, a successful Iranian intelligence-Hezbollah plot to assassinate dissidents in Germany. For general background on this and comparable foreign intelligence issues, see Federation of American Scientists (2007).

6   In strategic security relations, deterrence theory posits that adversary countries or blocs will avoid—or be "deterred" from—commencing hostilities with a country or bloc that has the capacity and will to respond with sufficiently damaging military means.

2006 Islamic terrorist plot to attack public buildings in Toronto, blow up Parliament, and behead the Prime Minister.[7]

The nuclear element

Let us consider the impact of nuclear weapons. One estimate suggests that a somewhat limited 150 kiloton nuclear ground burst in Manhattan would kill 800,000, and injure 900,000 (Atomic Archive, 2006; Glaser, 2006). Nothing suggests that Canadian municipalities would fare much better. Moreover, virtually no hospital, water, or energy facilities would survive in the region. Radiation and blast-effect would be catastrophic. A detonation above fifty kilometres in altitude would produce an electromagnetic pulse effect (EMP) likely to fry electrical and electronic equipment over a substantial area—perhaps nationwide, if exploded at above 400 kilometres[8]—paralyzing any surviving rescue vehicles, generators, communica-

---

7   These numbers are based on interpretations of an Environics poll of Canadian Muslims that was published February 13, 2007, by CBC Television. As columnist Licia Corbella reported, "Fully 12% of Muslim Canadians polled by Environics said the alleged terrorist plot—that included kidnapping and beheading the prime minister and blowing up Parliament and the CBC—was justified" (2007, Feb. 18). Based on the poll and a wish to be "really non-alarmist," Corbella reduced the estimate using the margin of error (4.4%) and conservatively "translated" the 12% to signify that between 49,000 and 84,000 of Canada's 700,000 Muslims would feel that an attack on Canada would be justified (Corbella, 2007, Feb. 18). A more statistically-proficient economist consulted by me reported that the 4.4% error margin is, in statistical terms, a "two-tailed error"—meaning that the statistical range should be between the mean plus 4.4% and the mean minus 4.4%. Thus, the true range of Muslim Canadians willing to justify terrorism against their country is between 49,000 to 119,000, with a mean of 84,000. As Corbella pointed out, however, denial springs eternal: "Predictably, the CBC managed to find a talking head—in this case York University sociology professor Haideh Moghissi—who dismissed this disturbing revelation. 'It's really negligible that 12% feel that the attacks would be justified,' said Moghissi. 'I don't think it even warrants attention'" (Corbella, 2007, Feb. 18).

8   This is an approximation assuming a one-megaton yield, and is based on the testimony of Dr. George W. Ullrich (1997), Deputy Director, Defense Special Weapons

tions equipment, and other life-saving apparatus. And what if this were to happen during a stifling summer or freezing winter?

This type of analysis is often portrayed by academics and others as irresponsible and alarmist,[9] yet it relies on facts and common knowledge (see International Atomic Energy Agency, 2007; Barnaby, 1997). Its message is bleak, but realistic, and its warning is clear: if we consider this kind of nuclear holocaust as a mere fraction of the overall threat that civilization faces, without the blinders of denial, we can see that survival is dependant on assessing the threat correctly before rushing in to determine the balance between liberty and security. How we respond in terms of our

---

Agency, US Department of Defense, before a US Congressional subcommittee, on July 16, 1997.

9   An example of such a tendency is found in a work by McGill University economics professor, R.T. Naylor. Jeffrey Breinholt, US Justice Department counterterrorist prosecutor, tersely summarized the worldview captured in Naylor's book, *Satanic Purses*: according to Naylor, "Al Qa'ida is a 'synaptic leap in some US prosecutor's brain,' and ... there is no such thing as a terrorist organization" (Breinholt, 2007). These sentiments are similar to those expressed in Benjamin R. Barber's *Fear's Empire*, in which Barber appears to claim that the fear of mass-casualty terrorism is at least as great a threat as terrorism itself. He argues that "[t]errorists otherwise bereft of power have bored into the American imagination," and that "it is not terrorism but fear that is the enemy" (2003: 15, 32). On the other hand, *The New York Times* reports that distinguished strategic thinker and Harvard University professor, Graham Allison, "offers a standing bet at 51-to-49 odds that, barring radical new anti-proliferation steps, a terrorist nuclear strike will occur somewhere in the world in the next 10 years" (Kristof, 2004, Aug. 11). In April 2008, Dr. Cham E. Dallas, Director of the University of Georgia's Institute for Health Management and Mass Destruction Defense, told the US Senate Committee on Homeland Security that a nuclear attack was "inevitable," adding, "it's wistful to think that it won't happen by 20 years" (Emerling, 2008, Apr. 16). Assessing the prospect of nuclear terrorism, former Speaker of the United States House of Representatives, Newt Gingrich, declared that "we are not very many mistakes away from a second Holocaust ... Our enemies would like to get those [nuclear] weapons as soon as they can, and they promise to use them as soon as they can" (Gingrich, 2007). As for the risk of a radiological "dirty" bomb terrorist attack, International Atomic Energy Agency chief Mohamed El Baradei has said, "Sometimes I think it's a miracle that it hasn't happened yet" (Bednarz and Follath, 2007, Sep. 3).

national security policy will define our long-term ability to enjoy liberty of any kind.

In light of these kinds of risks and consequences, we can begin to examine how our immigration-related national security policies threaten both our liberty and security.

Immigration and security

Despite the existence of the terrorist threat, the extent of which is only hinted at in the example of Iran, Canada welcomes more immigrants per capita than almost any other nation: 260,000 each year. Canada is also among the world's greatest per capita recipients of refugee claimants, accepting about 22,910 people in 2006 (United Nations High Commissioner for Refugees, 2007), compared to 500 in 1977 (Bissett, 1998).

An extremely powerful lobby of politicians, immigration lawyers, government-funded settlement organizations, non-governmental organizations (NGOs), and others claim various justifications for these high levels: aging population, growing economy, and so on. Principled social and economic thinkers who are not beholden to the immigration industry—such as Daniel Stoffman, Martin Collacott (2006), and many others—risk being called racist, anti-immigrant, or "Islamophobic,"[10] for saying that this is simply unjustified (Dhillon, 2003, Aug. 16). Canada's immigration and refugee system has become largely a vote-importing mechanism designed to play on identity politics. It gives no consideration to the kinds and scale of terrorist threats, subversion, and disruption that such massive population movements can facilitate, even at the best of times.

---

10   Many critics agree that the term "Islamophobia" is being used to censor debate on immigration. Dr. Sam C. Holliday (2007) of the Armiger Cromwell Center refers to Islamophobia as "a term invented to shut down legitimate and vital debate about the threat of the Third Jihad," his term for the present worldwide radical Islamist offensive and associated subversion. Kenan Malik (2005, Feb. 10) observes that "[t]he charge of 'Islamophobia' is all too often used not to highlight racism but to silence critics of Islam, or even Muslims fighting for reform of their communities."

Those of us who are concerned with terrorism, liberty, stability, and public safety recognize that, in today's world, sheer numbers can constitute a clear and present danger and threaten our liberty. Consider that some of the Canadian Security and Intelligence Services' (CSIS) 2,500 personnel and perhaps a few thousand other government employees are involved in screening approximately 250,000 newcomers every year (Singer, 2002, Dec. 6). Many of these people are coming from, for example, Pakistan, Iran, and Saudi Arabia—countries that are, to varying degrees, virtual enemy states.

Iran's leadership, for example, remains devoted to the memory of Ayatollah Ruhollah Khomeini, leader of the Iranian revolution that took place in the late 1970s, whose photo appears in Tehran government offices today. Listing "11 things which are impure" Khomeini included urine, excrement, the sweat of the excrement-eating camel, dogs, pigs, and non-Muslim men and women (Khomeini, 1980: 48; quoted in Harris, 2007, June 4: A11). In 1989, Khomeini issued a fatwa (a religious edict) calling for the assassination of writer Salman Rushdie because of his alleged blasphemy against Muhammed in his novel, *The Satanic Verses*.

As for Pakistan, the radicalism of some of the country's influential elements was illustrated when Rushdie, who was knighted in 2007 by Queen Elizabeth. Mohammed Ijaz ul-Haq, Pakistan's religious affairs minister, recently said that Rushdie's knighthood could justify suicide bombing: "If someone exploded a bomb on his body, he would be right to do so unless the British government apologizes and withdraws the 'sir' title" (Pennington, 2007, June 18). National Assembly opposition leader Maulana Fazlur Rehman told protestors that by knighting a "blasphemer," the British government had "hurt the religious sentiments of Muslims throughout the world" (*Daily Times*, 2007, June 23). Rehman also attacked the late Pakistan People's Party (PPP) chairwoman, Benazir Bhutto, for opposing suicide attacks on blasphemers (*Daily Times*, 2007, June 23).

Other Pakistani leaders are also hostile to non-Muslims, and to peaceful coexistence. Muhammed Taqi Usmani, a retired sharia judge of Pakistan's Supreme Court and a reported "moderate-leaning" Deobandi Muslim scholar, has expressed the view that "Muslims should live peacefully in countries … where they have the freedom to practise Islam, only until they gain enough power to engage in battle" (Norfolk, 2007, Sep. 8). This view is consistent with that of some Pakistani extremists who, according to Arnaud de Borchgrave (2002, Aug. 21), promised that "in the next 10 years, Americans will wake up to the existence of an Islamic army in their midst—an army of jihadis who will force America to abandon imperialism and listen to the voice of Allah."

Despite these threats, Canada's policy with respect to Pakistani immigrants remains lax. Only 10% of Pakistani immigrants are screened by CSIS. Moreover, based on United Nations figures, Martin Collacott (2006) concludes that "[a]ltogether in 2003, Canada granted refugee status to more than twice as many Pakistanis as did all other countries in the world combined."

Saudi Arabia has also shown hostility towards Canada. This largely Islamic country, which is home to a variant of sharia law that condones the stoning of women and the killing of homosexuals, injects money and its values into various Canadian Islamic and non-Islamic institutions in a process that has been subjected to increasingly critical scrutiny (Kaplan, 2004, Apr. 5). When Sheikh Abd Al-Rahman Al-Sudayyis, Saudi Arabia's highest ranking government-appointed cleric, has spoken to outreach-hungry churchgoers and naïve social justice advocates, he has talked about interfaith peace and dialogue (Stalinsky, 2004). But at home in Saudi mosques, he reportedly "refers to Jews as 'the scum of the Earth,' and ... exhorts his followers against the Christian 'worshippers of the cross' and the 'idol-worshipping Hindus.'"[11] When the Islamic Society of North America, a supposedly mainstream Islamic group, reportedly invited him to officiate at their conference in Canada, authorities were ready to bar his entry (B'Nai Brith Canada, 2004; United States Senate Committee on the Judiciary, 2006).[12]

In light of the seriousness of the threats noted above, Canada must reconsider its current immigration policies. The number and sources of

---

11   This quote has been attributed to Canadian Member of Parliament Jason Kenney, (Stalinsky, 2004).

12   For more information on the strange background to—and fallout from—this invitation, see Sharrif (2004, July 1).

immigrants to Canada are undermining the foundational requirements of our liberal-pluralist society: integration, stability, and public safety. The number and concentration of extremists increases, while the possibility of diluting such tendencies decreases. When immigrants arrive in Canada after being taught in the madrassas and mosques of certain countries that Hindus, Buddhists, Christians, Jews, and moderate Muslims are sub-human, one cannot expect a change in their thought patterns once they settle in Canada. A change is even more unlikely if they set up their own schools. With this development, an increase in the number of recruits to extremism becomes possible, and the probability of the realization of ghastly scenarios, similar to those already mentioned, increases.

Once again, it would seem reasonable to speculate that the bulk—quite possibly, the vast majority—of people entering Canada will contribute positively to the country. However, it would seem naïve to assume that none of the many newcomers would possess the training, conditioning, and values imparted in some of the world's illiberal and anti-liberal jurisdictions.

Meanwhile, none of this even begins to address the developing risk that chain migration involving radicalism may reinforce the growth of a dangerous political demographic in Canada. It is far from clear that politicians and other vote- and lobby-conscious authorities would be willing to challenge the demands of zealous blocs. In this regard, the recent openness of several public universities to radical demands for taxpayer-supported prayer rooms, footbaths, and even separate, gender apartheid-style female swimming hours, could be regarded as a compromising of basic, religiously-neutral standards in the face of fundamentalist pressure.[13] This unwillingness to "grasp the nettle" is also demonstrated by politicos and officials who are considering providing, in the tradition of Saudi-style gender separation, women-only government screeners to check beneath face-veils at polling stations. At recent Canadian House of Commons committee hearings on "burqua voting," moderate Muslims seemed startled to hear a Member of Parliament, who had recently observed Morocco's elections,

---

13   See Carrigg (2007, Aug. 14). See also CRARR (2006) for some insight into the role that human rights' commissions may play in related matters.

commending that country's gender-separated approach to the screening of veiled women as a model for Canada to consider emulating.[14]

Simply put, rational polities do not bring in large numbers of newcomers from such potentially "Western-hostile" source regions while a war is going on. But they might if their influential intellectual elite were bereft of a proper sense of the risks involved, and therefore, of the appropriate balance. If polities bring in large numbers of such immigrants during wartime, they must expect to see their freedoms curtailed as their government anticipates larger communities of hostile residents in their midst—and the infiltration of government, security, and emergency services.

This latter prospect is far from being a paranoid delusion. In *The Management of Savagery*, senior al-Qaeda strategic thinker Abu Bakr Naji (2006) calls for,

> infiltrating the adversaries and their fellow travelers and establishing a strong security apparatus that is more supportive of the security of the [revolutionary Islamic] movement now, and later the [resultant Islamic] state. (We) should infiltrate the police forces, the armies, the different political parties, the newspapers, the Islamic groups, the petroleum companies (as an employee or as an engineer), private security companies, sensitive civil institutions, etc.

Naji notes that this "actually began several decades ago," but adds, "we need to increase it in light of recent developments."

Indeed, it appears that a good start has been made on Naji's plan. The 9/11 Commission hearings were one forum in which American officials recounted enemy efforts to install operatives into various government and para-governmental positions, including those of FBI translator and defence contractor (*Washington Post*, 2004, June 16). From Britain (Leapman, 2007, Apr. 29; see pg. 143) to Spain (Jordán and Wesley, 2007) to India (*India Times News Network*, 2006, July 21), and beyond, there

---

14   As one of those testifying at the House of Commons' Standing Committee on Procedure and House Affairs hearing on September 13, 2007, the author was witness to the dismayed reactions of those described.

A Security Breach in the House of Lords

In the House of Lords in November 2005, Baroness Cox expressed concern about interference with the Lords' microphone system during her discourse on extremist Islam. She reported the advice of an independent specialist she had sought who "pointed out that such jamming is easy to achieve and that it demonstrates the ability to penetrate the security of Parliament, shows contempt for democracy, was a specific threat to me, and a general threat to anyone who dares to speak critically about Islamists" (United Kingdom House of Lords, 2005).

In her speech, Cox pointed to an article printed in the *Sunday Times* on July 30, 2000, which reported that,

> A Sudanese businessman who has been linked by the American CIA to the world's most wanted terrorist is the leading shareholder in a company that provides security systems to the House of Parliament … [This person's] pharmaceutical factory in Sudan was flattened by American cruise missiles after it was linked to Osama bin Laden … [The businessman] owns 25 per cent of IES, a company specialising in high-technology surveillance and security management.

The article claimed that IES had provided such equipment to New Scotland Yard, British Airways, Texaco, and other blue chip firms (United Kingdom House of Lords, 2005).

is growing evidence of actual and attempted radical fundamentalist and terrorist penetration of Western countries' machinery of government and national infrastructure.

In sum, if the government fails to restrict the enjoyment of some liberties in the face of infiltration and growing threats, one might expect to see other liberties ultimately going unenjoyed—perhaps even the right to life and security of the person, which is guaranteed under the Canadian Charter of Rights and Freedoms.[15] These are among the liberties that bombings and intimidation tend to remove.

This is a lesson in how a failure to take national security sufficiently seriously, and to translate this seriousness into immigration policy will

---

15   Canadian Charter of Rights and Freedoms, s. 7, Part I of the *Constitution Act, 1982*, being Schedule B to the *Canada Act 1982* (U.K.), 1982, c. 11.

lead, at best, to an unrealistic balance between liberty and security, and restricted freedoms. In an era of proliferating weapons and materials of mass destruction, the risk of social, economic, and political chaos and infrastructural collapse is not to be disregarded. In fact, chaos can create the worst form of unconstitutionality,[16] for, in a chaotic situation, there is no judiciary, no government, no rule of law, no liberty—and perhaps, for increasing numbers—no life. However, well before this point were to be reached, more subtle restrictions on freedom would be felt.

The radical traditions of *sharia*, as known in Saudi Arabia, Iran, and parts of Pakistan, are already pressed upon us in the form of "Islamic civil law," frequently in the teeth of objections from Canadian Arabs and Muslims who may have escaped the horrors of certain sharia jurisdictions. Hard-line immigré-based groups such as the Canadian Council on American-Islamic Relations (CAIR-CAN) and the Canadian Islamic Congress (CIC) are the leading advocates of adopting sharia law. These groups have caused alienation within the Muslim community with their improbable "studies" (see pg. 146) that allege Canadian Muslims are being victimized everywhere, and their calls for further "accommodation" of the fundamentalist view.

Challenging CAIR-CAN statistics, Fraser Institute CANSTAT Project Director Neil Seeman (2002, Sep. 14) concluded that "however much some in the media tried to imagine a 'backlash' against Muslim Canadians, the truth is there never really was one." In fact, Statistics Canada reports that the number-one target of hate crimes in 2001 and 2002 after 9/11 was not Muslims but Jews. Twenty-five percent of 1,000 hate crimes reported by 12 big-city police forces in Canada were committed against Jews. By comparison, Muslims (11%) were targeted in roughly the same numbers as South Asians (10%) and gays and lesbians (9%) (*The Globe and Mail*, 2005, July 14).

In the United States, FBI statistics have led the *Investor's Business Daily* to declare that "Muslim groups are crying wolf about exploding anti-Muslim abuses" (2007, Dec. 3):

---

16 On this subject, it is worth recalling the Canadian Supreme Court's warning to this effect in Reference re Manitoba Language Rights [1985] 1 S.C.R. 721.

A Closer Look at a CAIR-CAN survey

The credibility of one of CAIR-CAN's surveys on the treatment and perceptions of Canadian Muslims came into question when a representative of CAIR-CAN testified before the Maher Arar Commission regarding its curious statistical "survey," conducted in June 2005 and titled *Presumption of Guilt*.

Testifying about the survey, CAIR-CAN's Chair, Sheema Khan, faced only deferential questions from Commission staff. However, Simon Fothergill, Counsel for the Attorney General of Canada, exposed doubts about the survey's reliability and credibility (Commission of Inquiry into the Actions of Canadian Officials in Relation to Maher Arar, 2005: 6290ff). It turned out that the anonymous, questionnaire-based study had made response-forms available on the internet, making it possible for foreigners who had never even set foot in Canada to attest to the imaginary anti-Muslim abuse they had suffered in the country. Copies had also been emailed to those on the CAIR-CAN member list, raising issues of bias, given CAIR-CAN's *idée fixe* about "anti-Islamic" behaviour.

Fothergill pointed out that over half the respondents were connected to CAIR-CAN (6323, l. 3–6), and a "good proportion" were from those interested in Muslim and/or Arab advocacy or issues (6323, l. 17–22). In the end, the survey's credibility—and its implicit claims regarding anti-Islamic tides—were dashed as Khan proved unable to clarify fundamental aspects of the study, including the number of forms that were distributed: "I can't really say"; the number of hard copies that were distributed at centers and mosques: "I don't have the number on me right now"; and whether the ethnic make-up of respondents was statistically-representative of Muslim Canada: "I would have to look at the Census to speak to that" (6321, l. 16–21; 6322, l. 1–2; and, 6322, l. 25–6324, l. 1–2).

In 2006, a whopping 66% of religiously motivated attacks were on Jews, while just 11% targeted Muslims, even though the Jewish and Muslim populations are similar in size. Catholics and Protestants, who together account for 9% of victims, are subject to almost as much abuse as Muslims in the US (see also Salman, 2006, Aug. 31).

As mentioned, it is unclear why anyone would propagate unreliable information that might trigger upheavals, but this is part of the challenge Canada now faces (for a critical, annotated bibliography of the claims of anti-Muslim bias, see Appendix C to Canadian Coalition for Democracies, 2008).

Charter values as a defensive measure

Free speech rights have also been under pressure from hardliners. Despite constitutional guarantees, a number of Canadian and American research-ers, media outlets, and commentators have been sued for libel by the Canadian Council on American-Islamic Relations (CAIR-CAN) and its troubling American parent organization, the Council on American-Islamic Relations (CAIR).[17]

In general, these lawsuits were brought against media outlets and com-mentators who asked questions about the history, links, agendas, and leading personalities of CAIR and CAIR-CAN. Aware of the free speech issues raised by these suits, several defendants in these lawsuits made a principled stand and drove the plaintiffs—who then faced disclosure risks—to ask for the dismissal of their own suits, and, it seems, to leave the libel suit business entirely.

Unfortunately, those who struggled in defence of Canada's consti-tutional rights had to do so without any help from the intellectual and humanitarian organizations normally considered to be advocates for

---

17   The US government has CAIR on its "List of Unindicted Co-conspirators and/or Joint Venturers," under Section III ("individuals/entities who are and/or were mem-bers of the US Muslim Brotherhood's Palestine Committee and/or its organizations") (see *United States of America* v. *Holy Land Foundation for Relief and Development* as incorporated into the Government's Trial Brief by reference at Trial Brief, Section IV B.2). CAIR derives from the Islamic Association for Palestine (IAP), and, according to the US government, the IAP, "as well as its members, representatives and supporters were participants in the same joint venture or conspiracy—the conspiracy to support Hamas." Like CAIR, certain other organizations with a Canadian presence were iden-tified in the "List of Unindicted Co-conspirators and/or Joint Venturers," including the Islamic Society of North America (under Section VII: "individuals/entities who are and/or were members of the US Muslim Brotherhood"), and the Jerusalem Fund (IRFAN) (under Section VIII: "individuals/entities that are and/or were part of the Global HAMAS financing mechanism").

human rights. Well-known organizations in Canada such as Amnesty International, PEN, Reporters Without Borders, and the Canadian Civil Liberties Association (CCLA) did not come to anyone's aid, while, at the same time, many of these rights' groups pontificated about post-9/11 freedoms on platforms shared with CAIR-CAN and similar groups. Indeed, during these lawsuits, the CCLA stunned some observers by electing to its own board one of CAIR-CAN's leading plaintiffs, a development that, in the freedom of expression context, invited metaphors about foxes and henhouses. None of the free speech lawsuit victims dared approach the CCLA for assistance after this occurred.

Even presenters at the Fraser Institute's immigration conference in June 2007, the conference from which this chapter derives, were obliged to fight for free speech. Apparently uncomfortable with the prospect of a mainstream conference regarding immigration, security, and radicalism, the Canadian Islamic Congress and Canadian Arab Federation jointly—and implausibly—called upon the police to put the conference under surveillance. Though a number "free speech" organizations stayed selectively silent on this issue, journalists such as *Calgary Sun* Editor Licia Corbella (2004, Oct. 31; 2007, June 15) stepped into the gap and exposed the disturbing origins and implications of the attempts to shut down the Institute's learned and responsible exercise of the Charter-guaranteed right to free expression.

However, by the end of 2007, the prospects of those wishing to silence speech and warnings about radical Islam had improved. Media developments had led to fears that "silencers" could avoid the costs and disclosure-risks of the courtroom simply by appealing to one of Canada's human rights commissions—at the taxpayers' expense (Levant, 2007). In 2007, the Alberta Human Rights Commission moved forward with a Canadian imam's complaint against the *Western Standard* for reprinting controversial cartoons of Mohammed. In one fell swoop, expenses were forced on a media outlet, a deterrent effect was imposed on publishers, and—particularly in this case—Canadians had to contend with the possibility that government quasi-judicial "human rights'" bodies might be used indirectly to enforce sharia law bans on portrayals of the Islamic Prophet.

Ezra Levant, who was the publisher of the *Western Standard* at the time, has highlighted the attractiveness of appealing to a human rights board, rather than filing a civil law suit, for those wanting to control speech:

> After the *National Post* ran my column, the CIC served us with notice under the defamation laws. Of course, they had no case— we had the defences of truth, fair comment, etc.—so the CIC had to settle for a letter to the editor almost a year later.

> But the CIC learned their lesson: there's no point suing in defamation law, where the CIC would have to pay for their own lawyers, and our lawyers if we won, and where silly things like the rule of law apply. Better to go to the human rights commissions where the taxpayer pays for the prosecution, traditional rules of evidence and procedure don't apply, and free speech is not protected. It still has all of the down-sides for the defendant—the hassle, the cost, and a lower bar for a "conviction"—but none of the cost for the complainants. (Levant, 2007)[18]

At the end of the year, alarms were growing louder as federal and provincial human rights' commissions were simultaneously served with a formal complaint, supported by the Canadian Islamic Congress, against *Maclean's* magazine. *Maclean's* had published an excerpt from internationally-syndicated journalist Mark Steyn's best seller, *America Alone*, and this had been deemed unacceptable by those making the complaint (Levant, 2007). Levant suggests that the Canadian Islamic Congress' record in their libel law contretemps with him led that organization to

---

18   By early 2008, the complainant, Imam Soharwardy, was facing growing pressure from the media and the public, and, in a strange turnaround, was having to fend off formal complaints from certain members of his own mosque. This public relations' debacle was said to have led to his withdrawal of his "human rights'" complaint in February 2008. Levant contended that he would pursue Mr. Soharwardy for the costs involved in the commission exercise (see Levant, 2008, and Corbella, 2008, Feb. 16).

recognize the value of human rights' commissions to its campaign against *Maclean's* magazine.

Conclusion

Without an appropriate, proportionate understanding of the threat, our national community will continue to downplay the challenge of radicalism and terrorism, and to pursue a course of freewheeling laxity in immigration, refugee, and other social and security matters. The unrealistic belief that Canadians enjoy an unconstrained luxury of public policy choice—that virtually nothing can justify inconveniencing our freedoms—will paradoxically bring nearer and make more imposing the restrictions that our freedoms will eventually face. A naïve public policy—such as relatively open borders during wartime—means that we will see more "no-fly" lists, more agitation and instability, more crises, and more constraints.

Under current conditions, vast intakes of immigrants from a world at war—part of which is at war with us—is a recipe for non-assimilation, provocation, violence, genuine alienation, domestic chaos, panic, and reactive, if unavoidable, state inhibitions on civil liberties. Once we are very far down the road to chaos, reassuring government statements and human rights organizations' resolutions will have no more relevance than burnt-out courtrooms and judges in hiding. If we reach a state of panic and reaction, the essence of liberty will be undone.

"Liberty lies in the hearts of men and women," Learned Hand, the great American judge, once said. "[W]hen it dies there, no constitution, no law, no court can save it; no constitution, no law, no court can even do much to help it" (Hand, 1960, quoted in Mehta, 2007: 82). With this in mind, we must govern ourselves accordingly while there is still time.

References

Atomic Archive (2006). *Example scenarios*. Atomic Archive. <http://www.atomicarchive.com/Example/index.shtml>. Accessed December 17, 2007.

Barber, Benjamin R. (2003). *Fear's Empire*. W.W. Norton & Company.

Barnaby, Frank (1997). *Nuclear Legacy: Democracy in a Plutonium Economy*. Corner House Briefing 02. <http://www.thecornerhouse.org.uk/item.shtml?x=51956>. Accessed February 16, 2008.

Bednarz, Dieter, and Erich Follath (2007, September 3). 'We Are Moving Rapidly Towards an Abyss.' *Spiegel*. <http://www.spiegel.de/international/world/0,1518,503841,00.html>. Accessed September 3, 2007.

Bissett, James (1998). Background Implementation of the IRB. Unpublished paper, written for the Canadian Minister of Citizenship and Immigration.

B'Nai Brith Canada (2004). Toronto Conference Linked to Group on US Senate Terror Watch. News release (May 20). <http://www.bnaibrith.ca/prdisplay.php?id=423>. Accessed January 2, 2008.

Breinholt, Jeffrey (2007). Being Wrong About the Big Issues [Review of the book *Satanic Purses: Money, Myth and Misinformation in the War on Terror*]. International Assessment and Strategy Center. <http://www.strategycenter.net/research/pubID.155/pub_detail.asp>. Accessed December 14, 2007.

Canadian Coalition for Democracies [CCD] (2008). Recommendations of the Canadian Coalition for Democracies to the Commission of Inquiry into the Investigation of the Bombing of Air India Flight 182, March 4, 2008, Final Submission. Counsel for the Canadian

Coalition for Democracies <http://canadiancoalition.com/CCD_AirIndiaFinalSubmission.pdf>. Accessed 17, 2008.

Carrigg, David (2007, August 14). Muslim Students to Get Footbaths at UBC. *The Province*. <http://www.canada.com/theprovince/news/story.html?id=a68fe76d-2c5f-4e88-8fa8-9af2fdb3524e&k=62866>. Accessed August 14, 2007.

Collacott, Martin (2006). *Canada's Inadequate Response to Terrorism: The Need for Policy Reform*. Fraser Institute Digital Publication. Fraser Institute. <http://www.fraserinstitute.org/COMMERCE.WEB/product_files/TerrorismResponse6.pdf>.

Commission des droits de la personne et des droits de la jeunesse (2006). *Résolution COM-510.5.2.1.* <http://www.cdpdj.qc.ca/fr/publications/docs/ETS_resolution.pdf>. Accessed January 3, 2008.

Commission of Inquiry into the Actions of Canadian Officials in Relation to Maher Arar (2005). Transcript of public hearing, held at Old City Hall, Ottawa, Ontario, June 9, 2005. <http://epe.lac-bac.gc.ca/100/206/301/pco-bcp/commissions/maher_arar/07-09-13/www.stenotran.com/commission/maherarar/2005-06-09%20volume%2025.pdf>.

Corbella, Licia (2004, October 31). Elmasry Reveals True Colours. *Calgary Sun*. <http://www.canoe.ca/NewsStand/Columnists/Calgary/Licia_Corbella/2004/10/31/694019.html>. Accessed August 17, 2005.

Corbella, Licia (2007, February 18). Disturbing Reality Buried. *Calgary Sun*. <http://calsun.canoe.ca/News/Columnists/Corbella_Licia/2007/02/18/pf-3642930.html>. Accessed February 19, 2007.

Corbella, Licia (2007, June 15). Gotta Hate This Idea. *Toronto Sun*. <http://www.torontosun.com/Comment/2007/06/15/4262675-sun.html>. Accessed June 15, 2007.

Corbella, Licia (2008, February 16). Imam Undercuts Himself by Twisting His Own Words. *Calgary Herald*. <http://www.canada.com/calgaryherald/news/theeditorialpage/story.html?id=5162d29c-ffe4-4f4a-8d25-fe5e097c0963>. Accessed February 17, 2008.

Daily Times [Pakistan] (2007, June 23). PAT Leader Warns to Bomb UK Embassy. <http://www.dailytimes.com.pk/default.asp?page=2007\06\23\story_23-6-2007_pg7_6>. Accessed June 23, 2007.

Daniels, Ronald J., Patrick Macklem, and Kent Roach (eds.) (2001). *The Security of Freedom: Essays on Canada's Anti-Terrorism Bill*. University of Toronto Press.

de Borchgrave, Arnaud (2002, August 21). Criminals Recruited for 'Islamic Army' in America. *NewsMax.com*. <http://www.newsmax.com/archives/articles/2002/8/20/163711.shtml>. Accessed June 14, 2007.

Dhillon, R. Paul (2003, August 16). Indo-Canadians and Chinese Should Stand Up to People Like Martin Collacott and His Rightwing Friends. *The Link*.

Emerling, Gary (2008, April 16). Nuclear Attack on DC a Hypothetical Disaster. *Washington Times*. <http://www.washingtontimes.com/apps/pbcs.dll/article?AID=/20080416/METRO/556828862/1001&template=printart>. Accessed April 16, 2008.

Federation of American Scientists (1997). Operations: Ministry of Intelligence and Security [MOIS] Vezarat-e Ettela'at va Amniat-e Keshvar VEVAK. <http://www.fas.org/irp/world/iran/vevak/ops.htm>. Last updated December 8, 1997. Accessed December 18, 2007.

Gingrich, Newt (2007). *Sleepwalking Into a Nightmare*. Family Security Matters. <http://www.familysecuritymatters.org/terrorism.php?id=1385641>. Accessed December 1, 2007.

Glaser, Alexander (2006). *Effects of Nuclear Weapons*. Lecture Princeton University. <http://www.princeton.edu/~aglaser/lecture2006_nuclearweapons.pdf>. Accessed December 17, 2007.

The Globe and Mail (2005, July 14). First, Remember Who the Real Victims Were. A14. <http://www.theglobeandmail.com/servlet/story/RTGAM. 20050714.EMUSLIM14_COPY/BNStory/>. Accessed January 3, 2008.

Hand, Learned (1960). The Spirit of Liberty. In Irving Dillard (ed.), *The Spirit of Liberty: Papers and Addresses of Learned Hand*. Alfred A. Knopf.

Harris, David (2007, June 4). The Case for Bombing Iran. *Ottawa Citizen*. <http://www.canada.com/ottawacitizen/news/opinion/story.html?id=dbd924c7-33ab-4cbc-964e-59e006a4047c>. Accessed June 4, 2007.

Hitchens, Christopher (2007). Facing the Islamist Menace. *City Journal* (Winter). <http://www.city-journal.org/html/17_1_urbanities-steyn.html>. Accessed February 1, 2007.

Holliday, Sam C. (2007). Effectively Communicating Jihad: A Spade is a Spade. Blog. Politeia (October 21). <http://politeia-dbase.blogspot.com/2007/10/effective-communication-against-third.html>. Accessed October 23, 2007.

India Times News Network (2006, July 21). Lashkar Cadre in Indian Air Force? <http://timesofindia.indiatimes.com/articleshow/1789068.cms>. Accessed July 21, 2006.

International Atomic Energy Agency (2007). *Combating Illicit Trafficking in Nuclear and Other Radioactive Material*. IAEA Nuclear Security Series No. 6. International Atomic Energy Agency. <http://

www-pub.iaea.org/MTCD/publications/PDF/pub1309_web.pdf>.
Accessed February 16, 2008.

Investor's Business Daily (2007, December 3). Hyping Hate
Crime vs. Muslims. <http://www.ibdeditorials.com/IBDArticles.
aspx?id=281576932449479>. Accessed December 4, 2007.

Jafarzadeh, Alireza (2007). *The Iran Threat.* Palgrave Macmillan.

Johnson, Larry C. (2001, July 10). The Declining Terrorist Threat. *The
New York Times.* <http://query.nytimes.com/gst/fullpage.html?res=9A
02EEDF1138F933A25754C0A9679C8B63&n=Top/Reference/Times%20
Topics/Subjects/U/United%20States%20Foreign%20Service>. Accessed
December 17, 2007.

Jordán, Javier, and Robert Wesley (2007). The Threat of Grassroots
Jihadi Networks: A Case Study from Ceuta, Spain. *Terrorism Monitor*
5, 3 (February 15). <http://www.jamestown.org/terrorism/news/article.
php?articleid=2370249>. Accessed February 17, 2007.

Juan, Stephen (2006, September 29). Why Are People So Often in
Denial? *The Register.* <http://www.theregister.co.uk/2006/09/29/the_
odd_body_denial/>. Accessed September 8, 2007.

Kaplan, Lee (2004, April 5). The Saudi Fifth Column on Our Nation's
Campuses. *Frontpage Magazine.* <http://www.frontpagemag.com/
Articles/ReadArticle.asp?ID=12833>. Accessed May 12, 2007.

Khomeini, Ruhollah (1980). *Sayings of the Ayatollah Khomeini: Political,
Philosophical, Social and Religious.* Bantam Books.

Kristof, Nicholas D. (2004, August 11). An American Hiroshima. *The
New York Times.* <http://www.nytimes.com/2004/08/11/opinion/11kris.h
tml?ex=1249963200&en=81fb0a21e469c56a&ei=5088&partner=rssnyt>.

Leapman, Ben (2007, April 29). Al-Qaeda Supporters Working at Strategic Sites. *The Daily Telegraph*. <http://www.telegraph.co.uk/news/main.jhtml?xml=/news/2007/04/29/nterr29.xml>. Accessed May 1, 2007.

Levant, Ezra (2007). Elmasry vs. Steyn. Blog. The Shotgun Blog. (December 2). <http://westernstandard.blogs.com/shotgun/2007/12/elmasry-vs-stey.html>. Accessed January 2, 2008.

Levant, Ezra (2008). How Syed Soharwardy fights. Blog (February 16). <http://ezralevant.com/2008/02/how-syed-soharwardy-fights.html>.

Levitt, Matthew (2003). *Hezbollah: A Case Study of Global Reach*. The Washington Institute for Near East Policy. <http://www.washingtoninstitute.org/templateC07.php?CID=132>. Accessed December 18, 2007.

Malik, Kenan (2005, February 10). Islamophobia Myth. *Prospect Magazine*. <http://frontpagemag.com/Articles/ReadArticle.asp?ID=16735>. February 10, 2005.

Mansur, Salim (2007, September 8). Fickle Memories. *Toronto Sun*. <http://www.torontosun.com/News/Columnists/Mansur_Salim/2007/09/08/4478789.php>. Accessed September 14, 2007.

Mehta, Pratap Bhanu (2007). The Rise of Judicial Sovereignty. *Journal of Democracy* 18, 2 (April): 70–83.

Melman, Yossi, and Meir Javedanfar (2007). *The Nuclear Sphinx of Tehran*. Carroll & Graf Publishers.

Mia, Ziyaad E. (2002). Terrorizing the Rule of Law: Implications of the Anti-terrorism Act. *National Journal of Constitutional Law* 14, 1: 125–152.

Naji, Abu Bakr (2006). *The Management of Savagery: The Most Critical Stage Through Which the Umma Will Pass*. (William McCants, Trans.).

John M. Olin Institute for Strategic Studies, Harvard University. <http://ctc.usma.edu/publications/pdf/Management_of_Savagery.pdf>.

Norfolk, Andrew (2007, September 8). Our Followers 'Must Live in Peace until Strong Enough to Wage Jihad.' *The Times*. <http://www.timesonline.co.uk/tol/comment/faith/article2409833.ece>. Accessed September 8, 2007.

Orwell, George (1945). Notes on Nationalism. Charles' George Orwell Links. Originally published in *Polemic* (October, 1945). <http://www.netcharles.com/orwell/essays/notes-on-nationalism2.htm>. Accessed September 8, 2007.

Pennington, Matthew (2007, June 18). Pakistan Condemns Rushdie Honor. *Washington Post*. <http://www.washingtonpost.com/wp-dyn/content/article/2007/06/18/AR2007061800243.html>. Accessed June 21, 2007.

Reference re Manitoba Language Rights [1985] 1 S.C.R. 721.

Roach, Kent (2003). *September 11: Consequences for Canada*. McGill-Queen's University Press.

Rushdie, Salman (2006). Secular Values, Human Rights and Islamism. Presentation to Center of Inquiry, New York, October 11, 2006. <http://www.pointofinquiry.org/salman_rushdie_secular_values_human_rights_and_islamism/>.

Salman, Omran (2006, August 31). Misguided Muslim groups. *Philadelphia Daily News*. <http://www.philly.com/mld/inquirer/news/editorial/15401769>.htm?template=contentModules/printstory.jsp>. Accessed September 1, 2006.

Seeman, Neil (2002, September 14). Are We All Islamophobes? Not Really. *Free Republic*. <http://www.freerepublic.com/focus/news/750816/posts>. Accessed April 3, 2004.

Sharrif, Ali (2004, July 1). No-show Sheikh Rattles Jewish-Muslim Relations. *NOW Magazine*. <http://www.nowtoronto.com/ issues/2004-07-01/news_story7.php>. Accessed January 2, 2008.

Singer, Colin (2002, December 6). The Facts about Immigration. *National Post*. <http://www.immigration.ca/permres-nationalpost.asp>. Accessed April 18, 2008.

Stalinsky, Steven (2004). *Incitement to Jihad on Saudi Government-Controlled TV*. The Middle East Media Research Institute Special Report No. 29. The Middle East Media Research Institute. <http:// memri.org/bin/articles.cgi?Page=archives&Area=sr&ID=SR2904>. Accessed January 2, 2005.

Ulrich, George W. (1997). Threat Posed by Electromagnetic Pulse (EMP) to US Military Systems and Civil Infrastructure. Testimony before Military Research and Development Subcommittee, Committee on National Security, United States House of Representatives, July 16, 1997. <http://commdocs.house.gov/committees/security/has197010.000/ has197010_1.HTM>. Accessed 17 April 2008.

United Kingdom House of Lords (2005). *Daily Hansard*. The United Kingdom Parliament (November 21). <http://www.publications. parliament.uk/pa/ld200506/ldhansrd/vo051121/text/51121-13.htm>. Accessed April 17, 2008.

United Nations High Commissioner for Refugees (2007). *Asylum Levels and Trends in Industrialized Countries, 2006*. Field Information and Coordination Support Section, Division of Operational Services, UNHCR Geneva. <http://www.unhcr.org/statistics/ STATISTICS/460150272.pdf>. Accessed December 31, 2007.

United States of America v. *Holy Land Foundation for Relief and Development*, CR No. 3:04-CR-240-G Dist. Ct. for the Northern District of Texas, Dallas Division.

Washington Post (2004, June 16). Transcript: 9/11 Commission Hearings for June 16, 2004. <http://www.washingtonpost.com/wp-dyn/articles/A46525-2004Jun16.html>. Accessed January 19, 2007.

Woolsey, R. James (2006). Testimony before the Senate Committee on the Judiciary, Wartime Executive Power and the NSA's Surveillance Authority II, February 28, 2006. <http://judiciary.senate.gov/testimony.cfm?id=1770&wit_id=5227>. Accessed January 2, 2008.

Chapter 9

A Secure Border?
The Canadian View

John J. Noble

In a previous examination of the issues involved in a common security perimeter, I came out in favour of expanding the common security perimeter we have had since the 1950s—North American Aerospace Defence Command (NORAD)—to deal with the security challenges of the twenty-first century (Noble, 2005). Those challenges now include a sharper focus on who is allowed to cross national borders and who we let into Canada and the United States, both from across our common border and from outside North America. There have been and always will be segments of Canadian and American society that regard any sharing of sovereignty as bad thing, by definition, notwithstanding the end result. In this chapter, I review major developments in the past three years which affect the prospects for a common security perimeter and common security criteria for immigration and refugees. In the end, I conclude that while the prospects for more cooperation are good, the chances of a common security perimeter and common security criteria for immigration and refugees are not good on either side of the forty-ninth parallel. First, I will discuss several recent developments regarding the flow of people across our mutual border.

The Security and Prosperity Partnership

In late November 2004, Prime Minister Paul Martin and President George W. Bush agreed to a bilateral Security and Prosperity Partnership (SPP) during the latter's visit to Ottawa. This Partnership built on the Smart Border Declaration and 30-point Plan of Action which were established in December 2001. This bilateral SPP agreement was trilateralized in March 2005 during a meeting between President Bush, President Vicente Fox of Mexico, and Prime Minister Martin at Waco, Texas (White House, 2005b). A key element of the SPP is that it is trilateral in concept, but it allows any two countries to move forward on an issue, creating a path for the third to join later. Prime Minister Stephen Harper became part of the discussion at a leaders' meeting in Cancun in March 2006, and then hosted the SPP Trilateral Summit in Montebello in August 2007 (Office of the Prime Minister, 2007b). One of the five key priorities identified by the leaders at the Cancun meeting was the creation of "smart, secure Borders," with the objective of completing the following activities within 24 months:

- Collaborate to establish risk-based screening standards for goods and people, which rely on technology, information sharing, and biometrics;
- Develop and implement compatible electronic processes for supply chain security that use advanced electronic cargo information to analyze risk and ensure quick and efficient processing at the border;
- Develop standards and options for secure documents, to facilitate cross-border travel;
- Exchange additional law enforcement liaison officers to assist in criminal and security investigations; and,
- Develop coordinated business resumption plans at border crossings, to ensure legitimate trade continues (Office of the Prime Minister, 2006).

On February 23, 2007, ministers from the three countries met in Ottawa where they issued a final communiqué which established a senior level coordinating body to prioritize and oversee emergency management activities, including emergency response, critical infrastructure protection, border resumption in the event of an emergency, and border incident management (Ministers Responsible for the Security and Prosperity Partnership of North America, 2007).

The SPP will enhance and strengthen our ongoing security efforts, such as the Smart Border Accord, the Border Partnership Action Plan, and the Free and Secure Trade (FAST) Initiative. As a White House (2005a) news release states,

> The SPP builds upon, but is separate from, our long-standing trade and economic relationships, and it energizes other aspects of our cooperative relations, such as the protection of our environment, our food supply, and our public health. The issues of immigration and trade disputes will be dealt with outside the SPP through existing treaties and congressional action.

The SPP and its related programs are the platform on which more cooperation and greater confidence between Canada and the United States in the flow of people across our mutual border is being built. The SPP may also be the platform on which certain aspects of a common security perimeter can be built, but a formal common security perimeter is clearly outside the scope of the Partnership.

The Western Hemisphere Travel Initiative

The United States Congress passed the *Intelligence Reform and Terrorism Prevention Act* of 2004, which requires the development and implementation of a passport, other document, or combination of documents for all travel into the United States by American citizens and by other categories of individuals for whom documentation requirements had previously been waived (e.g., all Canadian citizens). The Western Hemisphere Travel Initiative (WHTI) of April 2005 is the proposed plan to implement this mandate (Abelson and Wood, 2007).

The WHTI has nothing whatsoever to do with illegal migration and is not expected to stem it in any way. In my view, a plan that is supposed to enhance the security of the United States, but does not deal with an annual illegal migration of some 500,000 people from Mexico seems to have a very big hole in it and makes a mockery of the whole process. When it comes to illegal migration from Mexico, the United States is faced with a difficult predicament: on the one hand, there is a strong security concern, and on the other, there is a strong demand for the labour provided by illegal migration. Canada faces a similar dilemma with respect to legal migration (Tibbetts, 2007, June 18; *The Economist*, 2007, May 31a; *The Economist*, 2007, May 31b). Both countries are confronted with the question of where to draw the line between meeting annual targets for migrants and refugees and maintaining national security. Not all of the illegal migrants entering the United States across the Rio Grande are Mexicans, and American security officials becoming increasingly worried about this. At least in Canada the authorities have an idea of who is entering the country.

There has been much talk about the possible development of an alternate secure ID document, such as a secure driver's license with biometric identifiers, and a United States smart pass card for traveling to Canada, which would be much cheaper than a full passport. To date, the Canadian government has focused almost exclusively on the development of a more secure driver's license as a satisfactory alternate ID that meets the criteria of the WHTI. Such as license would allow for a number of security options. For example, the duration of licenses issued to visitors with time-limited visas would not exceed the period of the visa (Vaughan, 2005).

In August 2007, the government of Canada asked the American administration to declare that it would accept enhanced driver's licenses as a passport substitute, and has asked for more time to introduce those licenses gradually, as existing licenses expire. However, an editorial in *The Globe and Mail* (2007, Sep. 4) suggested that this was unrealistic, and urged the government to expand its campaign to encourage Canadians to obtain passports. In addition, the editorial argued that the government should heavily advertise the NEXUS card, a high-security identity card available to Canadian and United States residents which expedites crossings at the land borders for low-risk, pre-approved travellers. The government should abandon its advocacy of the enhanced driver's license alternative, which would simply create more bureaucracy as provinces scrambled to give their licensing officials more security training, while dealing with privacy concerns.

In June 2007, the Department of Homeland Security (DHS) announced a further delay in the full implementation of the WHTI, which meant that the deadline after which citizens of both countries who want to enter or re-enter the United States would be required to have a passport had been postponed from January 31, 2008, to a yet to be determined date (DHS, 2007). A DHS news release noted that "on January 31, 2008, United States and Canadian citizens will need to present either a WHTI-compliant document or a government-issued photo ID, such as a driver's license, plus proof of citizenship, such as a birth certificate" (DHS, 2007).

The DHS announcement was due to a number of factors, the most important of which was pressure from border state legislators at the federal and state level who are concerned about the potential negative impact the passport requirement may have on the economy. The fact that passport offices on both sides of the border have been swamped with applications, causing considerable delays, is another factor. One unspoken factor is the clear desire of both countries to try to come up with a low-cost alternative to the passport that is still secure. While the WHTI is a unilateral American initiative, its implementation has various cross-border implications which have required, and will continue to require, extensive cooperation. The WHTI may yet result in some new form of secure ID which will be less than a full passport, such as the NEXUS card.

The Safe Third Country Agreement

Another recent development affecting the flow of people across our mutual border was the Agreement between the Government of Canada and the Government of the United States of America for Co-operation in the Examination of Refugee Status Claims from Nationals of Third Countries (known as the Safe Third Country Agreement). The Agreement reinforces refugee protection by establishing rules for the sharing of the responsibility between Canada and the United States to hear refugee claims made by persons at ports of entry (POEs) on the shared land border. Its objectives, as articulated in the Smart Border Action Plan, are to enhance the orderly handling of refugee claims, strengthen public confidence in the integrity of our asylum systems, and help reduce abuse of refugee programs.

The agreement applies only to land crossings of the Canada-United States borders, and not to arrivals by air or sea. In November 2006, a one year binational review of the implementation of the Agreement was completed (Citizenship and Immigration Canada, 2006). This review was conducted in cooperation with the United Nations High Commissioner for Refugees (UNHCR) and drew on input from non-governmental organizations (NGOs) in both countries, as mandated under section 8.3 of the Agreement. Overall, both governments' assessment of the implementation of the Agreement was positive. The Agreement also received the UNHCR's stamp of approval. The UNHCR's overall assessment was that "the Agreement has generally been implemented by the Parties according to its terms and, with regard to those terms, international refugee law" (Citizenship and Immigration Canada, 2006).

Over several years prior the Agreement, the number of refugee claims made in Canada declined steadily. In the 50 countries covered in a UNHCR report, there were 15% fewer applications for refugee status in 2005 (336,100) than there were in 2004 (394,600) (Citizenship and Immigration Canada, 2006).

In 2005, there was a 3% decrease in the number of refugee claims made at airports and a 6% decrease in the number of claims made at inland offices across the country, and a 55% decrease in the number of claims made at the land border. This led to an overall decrease of 23% in the number of refugee claims made in 2005, compared to the number made in 2004 (Citizenship and Immigration Canada, 2006).

In recent years, refugee claims made at the Canada-United States land border have comprised a significant portion of the total refugee claims received each year. On average, between 2002 and 2004, approximately 32% of the annual number of refugee claims were made at the land border. In 2005, this proportion fell to approximately 20%. In 2005, Canada received 4,033 refugee claims at the Canada-United States land border, 3,254 of which qualified for one of the exceptions to the Agreement. As a result, those people were able to pursue their claims for refugee protection in Canada. That acceptance rate (80.5%) is higher than the general

Canadian average mentioned below (Citizenship and Immigration Canada, 2006).

The Safe Third Country Agreement has reduced the number of unfounded refugee claimants coming to Canada across the land border, without becoming an impediment for genuine refugee claimants. Once word spreads about this agreement, perhaps the numbers of claimants will increase in future years.

The United States' experience with the Safe Third Country Agreement

Between 2000 and 2004, when the Agreement was not in place, an average of 58 asylum claimants arrived at one of the Canada-United States land border crossings each year. Of the 66 claimants during the first year of the Agreement, 62 were subject to the Agreement. The other four claimants were Canadian citizens, who are not subject to the Agreement. There were 39 cases in which United States Citizenship and Immigration Services (USCIS) determined that the applicant was subject to the Agreement. In 38 of the cases in which USCIS determined that an asylum seeker was subject to the Agreement, Asylum Officers found that an exception applied in 23 cases (60%). In 16 cases, there was a determination that an exception to the Agreement did not apply. In the 23 cases in which the applicant established an exception, all 23 were determined to have a family-based exception (Citizenship and Immigration Canada, 2006).

Reform of the refugee system in Canada

The Department of Citizenship and Immigration Canada (CIC) states that reform of Canada's refugee determination system is being explored so as to identify ways of streamlining the system to ensure protection is delivered efficiently to those in need. To support administrative reform of the system, additional funding was allocated to reduce the backlog in the refugee system. These new administrative measures continue to yield positive results in the form of an enhanced ability to manage access to the in-Canada refugee determination process and a reduction in the Immigration and Refugee Board (IRB) inventory by more than half since 2002 (from 51,600 in 2002 to 22,000 in 2005). In this context, CIC increased admissions from 15,901 in 2004 to 19,935 in 2005. CIC has also worked with other organizations—including the Department of Justice, the IRB, and the Canada Border Services Agency (CBSA)—to develop substantive proposals that will advance the refugee reform agenda (Citizenship and Immigration Canada, 2006).

However, a June 2007 article in the *Ottawa Citizen* reported that the "refugee backlog grows despite a flurry of appointments to IRB—Canada's backlog of refugee claims is growing by almost 1,000 cases a month as the Harper government continues to dawdle on filling vacancies at the Immigration and Refugee Board" (Bryden, 2007, June 16). The article pointed out that the backlog of claims has climbed to about 8,000, according to IRB records. Board spokesman Charles Hawkins said the number of pending cases is rising by about 900 a month, with each claim taking an average of 12.5 months to process. Furthermore, the *Citizen* reported that "when Prime Minister Stephen Harper took power 16 months ago, there were only five vacancies on the board, which at that time had 119 members .... [and] the backlog of claims had been effectively reduced to zero for the first time in a decade."

In August 2007, *Globe and Mail* columnist Jeffrey Simpson wrote about Canada's refugee system. He noted that,

> between January of 2005 and June of 2007, Mexico was the top source country for refugees to Canada. There were 6,745 Mexicans in the Canadian queue as of the end of June, more than Haitians, Chinese, Colombians and Sri Lankans combined. Yes, a majority of claimants are rejected, but given Canada's limited deportation success, even the unsuccessful ones can go underground and stay. Or, with a good lawyer, appeal to the minister. Or, as a last resort, a news outlet may provide a sympathetic front-page story. Because anybody who puts a toe on Canadian soil and claims to be a refugee has the right to Charter protection and the whole panoply of the refugee-determination system, the country is essentially helpless to do things more efficiently—and to assist genuine, certified refugees.

Helpless to deal with claimants when they land, the government has been forced to impose visas on all visitors from some friendly democratic countries, such as Costa Rica, Chile, and some countries in Eastern Europe. Mexico may be next. Today, Colombia (where Mr. Harper just made an official visit), India, the United States, and Israel are among the top 10 source countries for refugees. A majority of claimants from those countries, except Colombia, eventually are rejected, but they use up money and time, and send awful signals to other countries. We ought to have an annual list of countries from which Canada will not accept refugees, no matter the circumstances. Such a list could be compiled from a variety of public sources. But, of course, our laws would not allow it.

Election of the Conservative Party in January 2006

The election platform of the Conservative Party during their last campaign included a seven-page section entitled "Stand Up for Security," which included a section on "Securing our Borders" (Conservative Party of Canada, 2006: 26). The platform also included a section entitled, "Ensuring Effective Deportation Laws" (2006: 27). The platform contained a promise to hold "a comprehensive, independent judicial inquiry into the investigation of the Air India bombing of June 23, 1985," which, prior to the 9/11 attacks, was the largest single terrorist attack. That inquiry has been established and to date has heard considerable testimony and evidence which suggests the bombing could have been prevented.

Following its election, the Conservative government declared the Tamil Tigers a terrorist organization, resulting in favourable comments from Nicholas Burns, the United States Undersecretary of State. Burns made it clear that the State Department was tremendously excited to have an engaged, active new government as interlocutor. The government's early actions against Hamas, as well as its designation of Sri Lanka's Tamil Tigers as a terrorist group, were "indications of a very self-confident foreign policy and of a government not afraid to make very tough decisions," Burns said. "So we are very impressed. We are very impressed by the self-confidence and by the clarity of thinking in Canadian foreign policy" (Wells, 2006).

Need for further reforms to Canada's refugee system

The Canadian refugee system needs to be reformed for reasons other than issues of terrorism. Our concerns about possible terrorists slipping in as refugee claimants should not be the primary force driving this issue. But even if many Canadians are not concerned about terrorist threats to Canada, they should be concerned about the negative effects of a border closure in the aftermath of a terrorist attack with a Canadian connection. They should also be concerned about and want to rectify a two-tier system that many people use to try to circumvent the normal immigration process by claiming refugee status (Noble, 2003: 21). For example, the number of refugee claimants from Mexico continues to be very high, as noted above.

An Ipsos-Reid poll published by the *National Post* on June 18, 2007, concluded that "Canadians are split on refugee risks." Nearly one-half of those surveyed (48%) said immigration officials should be more worried about "accidentally letting someone stay in Canada when they are not a legitimate refugee." On the flip side, 43% said officials should be more concerned about "forcing someone to return to their country when in fact they really deserve to be considered a refugee." Nine percent said they did not know which prospect they find more worrisome (Tibbetts, 2007, June 18).

The same article noted that a separate Ipsos survey conducted among 1,002 Canadians between June 12–14 also found that over the past 20 years, Canadians have changed their attitudes regarding refugees. When asked whether Canada should be doing more than other similar countries, 41% said Canada should do more than other countries do to protect refugees, 1% said Canada should do less, and 48% said it should be about the same. In a 1987 survey, only one-quarter of Canadians said Canada should be doing more to protect refugees. However, in 1987, almost half said that Canada should be doing about the same as other countries, a figure that has held steady for two decades. The recent poll found that British Columbia residents were most likely (51%) to think Canada should be doing more than other Western countries. Québecers were the least likely (only 24%) to say Canada should be more active (Tibbetts, 2007, June 18).

Differences between the Canadian and American systems

There is no reason why Canada cannot continue to maintain its own policies on annual levels of immigration and its own regulations determining the selection of skilled immigrants, sponsored relatives, etc. Canada and the United States would only need to adopt common standards if they were to agree to combine their economies in a common market that included free movement of labour across their common border. If so, the reasons would be economic rather than security. Sovereignty concerns and jealousies in both Canada and the United States regarding the question of common standards for the selection and numbers of immigrants are not likely to abate.

In terms of law enforcement, prosecutions, and detention, the two countries differ in a substantial way. The United States uses detention much more aggressively than Canada does. Until recently, this indicated primarily a willingness to spend more money—much more money. However, since 9/11, the United States has also backed away from legal protections that still hold sway in Canada. In the United States, there is also a greater willingness to prosecute, a greater ability to convict, and harsher penalties imposed by the courts on smugglers and traffickers than is the case in Canada.

But does this mean that the American system is better than the Canadian system in terms of entry control and removals? In light of the number of asylum seekers from abroad coming to Canada via the United States, it seems that many people have not had difficulty getting past American entry controls. If Canada did not have to deal with the 10,000 to 15,000 additional refugee claimants per year who come from the United States, it would have considerably more resources to apply to enforcement, detention, and removals. That is why the Safe Third Country Agreement mentioned above was so important to Canada. It was supposed to relieve some of Canada's present burden, and force the United States to take some responsibility for the present flow of refugee claimants into Canada (Noble, 2005: 510–11).

A 2002 study entitled, *US and Canadian Immigration Policies: Marching Together to Different Tunes*, itemized problems with Canada's refugee determination system and American criticisms. It suggested that entry as a visitor would offer a terrorist the path of least resistance. The paper notes that "the modus operandi of the 9/11 terrorists suggest that they understood that the weakest link in North American border security lay in the admission and monitoring of tourists, international students, business people, and other temporary entrants, because there are no exit controls and no way of knowing whether those who were admitted temporarily ever leave" (Rekai, 2002: 15).

Schengen and the idea of a shared border for North America

A security perimeter, similar to the Schengen Treaty which covers most but not all European Union countries,[1] which would abolish the land border between Canada and the United States is not an option at this time for a number of reasons. First, Canada and the United States are not committed to the type of political and economic union that has developed in Europe. The Americans would worry that abolishing the border would make the United States more vulnerable to security threats. In addition to sharing those concerns, Canadians would worry about two things: the large number of illegal undocumented immigrants in the United States and the potential flow of guns into Canada. I must agree with James Laxer, long-standing nationalist and member of the New Democratic Party "Waffle Group," who wrote that an open border with the United States "would raise serious security concerns for Canada including importing the American gun culture into Canada, something most Canadians strongly oppose" (Laxer, 2003: 262, 318–19).

As Daniel Stoffman has written, there are two main problems with the idea of a security perimeter: "i) the Canadian immigration and refugee systems are in such disarray that American security would be compromised if border controls were removed; and ii) Canadian security would be at risk

---

1   The Treaty established the first provisions for a harmonized visa policy among signatory EU countries and established new policies to ensure the cooperation necessary to eliminate internal border checks for nationals of Schengen party states (Newland and Papademetriou, 1998-1999).

if Canada stopped checking people entering from the south" (2002: 48). Stoffman also wrote that "the major reason Canada should fear the United States is that the States is home to the greatest collection of unidentified illegal immigrants anywhere in the world" (2002: 66). Sidney Weintraub (2003) of the Center for Strategic and International Studies has also written about the problems associated with a security perimeter:

> the notion of perimeter screening to speed up the movement of goods and residents of the two countries is logical on the surface, but there are inherent problems that must be considered. Without any border screening, the two countries would need identical immigration laws to permit the free movement of people from one country to the other and a common tariff and other trade restrictions so that the transhipment [sic] of goods from one country to the other would not matter. These steps smack of sharing sovereignty rather than "mutual respect for sovereignty."

Moreover, in 2004, Christopher Rudolph concluded that "the unequal distribution of power among NAFTA states, disparate interests, and ideational factors make the establishment of a comprehensive harmonized regime governing migration and border policy in North America highly unlikely" (Rudolph, 2005: 457). Quoting Peter Andreas, Rudolph also noted that "to 'Schengenize' North Americas borders ... would require a level of formal institutionalization and policy harmonization that is difficult to imagine in the present context" (Andreas, 2003: 12, quoted in Rudolph, 2005).

When considering the possibility of a security perimeter, it is also useful to recall the assessment made by Gary Hufbauer and Jeffrey Schott (2004) that North American Free Trade Agreement (NAFTA) politics in the United States are far more sensitive to Mexico than to Canada. As such, a bilateral Canada-United States deal is less likely to garner the necessary support in Congress than a trilateral deal. Hufbauer and Schott suggested that,

> non-NAFTA visitors who threaten security can be better excluded if a few principal measures are adopted ... we believe that Ottawa,

Washington, and Mexico City can forge common visa standards for most non-NAFTA visitors and immigrants. The NAFTA partners should agree on visa-waiver country lists, length of stay, and watch lists for potentially troublesome visitors. Officials in each country should have electronic access to the immigration records of its partners. These suggestions seem obvious. However, US security agencies, such as the FBI, CIA, Customs, and Alcohol, Tobacco and Firearms (ATF), have yet to agree on a common watch list for potentially troublesome visitors to the United States, so it will take political energy to forge a common North American approach.

Furthermore, Hufbauer and Schott argue that NAFTA partners should create a special force to handle all third country immigration controls at the individual's first airport of entry into the NAFTA area. Common document and biometric identification standards should be applied (2004: 14). However, this kind of immigration control ignores the ongoing realities of illegal migration from Mexico into the United States and the unwillingness of both Canadian and American authorities to trust Mexican border officials.

Options for North American physical security

Previously, I have suggested various potential options for ensuring the security of North America (Noble, 2005: 520). The threat of a protectionist "Fortress America" mentality appears to have receded in the light of cooperation along the two American borders since 9/11. However, this assessment may be considered overly optimistic in light of a report tabled by North American business leaders at the Montebello Summit, which expressed concerns about the "need to make borders within North America as safe and transparent as possible" (North American Competitiveness Council, 2007). It is unknown what would happen in the event of another 9/11 type of attack on the United States, particularly if any of the terrorists gained access to the United States through Canada or Mexico. At a minimum, there would be the type of short-term interruptions which characterized the American response to 9/11. A Fortress America mentality would rely on existing borders as the best place to maintain controls. It could entail increased delays in the flow of people and goods from north and south of the United States, and thereby threaten the economic security of two large trading partners of the United States and a large amount of American investment in those countries.

Creating a Fortress America would be very expensive and would put the emphasis of control in the wrong area. Control should be maintained at the perimeter points of access to North America, which are not across the two land borders, but at airports and ports. I fear that the United States Congress has decided to spend a lot of money on controlling the two borders, for example, by building a physical fence along the southern border and an electronic fence along the northern border (or at least from the head of Lake Superior to the Pacific coast). As Michael Byers notes, "attempting to secure a frontier that is nearly nine thousand kilometres long is a fool's errand that will cost the American taxpayer dearly .... Fences might make for good neighbours, but barriers are not good for making or keeping friends" (Byers, 2007: 214).

The United States has recognized that it needs to expand the perimeters of its security at least to the edges of North America and, in many cases, beyond. Passengers destined for the United States and Canada from overseas countries must go through pre-clearance checks before they are allowed to board the aircraft. Canada and the United States are cooperating in this effort in various European airports and elsewhere. As well, container traffic bound for North America is being pre-cleared in ports outside the continent. Cooperation in this area was highlighted in the joint communiqué which came out of the Montebello SPP summit in late August 2007 (Office of the Prime Minister, 2007a).

Perimeter concepts for North America are not new and are best exemplified in the long standing Canada-United States defence partnership. Similar activities took place on the civilian side prior to 9/11 and have since become codified in the Smart Border Declaration and Action Plan. Various ideas have been put forward for concentric circles of perimeter security and some of these have been incorporated into the Smart Border plans, on which work is continuing alongside the Security and Prosperity Partnership.

The concept of a security perimeter could be limited strictly to a military or defence one in the face of traditional threats. But the new threats to North American security do not come from state actors, but non-state actors, and the most appropriate means of defence against these threats lies outside the traditional military pattern. Instead, it involves intelligence sharing, police cooperation, and tighter administration of refugee and asylum policies and visitor visas. Here, the past experiences of Canada and the United Sates, and Mexico and the United States are widely divergent. Defence cooperation between Canada and the United States has a long and ongoing history. However, cooperation between the United States and Mexico would be a new and very controversial matter.

Proposals for increased labour mobility within North America are being held hostage to the new security climate. The Canada-United States Free Trade Agreement (CUSFTA) and NAFTA introduced Trade NAFTA (TN) visas for certain categories of skilled professionals, with major differences in application between those issued by the United States for Mexicans and for Canadians.[2] Full scale labour mobility between Mexico and the United States is seen as a major threat to the United States and an economic drag. Whether or not it might be possible to envisage a widening of the categories for NAFTA, widening TN visas is another matter. In any event, full labour mobility inside the European Union did not come until after it had gone from a customs union to a common market and an economic union. Such a union would appear to be a pre-cursor to any Schengen type of agreement which governs admission from outside the borders of the European Union and has effectively abolished controls on the internal borders. Proposals to abolish all controls on the Canada-United States or Mexico-United States borders would run into strong opposition on both sides of the two borders for reasons mentioned in this chapter.

---

2   Until September 30, 2003, there was a yearly ceiling of 5,500 TN visas for Mexicans and no ceiling for Canadians. The ceiling on Mexican TN visas no longer exists. Mexicans have to apply for their TN visas at United States Consulates in Mexico. Canadians apply for their TN visas at the port of entry into the United States.

Conclusions

New initiatives with respect to the flow of people across our mutual border and for a common security perimeter are unlikely to find support from either the Canadian or the American government unless some fundamental decisions are made with respect to the nature of our future economic integration. Such a prospect is not in the cards at the present time, however much it might be in both countries' interests.

The two governments have committed themselves to the Security and Prosperity Partnership, which has as one of its key objectives a smart, secure border. However, the SPP has made it clear that no treaties are being negotiated under its mandate and that, in most respects, immigration is outside its purview, notwithstanding the relevance of border controls on some parts of immigration and refugee issues. The Safe Third Country Agreement appears to be working better than some thought, and with less impact than others feared. But it is not a panacea. Similar agreements are needed with other countries, especially those in the European Union. Alternatively, the Canadian government could just announce that it will return any refugee claimant arriving from a safe European Union country. All that is required to do this is a strong dose of political will from the federal government. The refugee system would also work better if the United States would agree to include refugee claimants arriving by air and sea in the Safe Third Country Agreement, rather than limiting its application to the land border.

Attempts to develop common security criteria for immigration and refugees could prove extremely problematic for a variety of reasons, including the sovereignty and criminal issues mentioned in this chapter. However, continued work and cooperation in this field will increase the confidence of the other party that the policies and their administration are being carried out in a manner which meets the common objective for smart, secure borders. Thus, more can be done without a formal common security perimeter and without common selection criteria for immigrants and refugees.

References

Abelson, Donald E., and Duncan Wood (2007). *People, Security and Borders: The Impact of the WHTI on North America*. Foundation for Educational Exchange between Canada and the United States of America and Accenture. <http://www.nnasc-renac.ca/People SecurityandBorders%20(English).pdf>. Accessed November 23, 2007.

Andreas, Peter (2003). *A Tale of Two Borders: The US-Mexico and US-Canada Lines after 9-11*. Working Paper No. 77. Centre for Comparative Immigration Studies, University of California, San Diego.

Bryden, Joan (2007, June 16). Refugee Backlog Grows Despite Flurry of Appointments to IRB. *The Globe and Mail*. <http:// www.theglobeandmail.com/servlet/Page/document/v5/content/ subscribe?user_URL=http://www.theglobeandmail.com%2Fservlet%2 Fstory%2FRTGAM.20070616.wrefugee0616%2FBNStory%2FNational %2Fhome&ord=4918699&brand=theglobeandmail&force_login=true>. Accessed November 23, 2007.

Byers, Michael (2007). *Lament for a Nation: What is Canada For? A Relentlessly Optimistic Manifesto for Canada's Role in the World*. Douglas & McIntyre.

Citizenship and Immigration Canada (2006). *A Partnership for Protection: Year One Review*. <http://www.cic.gc.ca/english/department/ laws-policy/partnership/index.asp>.

Conservative Party of Canada (2006). *Stand Up for Canada: Conservative Party of Canada Federal Election Platform*. <http://www.conservative.ca/ media/20060113-Platform.pdf>. Accessed November 23, 2007.

Department of Homeland Security [DHS] (2007). WHTI Land and Sea Notice of Proposed Rulemaking Published. News release (June 20). Department of Homeland Security, Office of the Press Secretary.

<http://www.dhs.gov/xnews/releases/pr_1182350422171.shtm>. Accessed November 23, 2007.

The Economist (2007, May 31a). Guests v Gatecrashers. <http://www.economist.com/research/articlesBySubject/displaystory.cfm?subjectid=894664&story_id=9256643>. Accessed January 24, 2008.

The Economist (2007, May 31b). In Search of an Immigration Policy. <http://www.economist.com/research/articlesBySubject/displaystory.cfm?subjectid=894664&story_id=9254520>. Accessed November 23, 2007.

The Globe and Mail (2007, September 4). The Pain of Getting Across the Border. <http://www.theglobeandmail.com/servlet/Page/document/v5/content/subscribe?user_URL=http://www.theglobeandmail.com%2Fservlet%2Fstory%2FRTGAM.20070904.wepassport04%2FBNStory%2FspecialComment%2Fhome&ord=4747861&brand=theglobeandmail&force_login=true>. Accessed November 23, 2007.

Hufbauer, Gary C., and Jeffrey J. Schott (2004). *Deeper North American Economic Integration: A US Perspective*. C.D. Howe Institute Commentary No. 195 (January). <http://www.iie.com/publications/papers/hufbauer0104.pdf>. Accessed November 23, 2007.

Laxer, James (2003). *The Border: Canada, the US and Dispatches from the 49th Parallel*. Doubleday Canada.

Ministers Responsible for the Security and Prosperity Partnership of North America (2007). Statement by Ministers Responsible for the Security and Prosperity Partnership of North America. Government of Canada. <http://www.spp-psp.gc.ca/progress/02_23_2007-en.aspx>. Accessed November 23, 2007.

Newland, Kathleen, and Demetrios G. Papademetriou (1998-1999). Managing Migration: Tracking the Emergence of a New International Regime? *UCLA Journal of International Law & Foreign Affairs* 3, 2 (Fall/Winter).

Noble, John J. (2003). Canada-US Relations in the Post-Iraq-War Era: Stop the Drift Towards Irrelevance. *Policy Options* (May). <http://www.irpp.org/po/index.htm>. Accessed November 23, 2007.

Noble, John J. (2005). Fortress America or Fortress North America? *Law and Business Review of the Americas* 15, 3/4 (Summer/Fall): 461–526.

North American Competitiveness Council (2007). Trilateral Business Council Urges Progress in Building a Secure and Competitive North America. News release (August 21). <http://www.ceocouncil.ca/publications/pdf/test_65b3c6bd19707985a7c5425b940da267/News_release_NACC_August_21_2007.pdf>. Accessed November 23, 2007.

Office of the Prime Minister (2006). Leaders' Joint Statement. News release (March 31). <http://www.pm.gc.ca/eng/media.asp?category=1&id=1085>. Accessed November 23, 2007.

Office of the Prime Minister (2007a). Joint Statement: Prime Minister Harper, President Bush and President Calderón. North American Leaders' Summit. News release (August 21). <http://pm.gc.ca/grfx/docs/statement-declaration-en.pdf>. Accessed November 23, 2007.

Office of the Prime Minister (2007b). Prime Minister Announces North American Leaders' Summit in Canada. News release (June 15). <http://www.pm.gc.ca/eng/media.asp?category=1&id=1698>. Accessed November 22, 2007.

Rekai, Peter (2002). *US and Canadian Immigration Policies: Marching Together to Different Tunes.* C.D. Howe Institute Commentary No. 171. <http://www.cdhowe.org/pdf/Rekai.pdf>. Accessed November 23, 2007.

Rudolph, Christopher (2005). International Migration and Homeland Security: Coordination and Collaboration in North America. *Law and Business Review of the Americas* 11, 3/4 (Summer/Fall).

Simpson, Jeffrey (2007, August 24). Canada's System is Failing Friends and Real Refugees Alike. *The Globe and Mail.* <http://www.theglobeandmail.com/servlet/Page/document/v5/content/subscribe?user_URL=http://www.theglobeandmail.com%2Fservlet%2Fstory%2FRTGAM.20070824.wcosimp24%2FBNStory%2FFront%2Fhome&ord=4992461&brand=theglobeandmail&force_login=true>. Accessed November 23, 2007.

Stoffman, Daniel (2002). *Who Gets In: What's Wrong with Canada's Immigration Program – and How to Fix It.* Macfarlane, Walter, & Ross.

Tibbetts, Janice (2007, June 18). Canadians Split on Refugee Risks: Poll. *National Post.* <http://www.canada.com/nationalpost/news/canada/story.html?id=b1929863-44d8-4246-87e7-c7a50e6d1838>. Accessed November 23, 2007.

United Nations High Commissioner for Refugees [UNHCR] (2006). *Asylum Levels and Trends in Industrialized Countries, 2005.* <http://www.unhcr.org/statistics/STATISTICS/44153f592.pdf>. Accessed November 23, 2007.

Vaughan, Jessica M. (2005). Secure Licenses Critical to Homeland Security. Testimony Prepared for the Joint Transportation Committee, Massachusetts State House, Boston, Massachusetts, October 25, 2005. Center for Immigration Studies. <http://www.cis.org/articles/2005/jmvtestimony102505.html>. Accessed November 23, 2007.

Weintraub, Sidney (2003). *Strains in the Canada-US Relationship.* Issues in International Political Economy No. 40. Center for Strategic and International Studies. <http://ctrc.sice.oas.org/geograph/north/causwein.pdf>.

Wells, Paul (2006). *Right Side Up: The Fall of Paul Martin and the Rise of Stephen Harper's New Conservatism.* McClelland & Stewart.

White House (2005a). Fact Sheet: Security and Prosperity Partnership of North America. News release (March 23). White House, Office of the Press Secretary. <http://www.whitehouse.gov/news/releases/2005/03/20050323-4.html>. Accessed November 23, 2007.

White House (2005b). Joint Statement by President Bush, President Fox, and Prime Minister Martin. News release (March 23). White House, Office of the Press Secretary. <http://www.whitehouse.gov/news/releases/2005/03/20050323-2.html>. Accessed November 22, 2007.

Chapter 10

A Smart Border?
The American View

Christopher Rudolph

Globalization has served to make immigration and border control an increasingly important priority for the state, affecting nearly all facets of security—geopolitical, economic, and societal (Rudolph, 2003a; 2006a; 2006b). Since September 11, 2001, the issue of immigration and border control has gained even more salience, as it now must be considered to constitute the front lines of homeland security (Camarota, 2002; Kephart, 2005). In Europe and North America—regions that attract the largest volume of migrants—states face a daunting challenge: to craft policy that will enable them to support the national interest along several security dimensions that often have contrasting policy preferences.

In terms of policy design, the European Union has been the most innovative in its attempts to deal with the issue of managing immigration and controlling borders (Papademetriou, 1996; Newland and Papademetriou, 1998; Meyers, 2002). In particular, the European approach of integrated border management sets it apart from most other states around the world, whose policies have traditionally been unilateral in orientation. Indeed, in North America, unilateral policies have dominated as policy makers have generally positioned the issue of immigration and border control as central to conceptions of sovereignty (Shanks, 2001; Rudolph, 2005b; 2006a).

Among the more significant elements of the European Union's integrated approach was the signing of the Schengen Agreement in 1985. Included in the Schengen Agreement were provisions to establish the Schengen Information System (SIS), which would provide authorities with needed information regarding who should and should not be admitted into the Schengen zone. Although not originally signed by all European Union member states, the Schengen Agreement and its provisions were later included in the Amsterdam Treaty (1997), which provided much of the political architecture employed in the European Union's process of regional integration. The European Union has also sought to utilize a multilateral approach to dealing with asylum claims. In 1997, most European Union member states signed the Dublin Convention in order to codify harmonized rules and procedures for asylum processing that were aimed to curtail the growing practice of "asylum shopping" (Koslowski, 2000).

This chapter briefly outlines the current developments and challenges in United States-Canada cooperation, focusing on the Smart Borders Agreement. It discusses the obstacles facing the quest for "smart borders" in an age of globalization and international terrorism, especially the challenge of intelligence sharing. Finally, it demonstrates that few of the conditions that led to Europe's Schengen regime are present within the current North American region.

North American integration and border management[1]

In contrast to Europe, integration and regional cooperation in North America was not initiated under extreme circumstances. Instead of a comprehensive "grand design," such as the one articulated in the Treaty of Rome, North American integration has been more measured and incremental. Recognition of regional—if not global—interdependence concerning international migration has pressed policy makers to shift political discourse from one solely rooted in a domestic perspective to one that moves beyond national borders. This does not necessarily mean that policy makers see management issues from a regional interest; rather, they see that

---

1   Portions of this section were published as Rudolph (2005a).

regional cooperation is necessary in order to achieve national interests. As United States Attorney General John Ashcroft (2003) explained to the Senate Judiciary Committee, "close working relationships with international allies" would allow the United States to "leverage our anti-terrorism efforts throughout the world."

Bilateral cooperation between the United States and Canada has a long tradition, and has been described as "the most extensive bilateral relationship in the world" (Johnson and Fitzgerald, 2003). In 2003, Tom Ridge, who was the United States Secretary of Homeland Security at the time, explained the desire for intergovernmental cooperation as an issue of common interests. He stated, "By working together we can better reach our common goals of ensuring the security and prosperity of our citizens" (Canadian Embassy in Washington, 2003). Yet when we examine the parameters of the existing bilateral measures taken concerning migration and border control, it appears that "common interests" have not generated movement toward a formal regime (Stein, 1983). Rather, the extension of egoistic self-interest (i.e., "leveraging" domestic efforts) has been the driving force behind the increased cooperation, especially since 9/11.

In the United States, cooperation with Canada is seen as increasingly important for United States security. First, there is concern about the possibility of terrorist activity and infiltration from the North. Suspicions rose with the apprehension of Ahmed Ressam, the "millennium bomber," in December 1999, and these were later bolstered by a 2003 report which suggested that some 50 terrorist groups were present and active in Canada at that time (*CBS News*, 2003, Sep. 7; Berry et al., 2003). Moreover, there is a wide spread belief that Canadian immigration and border policies are somewhat lax, especially those concerning refugees and asylum seekers (Gallagher, 2003). The 9/11 attacks increased the salience of counterterrorism as a policy imperative in Canada (from the standpoint of self-interest), but expressed interests continue to focus on building a more open border. An inability to increase security along the border and allay American concerns would no doubt put this goal in jeopardy. The tremendous back ups at key points along the border in the days following 9/11 made this perfectly clear.

The Smart Border Declaration

With mutual interest in increased cooperation, Canada and the United States signed the Smart Border Declaration on December 12, 2001. The declaration was accompanied by an action plan based on four pillars: the secure flow of people; the secure flow of goods; secure infrastructure; and, information sharing and coordination in the enforcement of these objectives (Foreign Affairs and International Trade Canada, 2001). What becomes evident quickly—even with only a cursory examination of the language used within the document—is that the Smart Border Declaration advances integration of border management more in terms of coordination, rather than collaboration.

Although programs such as NEXUS, FAST, and Integrated Border Enforcement Teams (IBET) have been touted as evidence of a more integrated approach, the level of "smart border" integration remains relatively shallow, with little effort made to formally link or harmonize policy in ways that would constrain independent decision making on things such as admissions criteria. Convergence in the domain of visa issuance has been informal—a "spontaneous regime," as Oran Young (1983) would say. As a result, the United States and Canada now share common visa policies with 175 countries, though they still differ with 18 other countries (*Migration News*, 2005). Negotiated collaboration has been more limited, and has focused on the issue of refugee and asylum processing.

Although harmonization of asylum policy is listed as part of the action plan of the Smart Border Declaration, a closer look at the issue warrants pessimism regarding the possibility of highly-integrated collaboration. In terms of current policy, several dimensions of the Canadian system make it disproportionately open relative to other advanced industrial states. These include high rates of approvals, a generous social welfare system, infrequent prosecutions, and lax deportation procedures. In 2002, the refugee recognition rate (for in-country determinations) in Canada was nearly double the American rate, while the per capita acceptance rate of refugees between 2000 and 2002 (in-country Convention refugee recognitions) was four times the American rate (United Nations High Commissioner for Refugees, 2003). In addition, authorities detain few refugees and asylum seekers while their claims are pending adjudication, even though

Canadian law permits the detention of applicants who may represent a possible security threat or flight risk.[2] In fact, generally only 5% of refugees entering Canada are detained; the remaining 95% are released until their immigration hearing is held (*CBS News*, 2003, Sep. 7; Bissett, 2002). Moreover, in Canada, there are few barriers to claimants working and accessing social entitlement programs while their claims are pending.

In contrast, the United States' *Illegal Immigration Reform and Immigrant Responsibility Act* (IIRAIRA) of 1996 added to existing restrictions on applicants' access to social welfare while their case is being adjudicated by requiring that employment authorization not be given for a period of at least six months. Because "first instance" determination of asylum status must be processed within 180 days according to American law, employment opportunities are reserved only for those who warrant an affirmative determination of their case. Moreover, in addition to detaining claimants pending a review of their case, the United States also has an "expedited removal" system in place which facilitates detention and removal of apprehended individuals who do not have proper immigration or travel documents. As well, out-of-status foreigners who are in the country for more than one year are barred from applying for asylum and are subject to deportation if apprehended (*Migration News*, 2003).

In contrast to its American usage, it has been argued that the use of the term "expedited" in Canada has meant "[to] speed positive claims toward recognition" (Gallagher, 2003: 14). In Canada, a failure to detain applicants pending what is often a lengthy judicial review process is coupled with a de facto policy of failing to deport those who either fail to appear at their hearing or are denied refugee status. As James Bissett writes, "not only does Canada permit anyone who arrives to make an asylum claim, but many of those eventually denied refugee status are never removed from the country. Only about 9,000 people are removed from Canada each year, and of these, approximately two-third[s] are failed asylum seekers" (2002: 5).

---

2   Peter Rekai notes that there are several factors leading to this failure to detain potential "high risk" applicants, including a lack of the intelligence necessary to identify "high risk" applicants, a lack of adequate detention facilities, and humanitarian considerations (Rekai, 2002: 13).

Canada's refugee and asylum policies have resulted in trends that are disconcerting to some security-minded American policy makers. Certainly, Canada's stance vis-à-vis asylum and refugees makes it a first choice for those seeking protection, as well as those seeking admission after failing to obtain it through other channels (Gallagher, 2003: 9). Unfortunately, this also creates conditions conducive for the infiltration of foreign terrorists. The Canadian Security Intelligence Service (CSIS) has confirmed the presence of some 50 active terrorist organizations operating in Canada, including the Irish Republican Army, Hezbollah, Hamas, and al-Qaeda (*CBS News*, 2003, Sep. 7). In addition, a number of known terrorists, including Hani Al-Sayegh, Gazi Ibrahim Abu Mezer, Nabil Al-Murabh, and Ahmed Ressam, have gained access to Canada by seeking political asylum upon entry. From an American point of view, this represents a potential threat to United States security, as terrorists can exploit Canadian policy and then use their Canadian base as a potential staging ground for terrorist attacks.

In the European Union, policy makers have sought to increase security through integration and policy harmonization, including "fast track" processing to dismiss "patently unfounded" asylum claims and applying "safe third country" principles in asylum processing to reduce the practice of asylum shopping. Applying this strategy in North America has proven to be politically challenging, even though a strong bilateral relationship exists between Canada and the United States. Canadian concerns with respect to protecting the human rights of bona fide refugees and asylum seekers fleeing persecution have made Canada wary of applying strict limitations on safe third country entrants. After a series of failed attempts since 1987 to apply safe third country protocols to asylum processing, new legislation was passed after 9/11. However, this has yet to change Canada's concerns regarding the practice of safe third country principles in asylum processing. The *Immigration and Refugee Protection Act* (IRPA), passed in November 2001, actually increased restrictions on applying the safe third country principle in the processing of asylum claims. A report released in December 2003 points out that "Article 102(2)(a) of the IRPA requires the government to 'consider' whether a 'responsibility-sharing' agreement exists between Canada and the transit country before a refugee claim can be considered 'ineligible' for determination in Canada" (Gallagher,

2003: 15). In contrast to American legislation passed after 9/11, which stresses security interests—e.g., *USA PATRIOT Act*, the *Enhanced Border Security and Visa Entry/Exit Reform Act*—the title of the 2001 legislation touts Canada's commitment to refugee protection, with no reference to security. Moreover, policy makers have made their discomfort regarding policy harmonization quite clear. In October 2001, the current Immigration Minister, Elinor Caplan, suggested that Canadian-American discussions concerning the development of a security perimeter should focus on information sharing rather than harmonization: "Let there not be any misunderstanding. Canadian laws will be made right here in the Canadian Parliament" (quoted in Adelman, 2002).

A Safe Third Country Agreement

There appears to be less of an incentive for the United States to enter a bilateral third country agreement with Canada, since the flow of asylum seekers generally moves toward Canada from the United States. Indeed, one United States State Department official suggested that the Safe Third Country Agreement is something that "Canada wants and that we are willing to agree to as a trade-off for other important counterterrorism measures" (United States House of Representatives, Subcommittee on Immigration, 2002; Gallagher, 2003: 15). Reluctance towards deeper integration and harmonization in this area is also evidenced in practice. For example, the United States' treatment of the Maher Arar case suggests a wariness with Canada's commitment to the war on terrorism and may also hint at a reluctance to turn over individuals who appear on American anti-terrorist watch lists. A report by the Center for Strategic and International Studies suggests that "by refusing to send [Arar] to Canada, the US government appears to have believed Canada would let Arar walk free, or at a minimum fail to gain any information from him" (Belelieu, 2003: 7).

The political inertia involved may explain the lag in implementing the Safe Third Country Agreement. The agreement was signed on December 5, 2002, but was not implemented until December 29, 2004. Under the terms of the agreement, refugees claimants are required to submit their claim in the first country they enter—either the United States or Canada (Citizenship and Immigration Canada, 2004). In addition to being limited in scope (including only Canada and the United States), the agreement had other limitations. For example, an exception to the agreement exists for refugee claimants attempting to enter Canada from the United States if they have family in Canada or if they are an unaccompanied minor. In addition, the agreement applies only to land border crossings. It does not include claims processed at airports or in the country's interior.

The Safe Third Country Agreement is a significant development in border management and it definitely suggests that increased collaboration between the United States and Canada is possible. However, there are many obstacles facing the creation of a more expansive North American security perimeter regime. For Canadians, immigration and border policy preferences are based on a number of goals: maximizing the economic gains from migration; upholding Canada's liberal humanitarian tradition by offering protection for refugees and for those who are fleeing persecution and require asylum; facilitating the social integration of new immigrants; and, maintaining border control as a component of homeland security. In Canada, liberal, open policies have strong domestic lobbies that have been instrumental in shaping both immigration and asylum policies. Moreover, the human rights and immigration law lobbies have successfully institutionalized protections for migrants within the judiciary (as well as the Immigration and Refugee Board) that constrain policy makers from enacting restrictive policies. Indeed, defense of the Canadian liberal identity is also evidenced in Canada's preference for the term "zone of confidence" rather than "security perimeter" when discussing bilateral cooperation (Andreas, 2003: 12). Moreover, further integration is also constrained by the notion that Canada's approach to immigration reflects its distinctiveness and sovereignty and thus should be protected. Member of Parliament John Manley has expressed this defense of Canadian sovereignty explicitly: "Working closely with the United States does not mean turning over to them the key to Canadian sovereignty" (quoted in Wells, 2003, Oct. 5: A6; Barry, 2003: 11).

The Americans also have an economic interest in having relatively liberal border policies. On this point, there is commonality between American and Canadian interests. However, the emphasis that the Bush administration has placed on security and the "War on Terror" has established that economic interests cannot be promoted at the expense of security. It is here that Canadian and American interests diverge. The Americans see coordination as a necessary means by which to increase security. From the United States' standpoint, maximizing the capacity to screen entrants is not only a homeland security imperative, but also a prerequisite for maintaining a relatively open stance regarding migration—both permanent and temporary. Coordination and collaboration would seem to advance this aim. However, similar to their Canadian counterparts, United States policy makers are also keenly defensive of their sovereignty in terms of migration policy, making policy integration politically difficult.

The Smart Border plan articulates several areas in which increased coordination could be cultivated, but few regarding policy harmonization or integration. In other words, the plan places few constraints on independent policy decision making. As Howard Adelman notes, "immigration and refugee policy has not been harmonized between Canada and the United States," and there are no indications that these policies will be (2002: 24). The fact that the driving force behind such a regime is one that is related more to a common aversion (terrorist alien infiltration) than a common interest (preference for a single common outcome), and that the regime is influenced by ideas regarding the goals and structures of such a regime causes deeper integration to remain politically challenging (Stein, 1983). The process of deepening integration in a way that is similar to the European Union is likely to be incremental, rather than the product of a comprehensive shift in grand strategy. In other words, policy makers will likely be "muddling through" the process in a piecemeal fashion, rather than reinventing the North American space.

Smart Borders and the challenges of intelligence sharing

If the existing Smart Borders agreements do represent the initial stages in the creation of a more expansive regional migration control regime in North America, what is necessary to make such a regime effective? To answer this question, we must first consider what the term "smart borders" means in the most basic sense: the ability to identify and filter potential threats while maintaining liberal flows to promote economic interests.

Figure 1: Basic elements of the smart borders regime

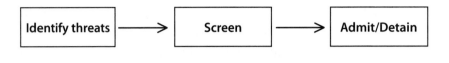

Whereas much of the existing cooperation of the Smart Borders regime has focused on the screening process (including cooperative border policing), effective screening requires us to be able to recognize and differentiate friend from foe. A 2004 report released by the Congressional Research Service points out that "[American] watch lists were only as good as the information contained in them, and the agencies responsible for producing these lookout records [to be used in the screening process] ... were dependent upon the information they received from the Intelligence Community and federal law enforcement" (Krouse, 2004: 6). A report released by the American Immigration Law Foundation concurred with this assessment (Stock and Johnson, 2003: 1):

If we are to succeed in reducing our vulnerability to terrorist attacks, we must focus our attention and resources on the gaps in intelligence gathering and information sharing that allowed the 19 terrorists responsible for 9/11 to enter the United States. National security is most effectively enhanced by improving the mechanisms by which we identify actual terrorists, not by merely implementing harsher immigration laws or blindly treating all foreigners as potential terrorists. This means that intelligence—especially that which concerns international terrorists and their supporters—and information management are the necessary foundations that must be built (Meyers, 2003; Salter, 2006).

The 9/11 attacks highlighted the challenges facing intelligence communities with regard to the global war on terrorism. Chief among these, perhaps, is the growing consensus regarding the need to share information in order to better identify potential threats. As the 9/11 Commission report states,

the US government cannot meet its own obligations to the American people to prevent the entry of terrorists without a major effort to collaborate with other governments. We should do more to exchange terrorist information with trusted allies, and raise US and global border security standards for travel and border crossing over the medium and long term through extensive cooperation. (United States National Commission on Terrorist Attacks Upon the United States, 2004: 390)

Canadian intelligence experts concur. Reid Morden, former Director of CSIS, has said, "If the overriding threat is terrorism, and terrorism transcends boundaries, then the ability of Canada's security and intelligence community to function effectively with its foreign partners has never been more important" (2003: 7). Morden also noted that "in this new world, nothing is more important than our overall relationship with the United States."

What makes this facet of an integrated border management regime so complicated is that the need for better intelligence creates interests for a regime within a regime. Pooling raw anti-terrorism data requires a high degree of cooperation in scale and scope, both within states (interagency sharing) and among them (interstate). The United States-Canada Smart Borders Action Plan specifically calls for a more integrated use of intelligence and includes provisions to establish Integrated National Security Enforcement Teams on a case-by-case basis. Though this is indeed a beginning for increased intelligence integration, at least on a bilateral basis, it does not come close to meeting the levels of integration and cooperation recommended by security experts (Markle Foundation Task Force, 2003). Because one can never know what piece of intelligence is vital for analysts to "connect the dots" in order to identify potential threats and keep terrorists from entering the country, it stands to reason that a wider net is necessary to maximize the potential uses of existing intelligence. The difficulties associated with creating such a multilateral intelligence-sharing regime are tactical, political, and procedural.

One key obstacle is the belief that expanding access to intelligence would necessarily incur a potentially significant cost in terms of system security. In other words, as more links are included in the chain of intelligence, the risk that such intelligence may be compromised increases. With respect to possible types of intelligence sharing arrangements, a United States congressional aide once said, "We don't want it to be in Interpol, because too many countries sit there and too much information can leak" (quoted in Farah and Eggen, 2003, Dec. 21: A25).

In the American intelligence community, risk involved in sharing information was minimized by including trusted partners in the loop. During the Cold War, for example, American and British intelligence services established a "special relationship," one that also extends to Canada and Australia. A former senior Central Intelligence Agency (CIA) official[3] suggested that, in practice, information sharing was the product of reciprocal ties and an established trust between corresponding agency representatives in each country—a practice that, he suggested, continues today. This seems to suggest that an intelligence sharing regime would be asymmetrical. Indeed, Peter Hoekstra, former Chairman of the United States House Intelligence Committee, described intelligence sharing as a system of "tiered relationships," based largely on the existing bilateral political relationship between the two countries involved, as well as the historical practice of sharing between agencies (personal communication, November 1, 2005). Indeed, the United States, Britain, Canada, Australia, and New Zealand probably share more information with each other than with other allies, as they are bound together by intelligence sharing agreements dating back to 1948 (Grant, 2000: 3).

While the historical legacy of close ties between Canada and the United States bodes well for increased bilateral cooperation and sharing, this does not necessarily mean that such practices would extend symmetrically throughout North America or with countries in other regions throughout the world. Even among close allies, some have suggested that the United States prefers a one-way approach to information sharing. As one European source explained, "It is a matter, in part, of culture. They believe strongly in the need-to-know operational function, and they usually believe we don't need to know" (quoted in Farah and Eggen, 2003, Dec. 21: A25; see also United States National Commission on Terrorist Attacks upon the United States, 2004: 417). An Indian intelligence analyst

---

3   The author personally interviewed this source, who wished to remain anonymous.

concurred: "Cooperation in counterterrorism has improved considerably since [9/11], but the US still calls the shots. It wants the agencies of other countries to share with it whatever it asks for, but gives them in return only what it thinks they should know" (Raman, 2003, Feb. 21). Moreover, Gregory Treverton, a senior policy analyst at RAND, points out that old intelligence relationships may not be the most advantageous when gathering information regarding terrorists and their organizations: "Even if the United States improved its HUMINT [Human Intelligence] dramatically, other nations and groups—including some that are not friends—would have more success against hard terrorist targets" (2003: 5). A Center for Defense Information Terrorism Project report seems to concur, suggesting that "if the United States is to penetrate international terrorist networks, it will need access to resources outside the purview of Western intelligence sources" (Donovan, 2001).

Since 9/11, the CIA has established a network of secret Counterterrorist Intelligence Centers (CTIC) in more than two dozen countries to foster cooperation between American and foreign intelligence officers (Priest, 2005, Nov. 18: A1). The extent of the existing cooperation is classified, but when we consider long-standing agency practices, it is likely that such sharing and cooperation is of a very limited nature. Indeed, although the deputy director of operations at the CIA told a Congressional committee that virtually every capture or termination of suspected terrorists since 9/11 was the result of a coordinated effort with foreign agencies, the CIA served as the primary intelligence source and foreign agents were largely responsible for apprehension (Priest, 2005, Nov. 18: A1).

Still, some analysts remain optimistic about the United States' cooperation with other nations. As Michael Herman writes,

> The move to more cooperation has not always been consistent. US policies vary between cultivating international support and going it alone. Nevertheless the increase in inter-governmental intelligence collaboration since 9/11, sometimes between unlikely allies, has been striking in what, despite foreign liaisons, had formerly been instinctively regarded as an essentially separate, reclusive national activity, deeply rooted in secrecy and national interests: waging a

zero-sum information contest between states, some far removed from the main fabric of international relationships, a matter for special people in special compartments. By contrast, intelligence cooperation is now regularly in the news, almost as often as the older elements of international relationships. (2003: 11)

The very nature of intelligence as it pertains to counterterrorism also presents formidable challenges to the effective pooling of information that is necessary to identify viable threats. It requires that long-standing oppositions within the intelligence community be integrated.

In addition to the opposition between foreign and domestic intelligence gathering, there is also the issue of the divide between "intelligence" and law enforcement information. Reid Morden, former Director of CSIS, once said, "The essence of the problem rests with the difference between the objectives of intelligence, especially security intelligence, and law enforcement. Simply put, security intelligence equals prevention and law enforcement equals prosecution" (2003: 11). In the United States, the separation of foreign and domestic information gathering was seen as necessary to protect civil liberties—in other words, to avoid a "big brother" scenario as was prevalent in the Cold War Soviet bloc. When the CIA was created in 1946, the current President, Harry Truman, worried that such an agency might evolve into a "Gestapo-like organization," and thus he sought to ensure that the agency would not engage in law enforcement or domestic activity (Treverton, 2003: 4). Indeed, this concern was so acute that, in the 1970s, policy makers established a legal "wall" between foreign and domestic intelligence through the provisions of the *Foreign Intelligence Surveillance Act* (FISA). Similar structural divisions were created in the Canadian intelligence bureaucracy, which was divided into foreign intelligence, security intelligence, military intelligence, and criminal intelligence functions (Morden, 2003). When we consider the history of the intelligence bureaucracy, it becomes clear that resistance to crossing jurisdictional lines and sharing information— even within a country, much less between countries—was created by design and that this culture evolved as standard operating procedure (Zegart, 1999).

The events of 9/11 provided a stark lesson regarding the costs of bureaucratic "stove-piping" within the intelligence bureaucracy, prompting policy makers to seek to make the institutional changes necessary to confront the new reality in a better way. In Canada, the *Anti-terrorism Act* sought to diminish due process protections to forward counterterrorism measures. In addition, the Act afforded the Solicitor General heightened powers to act on the advice of CSIS to define activities and organizations as "terrorist." Yet, such measures did little to alter the bureaucratic structure or the processes within and among it. As Reid Morden notes, "the Canadian intelligence community post 9/11 is structurally much the same as before, except buttressed with added powers and resources. Except for the creation of an ad hoc cabinet committee having overall responsibility for security matters, and chaired by the Deputy Prime Minister, little has changed" (2003: 9).

In the United States, a more ambitious agenda was attempted by policy makers. The process of intelligence reform in the United States began much like that in Canada—with new provisions that attempted to provide additional leverage to the existing intelligence and law enforcement community. First and foremost, the *USA PATRIOT Act* (2001) provided a legal mechanism by which the existing "wall" between domestic and foreign intelligence could be broached. In 2003, the current United States Attorney General, John Ashcroft, declared that "perhaps the most effective provisions of the *USA PATRIOT Act* are those that altered the outdated statutory restrictions so that intelligence and law enforcement agencies have greater freedom to coordinate their efforts and to share information gathered about terrorists" (2003; see also Goss, 2005). *The Intelligence Reform and Terrorist Prevention Act* of 2004 (IRTPA) was more expansive. It sought to address criticisms that 9/11 was at least in part the product of a failure of intelligence. Among its most significant provisions was the creation of a new Director of National Intelligence (DNI) to oversee the process of increasing coordination and cooperation among the nation's intelligence agencies. Policy makers and analysts also suggested that additional Congressional oversight was needed to promote an environment more conducive to cooperation (Markle Foundation Task Force, 2003). The culture of "ownership" of intelligence information at the agency level needed to change. To date, however, critics argue that much remains to be done along these lines. John Brennan, former interim director of the National Counterterrorism Center (NCTC), said,

> Sadly, the [IRTPA], which mandated many of the changes now underway, lacks a clear vision. A hurried and flawed piece of legislation, the act used ambiguous language to describe the authority of the czar [DNI] and other members of the intelligence community. The act also raised unrealistic expectations—for example, about sharing electronic databases. The legislation calls for the creation within two years of a terrorism information-sharing 'environment' that can be used by federal, state, local, and even Native American tribal officials. But it does nothing to make sure agencies develop information systems that meet not just their own needs, but those of their partners. (2005, Nov. 20: B5)

Jerry Berman, President of the Center for Democracy and Technology, offered much the same perspective, noting that "the sharing of terrorist-related information between relevant agencies at different levels of government has only been marginally improved in the last year, and remains haphazard" (2004: 3). Moreover, in December 2005, intelligence experts pointed out that "currently, no formal process exists for state, local, tribal, and private sector entities to task federal agencies with specific intelligence requirements" (LLIS, 2005: 1). Instead of federal oversight, for the most part these agencies have adopted their own informal and formal structures to share intelligence.

Clearly, there remain formidable structural challenges to information sharing and intelligence pooling at both the agency level and between states. William Nolte, Deputy Assistant Director of Central Intelligence for Analysis and Production, argues that "the end of the Cold War and the major changes which followed in both the operational and technical environments for intelligence did not produce sufficient momentum to overcome the institutional inertia that favored the status quo in the nature and structure of American intelligence" (2004: 1). Nolte also notes that "neither the significant budgetary austerity of the 1990s nor the attacks of 11 September 2001 produced enough shock to prompt major changes" (2004: 1).

Current President of the Markle Foundation Zoë Baird (2005), testifying before the United States House Permanent Select Committee on Intelligence, echoed this sentiment, but also pressed lawmakers to continue efforts to create reform: "While there has been some progress, we still have a long way to go [in terms of implementing the Executive and Congressionally mandated Information Sharing Environment] .... Without effective information sharing, information collection remains stove-piped and the importance of information held by different agencies or at different levels of government cannot be understood."

Conclusion

In March 2005, the leaders of the North American Free Trade Agreement countries adopted the Security and Prosperity Partnership of North America, in order to form a regional strategy to confront shared challenges, including border management (Independent Task Force, 2005). The question is whether such a regional approach to border management will work in North America. The European Union's extensive experience with regional approaches to policy serves as an appealing example of what is possible. However, when one recognizes the important differences that exist between Europe and North America, as well as the European Union's more recent challenges with expansion, two things become clear: first, the challenge is formidable—strategically, logistically, and politically; and second, the process of increasing the regionalization of border management will likely be an incremental one, rather than a giant leap forward.

As the evidence presented here shows, the creation of a regime of truly "smart borders" requires a fundamental reorganization of existing structures and procedures. The fact that this necessitates fundamental changes, both in border management and intelligence, makes this task all the more daunting. Moreover, when one considers the institutional inertia that is particularly acute in the intelligence community, one begins to see the magnitude of what a deeper integration of North America entails. The evidence presented here does not necessarily suggest that further integration is impossible. On the contrary, the need for both openness and security on our borders would seem to demonstrate that the creation of a cooperative regime is a necessity. What this chapter does reveal, however, is exactly how complicated the process will be as we move toward such a regime.

References

Adelman, Howard (2002). Governance, Globalization and Security: The Harmonization of Immigration Policy. Paper presented at the conference, "Globalization, Multilevel Governance, and Democracy: Continental, Comparative and Global Perspectives," at Queen's University, Kingston, Ontario, May 3-4, 2002.

Andreas, Peter (1999). *Border Games*. Cornell University Press.

Andreas, Peter (2003). *A Tale of Two Borders: The US-Mexico and US-Canada Lines After 9-11*. Working Paper No. 77. Center for Comparative Immigration Studies, University of California, San Diego.

Ashcroft, John (2003). The War Against Terrorism: Working Together to Protect America. Testimony presented before the Committee on the Judiciary, United States Senate, March 4, 2003. <http://www.globalsecurity.org/security/library/congress/2003_h/03-04-03_ashcroft.htm>. Accessed December 12, 2003.

Baird, Zoë (2005). Statement before the House Permanent Select Committee on Intelligence, United States House of Representatives, October 19, 2005. <http://www.fas.org/irp/congress/2005_hr/101905baird.pdf>. Accessed October 11, 2007.

Barry, Donald (2003). *Managing Canada-US Relations in the Post-9/11 Era: Do We Need a Big Idea?* Policy Paper on the Americas Volume 14, Study 11. Center for Strategic and International Studies. <http://canada.usembassy.gov/content/can_usa/csis_1103.pdf>. Accessed October 11, 2007.

Belelieu, Andre (2003). *Canada Alert: The Smart Border Process at Two: Losing Momentum?* Hemisphere Focus Volume 11, Issue 31. Center for Strategic and International Studies. <http://www.csis.org/media/csis/pubs/hf_v11_31.pdf>.

Berman, Jerry (2004). Prepared Statement of Jerry Berman, President of the Center For Democracy and Technology, before the Subcommittee on Crime, Terrorism and Homeland Security of the House Judiciary Committee, and the Subcommittee on Intelligence and Counterterrorism of the House Select Committee on Homeland Security, March 25, 2004. <http://www.cdt.org/testimony/20040325berman.shtml>. Accessed October 11, 2007.

Berry, LaVerle, Glenn E. Curtis, John N. Gibbs, Rex A. Hudson, Tara Karacan, Nina Kollars, and Ramón Miró (2003). *Nations Hospitable to Organized Crime and Terrorism.* Federal Research Division, Library of Congress. <http://www.loc.gov/rr/frd/pdf-files/Nats_Hospitable.pdf>. Accessed December 20, 2007.

Bissett, James (2002). *Canada's Asylum System: A Threat to American Security?* Backgrounder. Center for Immigration Studies.

Brennan, John (2005, November 20). Is this Intelligence? *Washington Post.* B1, B5.

Camarota, Steven A. (2002). *The Open Door: How Militant Islamic Terrorists Entered and Remained in the United States, 1993-2001.* Center Paper 21. Center for Immigration Studies.

Canadian Embassy in Washington (2003). Governor Ridge and Deputy Prime Minister Manley Issue One-Year Status Report on the Smart Border Action Plan – December 6, 2002. News release (October 3). <http://geo.international.gc.ca/can-am/main/border/smart_border_12_02-en.asp>. Accessed October 11, 2007.

CBS News (2003, September 7). North of the Border. <http://www.cbsnews.com/stories/2003/09/04/60minutes/printable571584.shtml>. Accessed February 18, 2004.

Citizenship and Immigration Canada (2004). *Fact Sheet: Safe Third Country Agreement.* Government of Canada. <http://www.cic.gc.ca/ english/about/laws-policy/safe-third-fact.asp>. Accessed October 11, 2007.

Cornelius, Wayne A., Takeyuki Tsuda, Philip L. Martin, and James F. Hollifield (eds.) (2004). *Controlling Immigration: A Global Perspective.* Second edition. Stanford University Press.

Donovan, Michael (2001). *Intelligence Cooperation on the Frontline of Terrorism: Easier Said Than Done.* Center for Defense Information. <http://www.cdi.org/terrorism/intell-sharing.cfm>. Accessed October 11, 2007.

Farah, Douglas, and Dan Eggen (2003, December 21). Joint Intelligence Center is Urged. *Washington Post.* A25.

Foreign Affairs and International Trade Canada (2001). Smart Border Declaration: Building a Smart Border for the 21st Century on the Foundation of a North American Zone of Confidence. News release (December 12). <http://geo.international.gc.ca/can-am/main/border/ smart_border_declaration-en.asp>. Accessed December 20, 2007.

Frank, Steven, and Stephen Handelman (2002, October 8). Drawing a Line. *Time* (Canadian edition).

Gallagher, Stephen (2003). *Canada's Dysfunctional Refugee Determination System.* Public Policy Sources 78. Fraser Institute.

Genson, Roland (1998). *The Schengen Agreements—Police Cooperation and Security Aspects.* Hume Papers on Public Policy 6, 1/2.

Goss, Porter J. (2005) Testimony of the Director of the Central Intelligence Agency before the Select Committee on Intelligence, United States Senate, February 16, 2005. <https://www.cia.gov/news-

information/speeches-testimony/2005/Goss-testimony_02162005.html>.
Accessed November 11, 2007.

Grabbe, Heather (2000). The Sharp Edges of Europe: Extending
Schengen Eastwards. *International Affairs* 76, 3 (July): 519–536.

Grant, Charles (2000). *Intimate Relations: Can Britain Play a
Leading Role in European Defence—and Keep Its Special Links to US
Intelligence?* Working Paper. Center for European Reform.

Hasenclever, Andreas, Peter Mayer, and Volker Rittberger (1997).
Theories of International Regimes. Cambridge University Press.

Hasenclever, Andreas, Peter Mayer, and Volker Rittberger (2000).
Integrating Theories of International Regimes. *Review of International
Studies* 26, 1: 3–33.

Herman, Michael (2003). *Intelligence After 9/11: A British View of the
Effects.* Commentary No. 83. Canadian Security Intelligence Service.
<http://www.csis-scrs.gc.ca/en/publications/commentary/com83.asp>.

Hollifield, James F. (1998). Migration, Trade, and the Nation-State: The
Myth of Globalization. *UCLA Journal of International Law & Foreign
Affairs*, 3, 2 (Fall/Winter): 595–636.

Independent Task Force (2005). *Building a North American Community.*
Task Force Report No. 53. Council on Foreign Relations.

Johnson, Stephen, and Sara J. Fitzgerald (2003). *The United States
and Mexico: Partners in Reform.* Backgrounder No. 1715. The
Heritage Foundation.

Kephart, Janice L. (2005). *Immigration and Terrorism: Moving Beyond
the 9/11 Staff Report on Terrorist Travel.* CIS Paper No. 24. Center for
Immigration Studies.

Koslowski, Rey (2000). *Migrants and Citizens*. Cornell University Press.

Krasner, Stephen D. (ed.) (1983). *International Regimes*. Cornell University Press.

Krouse, William J. (2004). *Terrorist Identification, Screening, and Tracking Under Homeland Security Presidential Directive 6*. Congressional Research Service.

Lessons Learned Information Sharing [LLIS] (2005). LLIS Intelligence and Information Sharing Initiative: Homeland Security Intelligence Requirements Process. United States Department of Homeland Security. <http://www.llis.gov>. Accessed October 11, 2007.

Markle Foundation Task Force (2003). *Creating a Trusted Network for Homeland Security*. Markle Foundation. <http://www.markletaskforce.org/Report2_Full_Report.pdf>. Accessed December 20, 2007.

Meyers, Deborah Waller (2003). Does 'Smarter' Lead to Safer? An Assessment of the US Border Accords with Canada and Mexico. *International Migration* 41, 4: 5–44.

Meyers, Eytan (2002). *Multilateral Cooperation, Integration and Regimes: The Case of Labor Mobility*. CCIS Working Paper No. 61. Center for Comparative Immigration Studies, University of California, San Diego.

Migration News (2003). *Migration News* 10, 2 (April). <http://migration.ucdavis.edu/mn/more_entireissue.php?idate=2003_04&number=2>.

Migration News (2005). *Migration News* 7, 3 (July). <http://migration.ucdavis.edu/mn/more_entireissue.php?idate-2005_07&number=3>.

Monar, Jörg (1999). *Flexibility and Closer Cooperation in an Emerging European Migration Policy: Opportunities and Risks*. Laboratorio CeSPI No. 1. Centro Studi di Politica Internazionale.

Morden, Reid (2003). *Spies, Not Soothsayers: Canadian Intelligence After 9/11*. Commentary No. 85. Canadian Security Intelligence Service. <http://www.csis.gc.ca/en/publications/commentary/com85.asp>. Accessed October 11, 2007.

Newland, Kathleen, and Demetrios G. Papademetriou (1998). Managing Migration: Tracking the Emergence of a New International Regime? *UCLA Journal of International Law & Foreign Affairs* 3, 2 (Fall/Winter): 637–57.

Nolte, William (2004). Preserving Central Intelligence: Assessment and Evaluation in Support of the DCI. *Studies in Intelligence* 48, 3: 21–25.

Nomikos, John M. (2005, June 17). The European Union's Proposed Intelligence Service. *Power and Interest News Report*.

Papademetriou, Demetrios G. (1996). *Coming Together or Pulling Apart?* Carnegie Endowment for International Peace.

Papademetriou, Demetrios G. (2002). *A Grand Bargain: Balancing National Security, Economic, and Immigration Interests of the US and Mexico*. Migration Policy Institute. <http://www.migrationpolicy.org/files/bargain.pdf>.

Priest, Dana (2005, November 18). Foreign Network at Front of CIA's Terror Fight. *Washington Post*. A1, A12.

Raman, B. (2003, February 21). The First War of the 21st Century. *Rediff*. <http://www.rediff.com/news/2001/sep/14spec.htm>. Accessed October 11, 2007.

Ranstorp, Magnus, and Jeffrey Cozzens (2004, March 24). The European Terror Challenge. *BBC News*. <http://news.bbc.co.uk/1/hi/world/europe/3563713.stm>. October 11, 2007.

Rekai, Peter (2002). *US and Canadia Immigration Policies: Marching Together to Different Tunes*. C.D. Howe Institute Commentary No. 171. C.D. Howe Institute.

Rudolph, Christopher (2003a). Globalization and Security: Migration and Evolving Conceptions of Security in Statecraft and Scholarship. *Security Studies* 13, 1 (Fall): 1–32.

Rudolph, Christopher (2003b). Security and the Political Economy of International Migration. *American Political Science Review* 97, 4 (Fall): 603–20.

Rudolph, Christopher (2005a). International Migration and Homeland Security: Cooperation and Collaboration in North America. *Law and Business Journal of the Americas* 11, 3/4 (Summer/Fall): 433–59.

Rudolph, Christopher (2005b). Sovereignty and Territorial Borders in a Global Age. *International Studies Review* 7, 1 (Spring): 1–20.

Rudolph, Christopher (2006a). Interdependence and Immigration: A Conceptual Framework. Unpublished paper, presented at the annual meeting of the International Studies Association, San Diego, California, March 22-25, 2006.

Rudolph, Christopher (2006b). *National Security and Immigration: Policy Development in the United States and Western Europe Since 1945*. Stanford University Press.

Salter, Mark B. (2006). Canadian Post-9/11 Border Policy: Smart, Safe, Sovereign? In Michael Orsini and Miriam Smith (eds.), *Critical Policy Studies: Contemporary Canadian Approaches*. University of British Columbia Press.

Sands, Christopher (2002). Terrorism, Border Reform, and Canada-United States Relations: Learning the Lessons of Section 110.

Unpublished paper, presented at the conference, "Linkages Across the Border: The Great Lakes Economy," Federal Reserve Bank of Chicago, Detroit Branch, April 4, 2002.

Seper, Jerry (2004, January 5). Cooperation at the Border Bolsters Law Enforcement. *Washington Times*. A1.

Shanks, Cheryl (2001). *Immigration and the Politics of American Sovereignty*. University of Michigan Press.

Stein, Arthur A. (1983). Coordination and Collaboration: Regimes in an Anarchic World. In Stephen D. Krasner (ed.), *International Regimes*. Cornell University Press.

Stock, Margaret D., and Benjamin Johnson (2003). *The Lessons of 9/11: A Failure of Intelligence, Not Immigration Law*. Immigration Policy Focus. American Immigration Law Foundation.

Treverton, Gregory F. (2003). *Reshaping Intelligence to Share with "Ourselves."* Commentary No. 82. Canadian Security Intelligence Service. <http://www.csis-scrs.gc.ca/en/publications/commentary/com82.asp>. Accessed December 20, 2007.

United Nations High Commissioner for Refugees (2003). *UNHCR Population Statistics*. United Nations High Commissioner for Refugees.

United States House of Representatives, Select Committee on Homeland Security (2004). *Information Sharing for Homeland Security: Obstacles to Effective Information Sharing Still Exist Post 9/11*. Issue Paper No. 1. Select Committee on Homeland Security.

United States House of Representatives, Subcommittee on Immigration, Judiciary Committee (2002). Hearing on the US and Canada Safe Third Country Pact, United States House of Representatives, Washington, DC, October 6, 2002.

United States National Commission on Terrorist Attacks Upon the United States (2004). *The 9/11 Commission Report.* <http://www.9-11commission.gov/report/911Report.pdf>. Accessed December 20, 2007.

Wells, Paul (2003, October 5). We Don't Pull Our Own Weight: Manley. *National Post.* A6.

Young, Oran (1983). Security Regimes. In Stephen D. Krasner (ed.), *International Regimes.* Cornell University Press.

Zegart, Amy (1999). *Flawed by Design: The Evolution of the CIA, JCS, and NSC.* Stanford University Press.

Chapter 11

Making Canada's Immigration System and Borders More Secure

Alexander Moens and Martin Collacott

In this volume, our contributors have examined the relationship between terrorist threats—particularly those from Islamist extremists—and Western countries, and the extent to which such threats have been made more real because of the nature of current immigration, asylum, and border control policies. The foregoing does not mean that all such threats are the direct result of inadequate selection or screening of immigrants, asylum seekers, and visa applicants. However, there is sufficient evidence of interconnections between threats and current policies, as described in the preceding chapters, that these policies need to be carefully examined and revised where appropriate.

Security implications of current Canadian immigration policies

A number of major themes that emerged in this book addressed the relationship between immigration and security. According to Mark Krikorian, mass immigration is essentially incompatible with security in the present era because it overwhelms our efforts (both American and Canadian) to screen out security threats, and it creates large immigrant communities that serve as the sea, as Mao might have said, "within which the terrorists swim as fish." In Krikorian's view, bringing security standards up to what is required because of current threats would require a huge increase in the resources devoted to screening immigrants. Krikorian argues that it would make more sense to reduce immigration levels substantially so as to bring them in line with the resources available for screening. Daniel Stoffman comes to a similar conclusion.

James Bissett notes that a large number of newcomers to Canada are from Muslim countries whose populations contain significant numbers of Islamist radicals. For example, he points out that between 1996 and 2005, Canada accepted over 118,000 immigrants from Pakistan, 62,000 from Iran, and 25,000 from Algeria, relatively few of whom received adequate security screening.

Stoffman also expresses concern over the large numbers of newcomers and the difficulty of screening them properly. He notes that, in the past, large-scale immigration came in waves. The periods in between these waves allowed newcomers and, in particular, their children to become integrated into Canadian society. However, immigration levels are relentlessly high (the highest per capita in the world), year after year, bringing immigrants from the same places to the same places. As a result, large, self-contained communities are developed and are constantly replenished, thereby reducing the need and opportunities for these immigrants to integrate into mainstream society.

Stoffman also points out that, while Canadians rightly pride themselves on the cultural diversity of their major cities, the reality is that Canadian cities are not diverse enough. Out of 194 countries in the world, just 10 of them account for 62% of current immigration to Canada. If the immigration intake were more diverse, the ethnic communities in Canada might be more numerous, but they would also be smaller and, perhaps, more integrated into the broader community.

In this respect, a Statistics Canada report issued in 2004 (Hou and Picot, 2004) revealed that, between 1981 and 2001, a significant change occurred in the number of visible minority neighbourhoods in Canada. The report indicated that the number of such neighbourhoods increased from six in 1981 to 254 in 2001. It also noted that such residential concentrations of minority groups may result in social isolation and reduce the incentives for those in such communities to learn the language of the host country or gain work experience and educational qualifications. Moreover, the report revealed that neighbourhoods with large concentrations of visible minorities tended to have a poor economic status and low income rates.

We completely agree with Stoffman when he points out that the majority of residents of immigrant communities are good people who want to build prosperous lives for their families as Canadian citizens. But some of them are not, and the larger an immigrant community is, the easier it is for groups that are hostile to Canada and the West to operate secretly within them and to develop support networks. In this regard, Krikorian adds that such enclaves not only shield terrorists, but they also facilitate the recruitment and incubation of new ones. Krikorian, along with Stoffman, asserts that continuous mass immigration seriously slows down the integration of newcomers.

With respect to criminal activity, he notes that during the great wave of immigration around the beginning of the twentieth century, and for some time after immigration was stopped in the 1920s, law enforcement had very little luck with penetrating the Mafia. This was because many immigrants lived in enclaves, had limited knowledge of English, were suspicious of government institutions, and clung to Old World prejudices and attitudes such as "omerta" (the Sicilian code of silence). When mass immigration ended, the assimilation of Italian immigrants and their children accelerated, and the offspring of these immigrants developed a sense of genuine membership and ownership in America. This is what John Fonte of the Hudson Institute calls "patriotic assimilation." This process drained the water within which the Mafia had been able to swim, allowing law enforcement to do its job more effectively and to eventually cripple the Mafia.

Krikorian notes that Muslim immigrant communities are not alone in exhibiting characteristics that may shield or even incubate criminality. For instance, as criminologist Ko-lin Chin has written, "the isolation of the Chinese community, the inability of American law enforcement authorities to penetrate the Chinese criminal underworld, and the reluctance of Chinese victims to come forward for help all conspire to enable Chinese gangs to endure." On this subject, Krikorian refers to William Kleinknecht, author of *The New Ethnic Mobs*, who notes that "if the mass immigration of Chinese should come to a halt, the Chinese gangster may disappear in a blaze of assimilation after a couple of decades." This solution to the problems associated with Chinese isolation can be applied to other ethnic groups as well.

In Krikorian's view, the same solution applies to immigrant-related terrorist activity. As long as immigrant communities are continuously buttressed with newcomers, the problems that some of them bring with them from their homeland, such as crime and terrorism, are likely to persist for much longer than they would otherwise. In this regard, Krikorian refers to the very rapid expansion of Muslim communities in the United States through immigration, and the effect that this could have on the creation of fertile soil for the recruitment of terrorists and sympathizers. He cites a disturbing example from Lackawanna, New York, where six Yemeni Americans—five of whom were born in the United States to immigrant parents and were raised in an immigrant community—were arrested in 2002 for operating an al-Qaeda terrorist sleeper cell. He points out that, between 1996 and 2005, more than 18,000 Yemenis immigrated legally to the United States. In Lackawanna alone, the Arab population ballooned by 175% during the 1990s. Yet the median household income in the Yemeni neighbourhood is 20% lower than in Lackawanna as a whole.

A rapid increase in the Muslim population is also taking place in Canada, mainly due to immigration rather than natural growth on the part of those who are already here. According to Statistics Canada, in 1981 the Muslim population was 98,165. By 2006, the population had increased to 783,700 and, based on mid-range projections, will reach 1,421,400 by 2017 (Statistics Canada, 2005). Thus, the Muslim population in Canada has grown six-fold in a period of 25 years, and over 36 years is projected to reach more than 14 times its 1981 size. As an illustration of the significance of this increase, the Muslim community will change from being one-third the size of the Jewish community, for example, to being four times the size. A further comparison of these two religious groups shows that in 2001, 69% of Jews in Canada were born in this country, while only 21% of Muslims were born here (Statistics Canada, 2001). The implications of these trends for Canadian foreign and domestic policies could be very important.

The continuing severity of the terrorist threat

Many of the chapters in this book clearly demonstrate that the ongoing terrorist threat to Canada remains serious. Christopher Rudolph notes that the Canadian Security Intelligence Service (CSIS) has confirmed the presence of some 50 active terrorist organizations operating in Canada. From an American point of view, this represents a potential threat to United States security as terrorists could exploit Canada's lax immigration policy and then use their Canadian base as a potential staging ground for terrorist attacks.

In addition to the threat that terrorists in Canada may pose to the United States, they may also plan to attack targets in this country. Stoffman points to the example of Ahmed Ressam, who was captured while trying to enter the United States for the purpose of bombing the Los Angeles Airport, admitted at his trial that he and an associate had also considered detonating a bomb in a Montreal area with a large Jewish population. As well, Stoffman notes that an al-Qaeda training manual published in 2004 states, "We must target and kill the Jews and the Christians .... The grades of importance are as follows: Americans, British, Spaniards, Australians, Canadians, Italians" (Bell, 2004, Mar. 31).

Even without considering the threat of attacks by terrorists from overseas, as was the case in the 9/11 attacks, neither Canadians nor Americans can be complacent about possible threats from within their countries. Jan C. Ting points out that, according to a poll released in May 2007, 47% of Muslim Americans think of themselves as Muslim first, rather than American, 8% think suicide bombing can often or sometimes be justified, and 5% have a favourable view of al-Qaeda. Among Muslim Americans between 18 and 29 years of age, 60% think of themselves as Muslim first, rather than American, 15% think suicide bombing is often or sometimes justified, and 7% have a favourable view of al-Qaeda.

The situation in Canada is not any more encouraging. Following the arrest of 18 Muslims in Ontario who allegedly were planning to carry out mass killings in the Toronto area, it was revealed that the RCMP had quietly broken up at least a dozen other terrorist groups in the previous two years (Sallot and Laghi, 2006, June 7). David B. Harris and Stoffman both point out that, in a poll released in February 2007, 12% of Canadian Muslims surveyed (almost 100,000 Muslims) believed that the plot was justified. A 2008 report regarding a Muslim university student from the Toronto area who called for the killing of Canadian troops in Afghanistan, as well as Jews, demonstrates a continuing cause for concern about such issues (Bell, 2008, Jan. 30).

While most of the focus in this volume has been on threats from Islamist extremists because they are the most likely to target Canadians and Americans, they are by no means the only terrorists within our borders. Sikh separatists were responsible for the Air India bombings in 1985—the largest single act of terrorism launched from Canadian soil. Since then, they have desisted from attempting large-scale operations in Canada. James Bissett and Stoffman both note the ongoing activities of Sikh and Tamil terrorist supporters in Canada, and express concern over the failure of our authorities to put a stop to their operations or to successfully prosecute those who have been apprehended. In recent months, there have been indications that extremists in both of these communities have become increasingly open in their efforts to build ties with political parties and to trade electoral support for more lenient treatment of their terrorist-related activities. For example, these activities include reported attempts at the Liberal Party leadership convention in December 2006 to offer delegate support to leadership candidates in exchange for a promise to remove the Liberation Tigers of Tamil Eelam from the list of designated terrorist groups in Canada. Meanwhile, Muslim delegates at the convention were advised by the Canadian Arab Federation not to support leadership candidate Bob Rae because his wife was a senior official with the Canadian Jewish Congress (Fatah, 2006, Dec. 6).

In spring 2007, a number of federal and provincial politicians attended a parade in Surrey, a suburb of Vancouver, where Talwinder Singh Parmar, the suspected mastermind of the Air India bombing, was held up as a "martyr" to the cause of an independent Sikh homeland (Brown, 2007, Nov. 22). Later that year, a three-day memorial service was held to commemorate

Parmar as a martyr at a Sikh temple in Surrey (Bolan, 2007, Oct. 31). In November, a number of federal Liberal Members of Parliament attended a memorial service held in Toronto for a senior leader of the Tamil Tiger terrorist group (Leong, 2007, Nov. 6).

Renewed doubts over whether Canada is able to deal effectively with terrorists and suspected terrorists on its own soil have also been raised in connection with the difficulty Canada had applying what appeared to be tough anti-terrorism legislation after 9/11. In recent months, opposition parties in Parliament have successfully prevented the extension of two important provisions of the *Anti-terrorism Act*, while, as Bissett notes, judicial decisions have placed in jeopardy the one remaining useful instrument for detaining and removing foreign terrorists: the immigration security certificate. Moreover, Canadian authorities have yet to lay a charge under legislation that was passed to curb terrorist fundraising, even though the agency that tracks such activities has reported transactions of $200 million annually under the category of suspected terrorist activity financing and other threats to the security of Canada (FINTRAC, 2007).

Despite the partial dismantling of the anti-terrorism law, the government has persisted in its efforts, begun in 2004, to bring to trial Mohammed Momin Khawaja, the first case under the remaining provisions. However, Khawaja's lawyers have been sufficiently successful at raising various legal and constitutional objections so that in January 2008 the presiding judge opined that the case may be nearly impossible to bring to trial. In the meantime, five of his alleged co-conspirators in the United Kingdom bomb plot in which he is accused of participating, were tried, convicted, and sentenced by a British court months ago (MacLeod, 2008, Jan. 25).

Assessing the economic and demographic benefits of immigration against the security risks

While issues concerning the benefits and costs of immigration in general were not addressed in any detail in this volume (but will be at a conference in Montreal in June 2008 which is being organized by the Fraser Institute), a few words have to be said about whether the security risks entailed by

Canada's current large-scale immigration policies must be accepted simply because of the major gains we realize through immigration. Stoffman, in particular, challenges the assumptions on which such claims are based. He points out that neither economic nor demographic justifications exist for accepting any negative consequences resulting from the Canadian immigration program. Stoffman points to major studies by the Economic Council of Canada and the US National Academy of Sciences which have found that, as a fraction of gross domestic product, the economic gains from immigration are minuscule. He also rejects claims that Canada will benefit economically from having a larger population, or that immigration can have a significant effect on mitigating the challenges associated with Canada's aging population.

Another issue that needs to be examined in relation to the benefits of large-scale immigration is whether it is necessary to fill labour shortages. The Economic Council of Canada report cited above, along with other more recent studies, concluded that immigration is not an effective way to fill gaps in the labour force and that cases where immigration had been successfully used to fill such gaps were rare.

One of Canada's most eminent experts on the economic and demographic impacts of immigration, Professor (Emeritus) Alan G. Green of Queen's University, points out that, in addition to the absence of any general economic gains from immigration, as well as the fact that immigration will not solve problems related to an aging population or to regional inequality, immigration is not the best way to address labour shortages. According to Green, Canada has the educational facilities to meet our domestic needs for skilled workers in all but extreme circumstances (Green, 2003). Whether Canada makes full use of this capacity and, if not, why does it not do so are questions that require further examination.

Security implications of the Canadian refugee system

In addition to security issues raised in relation to Canada's large-scale immigration intake, many of the chapters in the volume cited Canada's refugee determination system as a source of major problems. In particular, Stephen Gallagher, Bissett, and Stoffman examine, in considerable detail, the shortcomings of the system, including the extent to which it has been used by terrorists and their supporters. Harris also expresses concern over the system's laxity from a security point of view, while Noble identifies areas in which improvements are needed. Rudolph notes that, from an American perspective, Canada's refugee and asylum policies have resulted in trends that are disconcerting to some security-minded American policy makers, while Glynn Custred makes reference to the ease with which the "millennium bomber," Ahmed Ressam, had been able to make use of the Canadian refugee system.

In addition to the various points made in each chapter, it should be noted that the very large numbers of refugee claimants (or "asylum seek-ers," as they are called in most countries) that Canada has accepted—four times the per capita average of other countries—and its generous rates of approval—three times the average of other countries—have contributed substantially to the formation of large communities of ethnic minorities, many members of which are below the poverty line (Collacott, 2006).

Moreover, a number of developments since these chapters were writ-ten have cast serious doubts regarding Canada's ability to deal with the shortcomings of the system. A significant case in point is the Safe Third Country Agreement (STCA) between Canada and the United States, under which asylum seekers in the United States must make their claims in that country, rather than coming to Canada to do so. Similar restric-tions under the STCA apply to those in Canada. A number of the chapters in this volume voiced support for the STCA in principle, but argued that it needs to be strengthened by eliminating some of the exceptions under which, as Gallagher points out, the vast majority of asylum seekers in the United States who have come to the Canadian border since the agreement went into effect have been able to qualify. However, instead of closing the loopholes, a Canadian Federal Court judge, following representations from refugee advocacy groups, recently ruled that the entire STCA was invalid, essentially because no other country provided the same level of protection for refugee claimants as Canada did. The government, however, was not about to give up on the STCA and obtained a Court of Appeal decision in January 2008, allowing the agreement to remain in effect until a full review could be carried out.

Another recent development of concern in the area of refugee policy is the current initiative put forth by opposition parties in Parliament to create a body that would provide a further opportunity for appeal (the Refugee Appeal Division of the Immigration and Refugee Board) for failed refugee claimants who are seeking to avoid removal from the country. The current Conservative government, as well as its Liberal predecessors, has resisted pressure to create this additional level, given the already existing range of appeals and reviews which some failed claimants have been able to use to stay in Canada for years and even decades. If the opposition parties successfully establish this new level of appeal, they will make an already highly dysfunctional system even worse.

Obstacles to policy reform

While outlining the shortcomings of Canadian immigration and security policies from a security point of view, a number of chapters also examined the factors that make reforms difficult. Harris notes that "an extremely powerful lobby of politicians, immigration lawyers, government funded settlement organizations, NGOs and others" plays a role in impeding reform. Reform is also slowed by an absence of political debate regarding the abuse of the refugee system, as well as immigration policy in general. Gallagher points out that well-funded and well-organized advocacy and special interest groups connected to the immigration file work tirelessly to ensure that the government lives up to all of its pro-immigration rhetoric.

One of the chief obstacles to reform, according to Bissett, is the extent to which political parties solicit support from ethnic or religious groups and offer rewards in return for votes: "Block voting by new immigrant groups is an old phenomenon—these groups tend to vote for the party that promises them the most benefits." As Bissett writes, the government ended its former policy of adjusting the number of immigrants based on the ups and downs of the labour force, and decided that Canada should aim for an annual intake equivalent to 1% of the country's population. No convincing explanation was provided for establishing such levels, leading Bissett to suspect that the real reason behind this decision was the assumption that larger numbers of newcomers would mean more potential voters for the party in power.

In 1977, the *Citizenship Act* was passed, reducing the waiting time for citizenship eligibility from five to three years. Voting patterns show that new immigrants often vote for the party in power at the time the immigrant was admitted to the country. Bissett notes that, in return for the immigrants' votes, the party in power usually becomes a powerful advocate for large scale immigration.

Stoffman points to the influence that ethno-politics can have, not only on immigration, but on security issues as well. A steady stream of supporters of the Tamil Tigers, one of the world's most murderous terrorist organizations, have found a haven in Canada, largely because we accept a far higher percentage of asylum seekers claiming to be Sri Lankan Tamils than any other country in the world. Yet, as Stoffman argues, federal Liberal governments were so eager to cultivate support among the fast-growing Tamil community that they refused to ban the Tigers as a terrorist organization, even though the United States and the United Kingdom had already done so. When Paul Martin, who would later become Prime Minister, was criticized for attending a dinner sponsored by a group associated with the Tamil Tigers, he was unapologetic. Such criticism was "un-Canadian," Martin was reported as saying. In Stoffman's view, this is how a dysfunctional immigration and refugee system, in combination with the notion that minority cultural groups are immune from criticism, makes it all but impossible to control unwanted immigration.

Other actors with a vested interest in opening Canada's borders even wider and with little interest in impeding such a process by introducing more effective security measures include the immigration lawyers and immigrant settlement organizations mentioned by Harris. Many of them are government-supported organizations that lobby for diversity, human rights, and related causes.

In addition to vested interest groups lobbying for increased immigration, several of the chapters identify additional factors that impede reforms to our immigration and refugee policies. One of the most important of these is Canada's multiculturalism policy. Bissett argues that this policy is often used by political parties to shore up electoral support among

immigrant groups. He points out that, in the 1970s, political parties discovered that they could gain and maintain the allegiance of ethnic voters
by formalizing the concept of multiculturalism. Thus, it was no longer
necessary to use party funds to entice ethnic voters. Once in power, a
party was able to expend large sums of the taxpayers' money in support
of ethnic organizations, including newspapers and media outlets, and
ethnic or religious celebrations and related events. All of this was done in
the name of multiculturalism—and with the expectation of block voting
from ethnic groups.

Mansur examines how Western countries have made themselves vulnerable to penetration and exploitation by extremist groups through the
adoption of multiculturalism policies. He argues that these groups have
made use of opportunities to claim that they are being treated unfairly and,
therefore, should receive concessions in compensation. This assessment has
been born out by recent initiatives on the part of Islamic organizations to
use Canadian human rights tribunals to shut down media coverage of issues
that they consider unsympathetic to their cause (Steyn, 2008, Jan. 14).

In a similar vein, Harris documents how organizations such as the
Council for American Islamic Relations of Canada (CAIR-CAN), whose
parent organization in the United States has been associated with Islamist
extremist activities, have been able to promote the notion that Muslims
have been victimized by Canadian efforts to strengthen counterterrorism
measures. Such groups have made a careful study of Canadian law, including human rights provisions, and make maximum use of this knowledge
to advance their agendas.

Balancing freedom and security

A question that is frequently raised when new security measures are proposed is whether they will infringe unduly on the rights and freedoms of
individuals. Ting examines in detail various factors that must be considered when one tries to answer this question. While citing the declaration of
the US Supreme Court that "distinctions between citizens solely because
of their ancestry are by their very nature odious to a free people whose
institutions are founded upon the doctrine of equality," he notes that, in

certain circumstances, even the Court recognizes that security measures that focus on certain groups are justified. However, such measures should be restricted to situations where they are particularly warranted because of serious security risks. Ting argues that, for example, stopping and questioning drivers of a certain ethnicity on the New Jersey Turnpike with the hope of identifying a threat to national security ought not to be permitted. However, subjecting passengers boarding an airplane to closer inspection because of their ethnicity, if officially authorized, ought not to be rejected automatically as a violation of civil liberties. Ting challenges the claim that any compromises in relation to civil liberties carry a serious risk of being the beginning of a slide down a slippery slope towards the erosion of basic freedoms in general. In this regard, he points to the example of the restrictions placed on people of Japanese origin in the United States during World War II, and the fact that these restrictions were completely removed when the war was over.

Harris looks at the debate on these issues in Canada. He argues that most academics and lawyers who have taken a position on the subject have been ardent supporters of the primacy of human rights and have limited knowledge of the nature of the terrorist threat or the challenges associated with effectively dealing with it. In effect, they take the position that if there are any compromises in relation to civil liberties, then the terrorists will have "won."

Securing our borders

A number of chapters focused on the importance of border security and the possibility of establishing a common security perimeter around North America, or at least around Canada and the United States. Such a perimeter would enhance security and facilitate the movement of people and goods across our common borders.

Considering the issue from an American perspective, Custred raises concerns in relation to the potential threats to American security that may come from the Canadian side of the border. He notes that this danger does not come from a hostile country to the north, but rather from immigration and refugee policies that make it easier for aliens who are hostile to the

United States to enter Canada, disappear into the general population, and connect with networks submerged in its large immigrant communities.

Custred's strongest criticism, however, is reserved for the situation along the southern border of the United States. Noting the mass influx of illegal migrants, the level of lawlessness and violence (particularly on the Mexican side), and the large-scale smuggling of narcotics into the United States, Custred is highly critical of the Mexican authorities for allowing it to happen and of Washington for its lack of resolve in terms of controlling the situation. Given this lack of border security, Custred remains skeptical of North American attempts to facilitate trade and border flows.

Bissett, on the other hand, is in favour of the establishment of a common security perimeter by the United States and Canada, given the benefits to our country. He doubts that the increasingly robust measures being taken by the Americans to strengthen their side of the border will prevent determined terrorists from crossing it. However, he recognizes that to establish a common perimeter, our two countries would have to harmonize policies in a number of areas. For example, Canada and the United States would need to create a common list of countries for which visas are waived, and establish common policies regarding the detention of people arriving without travel documents, the acceptance of asylum claims, and the removal of foreign criminals and terrorists.

Bissett is not optimistic, however, that Canadian political parties would be prepared to make the changes to our immigration and refugee policies that would be necessary for any harmonization to take place and for the Americans to be interested in a common security perimeter. Similarly, Noble is not overly sanguine about the prospect of establishing a common security perimeter, even though it might be in both countries' interests to do so. Before a common perimeter could be established, Canada and the United States would first need to make some fundamental decisions with respect to the nature of our future economic integration, and a number of areas, including our porous refugee system, would need to be dealt with before the Americans would be interested in such a perimeter. As well, Noble does not think that the relatively unfettered movement of people and goods between our two countries would be entirely a blessing for Canada if, for example, it allowed greater freedom for more illegal firearms or more of the illegal immigrants presently flooding into the United States to enter our territory.

Noble also reviews the two countries' progress in terms of their increased cooperation to date in such areas as the implementation of the Smart Border Declaration and Action Plan and the Safe Third Country Agreement (with respect to asylum seekers). In doing so, he questions the value of some of the United States' attempts to strengthen security along our common border, particularly when the United States is clearly doing such an inadequate job of controlling its border with Mexico.

In Noble's view, Canadian interests would be best served by continuing to work with the Americans to find ways to make our border both smarter and more secure, while at the same time correcting some of our policies and programs. For example, one area that needs improvement is our refugee determination system, which is highly dysfunctional from a Canadian perspective. Such policies and programs undermine the United States' confidence in our ability and resolve to exercise effective control over our borders.

Rudolph also examines, in considerable detail, our prospects for greater progress in terms of Canadian and American efforts to create a "smart borders" regime. He argues that such a regime would require a fundamental reorganization of existing structures and procedures. Similar to some of the other authors, he has concerns about the Canadian refugee system and expresses doubts regarding the extent to which harmonization could be achieved with the United States in the area of asylum policy as envisioned under the 30-point smart border plan.

As well, Rudolph identifies features of the Canadian system that make it disproportionately open in comparison to those of other advanced industrial states. These features include high rates of approvals, a generous social welfare system, infrequent prosecutions, and lax deportation procedures. He notes that strong domestic lobbies in Canada have been instrumental in shaping both immigration and asylum policies, as human rights and immigration law lobbies have successfully institutionalized protections for migrants within the judiciary (as well as the Immigration and Refugee Board) that constrain policy makers from enacting restrictive policies.

To realize further progress in terms of border security cooperation, Rudolph argues that improvements in intelligence sharing must
be made. What makes this facet of an integrated border management
regime so complicated, according to Rudolph, is that the need for better intelligence creates interests for a regime within a regime. Pooling
raw anti-terrorism data requires a high degree of cooperation in scale
and scope, both within states (interagency sharing) and among them
(interstate). In the United States, major initiatives were taken to ensure
better integration among intelligence gathering agencies to eliminate the
kind of coordination failures that may have prevented the events of 9/11.
However, there is still much to be done in this area. In Canada, steps
have been taken to achieve greater integration in the handling of intelligence, and the intelligence community has been given additional powers
and resources. Yet, according to Rudolph, little has been accomplished
in terms of altering the bureaucratic structure and its processes, within
or among members of the intelligence community. These impediments
notwithstanding, Rudolph believes that the need for both openness and
security on our borders would seem to demonstrate that the creation of
a cooperative regime is a necessity. He advises, however, that we should
not underestimate just how complicated the process will be as we move
toward such a regime.

Conclusion

In the preceding chapters, each contributor outlined their concerns with
respect to the shortcomings in Canadian immigration and refugee policy
system as they relate to security issues and, in particular, the threat of terrorism. The authors point out that these problems not only involve risks to
the security of Canadians, but they also undermine American confidence
in the ability and resolve of Canada to exercise adequate control over
who is allowed to enter and remain in its territory. As such, the United
States will likely continue to impose tighter controls over the movement
of people and goods across its common border with Canada. This could
have serious implications for the Canadian economy since it is heavily
dependent on trade with the United States.

One of the major problems with Canadian immigration policy identified by the authors is the unrelentingly high level of intake that is resulting in an increase in both the number and size of separate immigrant communities. The formation of such communities tends to slow down the integration of newcomers and provides an environment in which extremists can operate relatively unnoticed and have increased opportunities to recruit supporters. Questions were raised as to why Canada maintains such high immigration levels, since they do not result in economic benefits of any significance and are not the most effective means of meeting most labour shortages. While Canada does have an aging population, it is clear that immigration will do little to mitigate the challenges associated with this phenomenon.

The authors who pursued this issue concluded that the most important factor contributing to the continuation of high immigrant intake levels was the influence of organizations and individuals who have a vested interest in seeing it continue. Prominent among them are political parties, which count on newcomers who arrive while they are in office to provide them with electoral support once they become eligible to vote. Other players include immigration lawyers, immigrant settlement organizations, and others such as groups that lobby for diversity or human rights, for example. While some chapters concluded that, at least in Canada's case, human rights and civil liberties had often been given undue priority over security concerns, it was also clearly accepted that the former were of fundamental importance and that a reasonable balance had to be established between liberty and security.

Related to Canada's high intake levels is the issue of the lack of resources available for the adequate security screening of individuals who are accepted as immigrants. To ensure reasonable standards of security, the resources available for screening must be increased or the number of immigrants admitted must be decreased.

Canada's refugee determination system was also cited as a source of major concern from a security point of view because it has been used as a means for terrorists and their supporters to enter Canada and to delay their removal from the country. American contributors noted that the weaknesses of the system are among the major reasons why the United

States continues to have serious concerns about Canada's ability to deal with security issues. With respect to Canada's refugee system, the authors identified the need to ensure that the system does not continue to be clogged with large numbers of asylum seekers who would be rejected or prohibited from applying for protection in other countries. To a great extent, this could be achieved through the application of "safe third country" and "safe country of origin" rules, as other countries have done.

Action also needs to be taken in other areas of our refugee system. For example, there is a need for more frequent use of detention in the case of claimants whose identity is in doubt and who may pose a security threat to Canada, as well as claimants whose applications have been rejected and who have been ordered removed but frequently fail to show up for their departure unless kept in custody. Another area that requires correction is the appeal process. Currently, refused claimants have the ability to delay their removal almost indefinitely through various appeals and reviews.

While not specifically proposed in any of the chapters, one of the obvious conclusions to be drawn from this volume is that a thorough and comprehensive review of both immigration and refugee policy is long overdue in Canada. Such a review must determine what the objectives of Canada's immigration policy should be, and must look critically at the extent to which current programs are achieving these objectives and the extent to which immigration policy and national security policy can pursue complementary objectives. Moreover, the review should not be done by any of Canada's political parties, which have a strong tendency to treat immigration policy as means of shoring up electoral support, or by organizations that will advocate policies that serve their own interests. While all interested groups should have an opportunity to present their views, it is important that an independent review be organized in such a way that the interests of Canadians in general are paramount.

A final topic discussed by the contributors was the importance of continued cooperation between Canada and the United States. Both countries should look for ways in which they can harmonize standards and procedures, in order to ensure that the measures in place along our common border provide an adequate level of security while facilitating the movement of goods and people. Such harmonization could include the establishment of common lists of visa-exempt countries, as well as common security screening standards and procedures for visa applicants. The contributors recommended that the two countries work towards a better integration of the work of intelligence gathering agencies from each country.

With a comprehensive and fundamental review of Canadian immigration and refugee policy that takes into account the various issues and recommendations made in the chapters in this volume, Canadians could ensure that the programs in these areas achieve their stated objectives, while contributing to, rather than detracting from, the security, economic, and humanitarian interests of Canadians at large.

References

Bell, Stewart (2004, March 31). Al-Qaeda Urges Attacks on Canadians. *National Post.*

Bell, Stewart (2008, January 30). Killing Canadians 'Best Way': Student. *National Post.*

Bolan, Kim (2007, October 31). Air India Blast Mastermind Called 'Martyr' at Sikh Service. *Vancouver Sun.*

Brown, Jim (2007, November 22). 'The Reign of Terror is Still There': Liberal MP Describes Beatings, Death Threats Faced by Opponents of Sikh Extremism. *Toronto Star.*

Collacott, Martin (2006). *Canada's Inadequate Response to Terrorism: The Need for Policy Reform.* Fraser Institute Digital Publication. Fraser Institute. <http://www.fraserinstitute.org/COMMERCE.WEB/product_files/Terrorism%20Response5.pdf>.

Demographia (2001). *Canada: Religious Affiliation.* Demographia. <http://www.demographia.com/db-canrelig.htm>.

Fatah, Tarek (2006, December 6). Race and Religion at the Liberal Party Convention. *The Globe and Mail.*

Financial Transactions and Reports Analysis Centre of Canada [FINTRAC] (2007). *FINTRAC Annual Report 2007.* <http://www.fintrac.gc.ca/publications/ar/2007/41-eng.asp>. Accessed February 1, 2008.

Green, Alan G. (2003). *What is the Role of Immigration in Canada's Future? Canadian Immigration Policy for the 21st Century.* McGill-Queen's University Press.

Hou, Feng, and Garnett Picot (2004). Visible Minority Neighbourhoods in Toronto, Montréal, and Vancouver. *Canadian Social Trends* (Spring): 8–13. <http://www.statcan.ca/english/freepub/11-008-XIE/2003004/articles/6803.pdf>.

Leong, Melissa (2007, November 6). Liberal MPs Attend Vigil for Slain Tamil Tiger. *National Post.*

MacLeod, Ian (2008, January 25). Terror Trial Delay Angers Judge. *Ottawa Citizen.*

Sallot, Jeff, and Brian Laghi (2006, June 7). RCMP Foiled Dozen Plots in Past Two Years. *The Globe and Mail.*

Statistics Canada (2001). *2001 Census of Canada.* Catalogue No. 97F0022XIE2001004. Statistics Canada.

Statistics Canada (2005). *Population Projections of Visible Minority Groups, Canada, Provinces and Regions.* Catalogue No. 91-541-XIE. Statistics Canada. <http://www.statcan.ca/english/freepub/91-541-XIE/91-541-XIE2005001.pdf>.

Steyn, Mark (2008, January 14). Here is What Offends This Writer. *Maclean's.* 76–77.

Publishing information

Distribution

This publication is also available from <http://www.fraserinstitute.org> in Portable Document Format (PDF) and can be read with Adobe Acrobat® or with Adobe Reader®, which is available free of charge from Adobe Systems Inc. To download Adobe Reader, go to this link: <http://www.adobe.com/products/acrobat/readstep2.html> with your browser. We encourage you to install the most recent version.

Ordering publications

For information about ordering the printed publications of the Fraser Institute, please contact the publications coordinator
- e-mail: sales@fraserinstitute.org
- telephone: 604.688.0221 ext. 580 or, toll free, 1.800.665.3558 ext. 580
- fax: 604.688.8539.

Media

For media enquiries, please contact our Communications Department
- telephone: 604.714.4582
- e-mail: communications@fraserinstitute.org.

Website

To learn more about the Fraser Institute and to read our publications online, please visit our website at <http://www.fraserinstitute.org>.

Copyright

About the Fraser Institute

Our vision is a free and prosperous world where individuals benefit from greater choice, competitive markets, and personal responsibility. Our mission is to measure, study, and communicate the impact of competitive markets and government interventions on the welfare of individuals.

Founded in 1974, we are an independent research and educational organization with offices in Calgary, Montréal, Tampa, Toronto, and Vancouver, and international partners in over 70 countries. Our work is financed by tax-deductible contributions from thousands of individuals, organizations, and foundations. In order to protect its independence, the Institute does not accept grants from government or contracts for research.

關於 菲沙研究所

菲沙研究所的願景乃一自由而昌盛的世界，當中每個人得以從更豐富的選擇、具競爭性的市場及自我承擔責任而獲益。我們的使命在於量度、研究並使人知悉競爭市場及政府干預對個人福祉的影響。

創辦於1974年，我們乃一獨立的研究及教育機構，在卡加利、滿地可、坦帕、多倫多及溫哥華均設有辦事處，並在超過七十個國家擁有國際伙伴。我們的工作得到不同人仕、機構及基金透過可免稅捐獻資助。為了保持其獨立性，本研究所不接受政府的撥款或研究合約。

Sur l'Institut Fraser

Nous envisageons un monde libre et prospère, où chaque personne bénéficie d'un plus grand choix, de marchés concurrentiels et de responsabilités individuelles. Notre mission consiste à mesurer, à étudier et à communiquer l'effet des marchés concurrentiels et des interventions gouvernementales sur le bien-être des individus.

Fondé en 1974, notre Institut existe en tant qu'organisme indépendant de recherches et établissement éducatif. Nous avons des bureaux à Calgary, à Montréal, à Tampa, à Toronto, et à Vancouver, ainsi que des associés internationaux dans plus de 70 pays. Notre œuvre est financée par la contribution déductible d'impôt de milliers de personnes, d'organismes et de fondations. Pour protéger son indépendance, l'Institut Fraser n'accepte ni subvention gouvernementale ni recherche sous contrat.

Sobre el Instituto Fraser

Nuestra visión es un mundo libre y próspero donde los individuos se benefician de una mayor oferta, la competencia en los mercados y la responsabilidad individual. Nuestra misión es medir, estudiar y comunicar el impacto de la competencia en los mercados y la intervención gubernamental en el bienestar de los individuos.

Fundado en 1974, nuestro instituto es una organización independiente dedicada a la investigación y educación, con oficinas en Calgary, Montréal, Tampa, Toronto y Vancouver; además de contar con asociados internacionales en más de 70 países. Nuestro trabajo es financiado por donaciones voluntarias de miles de individuos, organizaciones y fundaciones. A fin de mantener nuestra independencia, el Instituto no acepta subvenciones del gobierno ni contratos para realizar trabajos de investigación.

Supporting the Fraser Institute

For information about how to support the Fraser Institute,
please contact

- Development Department, Fraser Institute
  Fourth Floor, 1770 Burrard Street
  Vancouver, British Columbia, V6J 3G7 Canada
- telephone, toll-free: 1.800.665.3558 ext. 586
- e-mail: development@fraserinstitute.org

Calgary
- telephone: 403.216.7175 ext. 227
- fax: 403.234.9010

Montréal
- telephone: 514.281.9550 ext. 303
- fax: 514.281.9464
- e-mail: montreal@fraserinstitute.org.

Toronto
- telephone: 416.363.6575 ext. 232
- fax: 416.934.1639.

Vancouver
- telephone: 604.688.0221 ext. 586
- fax: 604.688.8539